PRAISE FOR
Lives of American Women

"Finally! The majority of students—by which I mean women—will have the opportunity to read biographies of women from our nation's past. (Men can read them too, of course!) The Lives of American Women series features an eclectic collection of books, readily accessible to students who will be able to see the contributions of women in many fields over the course of our history. Long overdue, these books will be a valuable resource for teachers, students, and the public at large."

—COKIE ROBERTS,
author of *Founding Mothers* and *Ladies of Liberty*

"Just what any professor wants: books that will intrigue, inform, and fascinate students! These short, readable biographies of American women—specifically designed for classroom use—give instructors an appealing new option to assign to their history students."

—MARY BETH NORTON,
**Mary Donlon Alger Professor of American History,
Cornell University**

"For educators keen to include women in the American story, but hampered by the lack of thoughtful, concise scholarship, here comes Lives of American Women, embracing Abigail Adams's counsel to John—'remember the ladies.' And high time, too!"

—LESLEY S. HERRMANN,
**Executive Director, The Gilder Lehrman
Institute of American History**

"Students both in the general survey course and in specialized offerings like my course on U.S. women's history can get a great understanding of an era from a short biography. Learning a lot about a single but complex character really helps to deepen appreciation of what women's lives were like in the past."

—PATRICIA CLINE COHEN,
University of California, Santa Barbara

D1120308

"Biographies are, indeed, back. Not only will students read them, biographies provide an easy way to demonstrate particularly important historical themes or ideas. . . . Undergraduate readers will be challenged to think more deeply about what it means to be a woman, citizen, and political actor. . . . I am eager to use this in my undergraduate survey and specialty course."

—JENNIFER THIGPEN,
Washington State University, Pullman

"These books are, above all, fascinating stories that will engage and inspire readers. They offer a glimpse into the lives of key women in history who either defied tradition or who successfully maneuvered in a man's world to make an impact. The stories of these vital contributors to American history deliver just the right formula for instructors looking to provide a more complicated and nuanced view of history."

—ROSANNE LICHATIN,
2005 Gilder Lehrman Preserve American History
Teacher of the Year

"The Lives of American Women authors raise all of the big issues I want my classes to confront—and deftly fold their arguments into riveting narratives that maintain students' excitement."

—WOODY HOLTON,
author of *Abigail Adams*

Lives of American Women

Carol Berkin, Series Editor

Westview Press is pleased to launch Lives of American Women. Selected and edited by renowned women's historian Carol Berkin, these brief, affordably priced biographies are designed for use in undergraduate courses. Rather than a comprehensive approach, each biography focuses instead on a particular aspect of a woman's life that is emblematic of her time, or which made her a pivotal figure in the era. The emphasis is on a "good read," featuring accessible writing and compelling narratives, without sacrificing sound scholarship and academic integrity. Primary sources at the end of each biography reveal the subject's perspective in her own words. Study Questions and an Annotated Bibliography support the student reader.

Elizabeth Gurley Flynn

Modern American Revolutionary

LARA VAPNEK

St. John's University

LIVES OF AMERICAN WOMEN
Carol Berkin, Series Editor

WESTVIEW PRESS

A Member of the Perseus Books Group

To my parents,
Daniel and Dianne Vapnek,
who taught me to ask questions

WESTVIEW PRESS was founded in 1975 in Boulder, Colorado, by notable publisher and intellectual Fred Praeger. Westview Press continues to publish scholarly titles and high-quality undergraduate- and graduate-level textbooks in core social science disciplines. With books developed, written, and edited with the needs of serious nonfiction readers, professors, and students in mind, Westview Press honors its long history of publishing books that matter.

Find us on the World Wide Web at www.westviewpress.com.

Every effort has been made to secure required permissions for all text, images, maps, and other art reprinted in this volume.

Westview Press books are available at special discounts for bulk purchases in the United States by corporations, institutions, and other organizations. For more information, please contact the Special Markets Department at the Perseus Books Group, 2300 Chestnut Street, Suite 200, Philadelphia, PA 19103, or call (800) 810-4145, ext. 5000, or e-mail special.markets@perseusbooks.com.

Series design by Brent Wilcox

Library of Congress Cataloging-in-Publication Data
Vapnek, Lara, 1967–
  Elizabeth Gurley Flynn : modern American revolutionary / Lara Vapnek.
        pages cm. — (Lives of American women)
  Includes bibliographical references and index.
    ISBN 978-0-8133-4809-4 (paperback) — ISBN 978-0-8133-4810-0 (e-book)
1. Flynn, Elizabeth Gurley.   2. Women labor leaders—United States—Biography.
3. Communists—United States—Biography.   4. Women revolutionaries—United States—Biography.   I. Title.
HX84.F5V37 2015
335.00092—dc23
[B]
                                                    2014027690

10 9 8 7 6 5 4 3 2 1

CONTENTS

Contents

SERIES EDITOR'S FOREWORD

American society underwent dramatic changes in the decades following the Civil War. Industrialization altered the workplace; immigration altered the cultural and religious profile of the nation's citizenry; cities came to dominate the landscape—and serious questions about the benefits of capitalism began to emerge. Reformers called for improved conditions in the workplace, aid to arriving immigrants, and more democratic practices in government on every level. But more radical ideas also began to circulate, ideas that challenged core elements of capitalism, such as private ownership of the nation's resources, and class and gender inequalities. The radical critique of American capitalism emerged as a central theme of the twentieth century.

Spurred by the Russian Revolution in the early twentieth century, the call for a radical alternative to capitalism grew in America. The rise—and decline—of this radical vision can be traced in the life of Elizabeth Gurley Flynn. As Lara Vapnek shows us in her biography of this remarkable woman, Flynn responded to the political currents of her long life, sometimes adopting a moderate approach, sometimes building alliances with liberal reformers, and sometimes tirelessly defending the rights of fellow dissidents and revolutionaries. As a committed radical, Flynn rejected the idea that meaningful change could come through the suffrage or unionization movements. Liberation would only come through a revolution that overthrew capitalism entirely.

Like many leading radicals, Flynn embraced the American Communist Party. She grasped the failures of capitalism and the wide gaps between the promises of democracy and its realities, but tragically, she never applied the same critical eye to the Soviet Union or to the communist system. She uncritically supported the Soviet Union during World War II and the Cold War, insisting on the success of communism until her death in 1964.

Flynn began her public career in New York City in the 1910s. Over the course of her lifetime, she paid a high price for her outspoken radicalism. In 1951, as American anticommunism raged, the aging Flynn was arrested and charged with conspiracy "to unlawfully, willfully, and knowingly . . . advocate and teach the duty and necessity of overthrowing the Government of the United States by force and violence." She was one of 109 members of the Communist Party to be indicted that year, and she served for twenty-eight months behind bars.

The greatest blow Flynn suffered was not her imprisonment, however, but the declining support for the Communist Party in America after 1950 and the growing evidence that the communist dream had failed in the Soviet Union. Although she could not close her eyes to the atrocities committed under Joseph Stalin, Flynn remained steadfast in support of the Soviet Union. In 1960, she traveled to Moscow, prepared, as Vapnek notes, to "love the Soviet Union." The Russian leaders, treating her as a celebrity, managed to paint a wildly positive portrait of life under communism. Flynn spoke glowingly about the success of communism, especially the alleged end of male domination of women in the Soviet Union.

The trip proved costly to Flynn, for soon after she returned to the United States, she learned that her passport had been revoked. It would take years before this decision was overturned by the US Court of Appeals. Free at last to travel, she returned to the Soviet Union, where she celebrated her seventy-fourth birthday. Soon afterward, she collapsed, fell into a diabetic coma, and died in a Russian hospital. The Soviet Union honored Flynn with a huge state funeral. Nikita Khrushchev himself joined her honor guard and 25,000 people filed past her coffin. But in America, she was quickly forgotten.

Lara Vapnek's sympathetic study of Flynn restores her to our national memory. Vapnek focuses on the historical context that fostered Flynn's radicalism, painting a vivid picture of the social and economic problems that plagued America during Flynn's lifetime. And although Vapnek finds much to admire in Flynn's effort to improve the lives of America's workers and women, she does not ignore Flynn's tragic flaw: her blind commitment to the Soviet Union. The rise and fall of an important strand of modern radicalism can be traced in this fascinating portrayal of the "rebel girl."

In examining and narrating the lives of women both famous and obscure, Westview's "Lives of American Women" series populates our national past more fully and more richly. Each story told is that not simply of an individual but of the era in which she lived, the events in which she participated and the experiences she shared with her contemporaries. Some of these women will be familiar to the reader; others may not appear at all in the history books that often focus on the powerful, the brilliant, or the privileged. But each of these women is worth knowing. American history comes alive through their personal odysseys.

—*Carol Berkin*

ACKNOWLEDGMENTS

My sincere thanks to the many people who have offered their insight and support. Conversations with Rosalyn Baxandall and Nick Unger helped me picture Flynn. The Washington, DC, Labor and Working-Class History Seminar encouraged me to think about American communism more critically. Generous comments from the following scholars enriched the manuscript immeasurably: Betsy Blackmar, Charlotte Brooks, Kristin Celello, Vanessa May, Tony Michels, Jonathan Soffer, and Randi Storch. Readers for Westview Press provided thoughtful suggestions for revision. Derek Denckla never tired of discussing Flynn. Zoe and Violet Denckla made me smile.

The Frederick Lewis Allen Memorial Room at New York Public Library provided an ideal place to write. Archivists and librarians offered untiring assistance. Many thanks to Jay Barksdale, New York Public Library; Kate Donovan, Peter Filardo, and Erika Gottfried, Tamiment Library, New York University; Kathleen Nutter, Sophia Smith Collection, Smith College; William W. Lefevre, Walter P. Reuther Library, Wayne State University; Julie Herrada and Kate Hutchens, Special Collections Library, University of Michigan; and Bonnie Foster, Syracuse University Library.

A research leave from St. John's University enabled me to complete this book. My colleagues in the History Department offered their support and encouragement. Special thanks to the Communist Party USA and the Estate of Michael Gold and of Elizabeth Gurley Flynn for permission to reproduce images and documents.

Introduction

Elizabeth Gurley Flynn's life (1890–1964) illuminates the history of American radicalism. Flynn devoted her life to two major causes: workers' empowerment and women's equality. She demanded the right to speak freely in order to pursue both of these goals. Flynn changed with the times, and time changed her. During the early 1900s, she played the part of the "East Side Joan of Arc," a beautiful young revolutionary demanding "bread and roses" for immigrant workers. Defending political prisoners during the Red Scare that began during World War I, she adopted a more moderate, professional persona. In middle age, she became a leading member of the American Communist Party. Flynn followed the twists and turns of the party line, building coalitions to support labor and the New Deal in the 1930s, and advocating an all-out fight against fascism during World War II. Flynn lived as a communist during the Cold War era. Prosecuted in the United States, she became a heroine in the Soviet Union.

Flynn was an outstanding orator. People who saw her speak never forgot the experience. Dorothy Healey, a communist organizer from California, marveled at Flynn's "remarkable ability to speak in plain language" and "establish immediate rapport" with her audience, no matter how large.[1] When Max Eastman, a writer and editor, first heard Flynn, during a 1913 strike in Paterson, New Jersey, he felt "strongly the likeness of all human beings and their problems." Anita Whitney, a California suffragist and socialist, describing Flynn's effect on her audience, remarked, "You feel that working class solidarity against the capitalist plot to undermine and destroy American civil liberties and the traditional American freedom is very definitely your problem."[2] The sheer power of Flynn's oratory moved her listeners.

The radicalism of a woman taking the stage to expound on politics, economics, and power hardly diminished over time. In some ways, Flynn seemed more extraordinary in the 1950s than she had been in the 1910s, when many working-class women took to the streets to demand equal rights as citizens and as workers. Flynn's speaking tours took her across the country and around the world. She inspired all sorts of women to step forward, speak their minds, and become politically active. Her feminism encompassed material as well as political equality: the right to vote was not enough; women needed equality at work, and they needed social support for motherhood, such as paid maternity leave and affordable daycare.

Many women joined movements devoted to social reform in the early decades of the twentieth century. Flynn was one of the few to call for revolution. She viewed capitalism, an economic system characterized by private ownership of property and profitability gained by minimizing labor costs, as incompatible with democracy. She embraced socialism—with collective ownership of manufacturing, land, and natural resources—as a necessary alternative. Flynn's ideas about socialism evolved, but certain themes remained constant. Capitalism, she believed, enabled a small number of people—those who controlled large corporations—to become ridiculously rich and to exercise a disproportionate share of political power. Workers, who created wealth through their labor, got far less than they deserved. Socialism would redistribute wealth based on people's need rather than their ability to make a profit. Poverty would disappear. Gender relations would be revolutionized, because women could stop relying on men for financial support. Flynn's socialist vision stayed steady, even if her ideas for how to achieve it evolved with her membership in two key organizations, the Industrial Workers of the World (IWW), from 1907 to 1916, and the Communist Party (CP), from 1937 to 1964.

Socialist ideas were never popular in the United States. Politicians, businessmen, and even labor leaders characterized socialism as "un-American." Flynn fought fiercely for the right to advocate controversial ideas. Her battles for free speech began in Missoula, Montana

(1909), and Spokane, Washington (1910). Speaking on city streets in Missoula and Spokane, she led battles for the right of the IWW to recruit members and stage protests. Flynn helped to pioneer new ideas of civil rights and new techniques of civil disobedience. She used arrests and trials to bring publicity to the IWW. The orgainzation became a target of government repression during World War I and the Red Scare. Flynn fought against wartime legislation classifying opposition to the war as sedition. She protested the deportation of foreign-born radicals. Likewise, the CP became a target for prosecution during the Cold War. In the 1950s, Flynn was one of more than a hundred communist leaders who were imprisoned for their beliefs.

Flynn formed alliances with liberals who shared her concern for preserving civil liberties, even if they disagreed with her ultimate goal of building a socialist America. As an agitator for the IWW and the CP, Flynn used the rhetoric of class conflict to convince workers to band together in order to exercise power over their wages and working conditions. However, she recognized the need for allies, including journalists, lawyers, and reformers, willing to campaign for free speech, or to aid workers in their battles with employers. In the 1920s, Flynn created a strong "united front" of people opposed to the excesses of government power embodied in the Red Scare. During the 1930s, she continued to pursue alliances with noncommunists in support of civil liberties. But liberal disillusionment with communism made these relationships difficult to sustain, as did the criminalization of the CP in the late 1940s. Flynn fought this trend by rebuilding alliances with liberals around the right to travel in the early 1960s.

Flynn worked mostly with men. She had no interest in all-female organizations, such as the Women's Trade Union League. She famously pronounced "the sisterhood of woman," like "the brotherhood of man," to be a "hollow sham." But women were often Flynn's strongest supporters. A small but dedicated group of female allies admired her bold public persona as the "rebel girl" and appreciated her deep concern for working-class women. Mary Heaton Vorse, a labor journalist who first met Flynn during a strike in Lawrence, Massachusetts, in 1912, became a lifelong friend. Mary van Kleeck, the first director of the US Women's Bureau, supported Flynn's battles for civil liberties. Alice Hamilton, a pioneer in establishing the field of industrial medicine, objected to Flynn's incarceration during the Cold War and corresponded with Flynn while she was in prison (1955–1957). Working-class women proudly claimed Flynn as one of their own. Letters in Flynn's papers testify to their admiration of her refusal to back down in the face of adversity.

Throughout her life, Flynn confounded expectations for women, but she did not do it alone. Her family provided a crucial source of support. Her father, Tom Flynn, schooled his family in socialism. Her mother, Annie Gurley Flynn, encouraged her daughters to pursue meaningful careers. The Flynn family drew strength from their Irish identity. Hating British rule, they identified with all sorts of fights against unjust power. Elizabeth Gurley Flynn married briefly, at age nineteen, but she left her husband while she was pregnant with her son, Fred, to return home to her family in New York City. She never found an entirely satisfying long-term romantic partner. A twelve-year relationship with Carlo Tresca, an Italian anarchist, ended badly, as did a ten-year relationship with Marie Equi, a lesbian physician.

Flynn fought for women's equality, but she could not escape certain fundamental inequalities of gender. A man who was a public figure on a par with Flynn would have found a wife to keep house and provide emotional support. Flynn made do with her family's help. After her relationships with Tresca and Equi ended, Flynn had a string of intense but temporary relationships with younger men. She hid these romances, knowing that sex outside of marriage was much less acceptable for a woman than a man. Flynn faced greater public scrutiny of her appearance than a man, too. As she aged, she gained weight and no longer conformed to youthful standards of feminine beauty. Although she remained sharp until the end, reporters often belittled her by describing her as "grandmotherly." Flynn was not afraid to state her positions strongly. But the men with whom she worked in both the IWW and the CP sometimes discounted her opinions because she was a woman, even though they valued her ability to reach the masses, her organizational skills, and her knack for publicity.

Flynn never lived to see her dream of a socialist America fulfilled, of course. Communism, the cause to which she devoted the second half of her life, collapsed in 1989 in the Soviet Union. Since then, capitalism has triumphed as a global system of economic organization. However, Flynn's life story foreshadows many of the problems of the early twenty-first century, including growing income inequality, continued imbalances of power between men and women, and tradeoffs between democracy and security. Flynn was active and engaged in the major battles of the twentieth century, and her life has much to tell us about our own times. Her critique of capitalism remains relevant and thought provoking even in the postcommunist era.

1

East Side Joan of Arc—
Early Life

On the evening of August 22, 1906, a ragtag group of New York City socialists raised a red flag atop a horse-drawn caravan at 38th Street and Broadway. Red flares illuminated the improvised stage where speakers took turns blasting the inequities of capitalism. They included Elizabeth Gurley Flynn, "a mere slip of a girl," just sixteen years old, "with large grey eyes," fair skin, and "a sensitive mouth." She wore her black hair in braids down her back. Her plaid dress skimmed the tops of her high-buttoned shoes, making her look more like a schoolgirl than a public speaker. This "delicate girl" delivered a shockingly radical message: workers must unite to overthrow capitalism. The crowd swelled as the Broadway shows ended and onlookers in evening clothes joined the "riff raff" of the tenderloin. Alarmed by the red flag and the swelling crowd, police broke up the gathering and arrested the speakers for blocking traffic. It was the first of at least a dozen arrests for Flynn, who devoted the rest of her life to movements to create a socialist America, "free," in her words, "from poverty, exploitation, greed and injustice."[1]

By age sixteen, Flynn was a precocious critic of American capitalism. America's economic system, based on production for profit, was a dynamic force driving industrial expansion, but in her eyes it was also

Flynn around the time she began speaking publicly (1906).

NP18-1A, EGF Photographs, Tamiment Library, NYU

responsible for creating social inequalities. Flynn's radical family background, distinctive childhood experience, and close reading of American and European protest literature ignited her passion to transform the United States. She identified with exploited workers and she believed their best chance for freedom lay with socialism. Flynn envisioned socialism as transforming the lives of men and women and ending both poverty and gender inequality.

Flynn and her fellow speakers on Broadway that summer evening in 1906 believed that capitalism warped the American dream of creating a new, more egalitarian society. They called for an end to private ownership of factories, farms, and mines. They wanted the state to take over public utilities such as water, railroads, and electricity and run them to benefit the public. American socialism drew on eighteenth-century British and nineteenth-century American critiques of the ways in which concentrated wealth and power undermined democracy. Informed by the German thinker Karl Marx, American socialists viewed capitalist employers as members of a parasitic class who essentially stole from their workers by paying them a wage far below the value of the goods they produced and then accumulating the profit. They drew on abundant examples of income disparities in the United States to argue that capitalism made employers rich and workers poor. American socialists called for a redistribution of wealth and resources to benefit the many instead of the few.

Elizabeth Gurley Flynn's parents, Tom and Annie Gurley Flynn, fostered her radicalism. They hailed from Irish families that hated British rule and insisted on the right of the Irish "to be independent and self-governing." Elizabeth felt that she and her three younger siblings "drew in a burning hatred of British rule with our mother's milk." Her mother became a proud member of Sinn Féin, which worked to establish Irish independence. Her father, who lived into his eighties, never uttered the word "England" without adding "God damn her."[2] This sensitivity to unjust power fed Flynn's hostility toward capitalism, which she viewed as fundamentally unfair to working people. The Flynn family identified with other oppressed and oppositional groups. They celebrated the Filipino freedom fighter Eduardo Aguinaldo and sympathized with Jewish socialists fleeing persecution in Russia and Eastern Europe.

Annie Gurley and Tom Flynn reared their children with Irish songs and stories, glorifying rebellion against unjust rule. Annie was raised Presbyterian and Tom Catholic, but, like many other free thinkers, they rejected organized religion and considered themselves atheists. Annie Gurley arrived in Boston from Galway, Ireland, in

1877 at the age of seventeen. Like many young Irish women who migrated to America, she had a strong sense of responsibility to provide for her family. The eldest daughter in a family of thirteen children, Annie labored as a skilled seamstress for thirteen years. The income that she provided proved crucial, especially when her father died and her mother moved their large family to Concord, New Hampshire. With Annie's support, her brothers learned trades such as leather- and metalworking and her sisters became skilled dressmakers.[3] Even after she married at age thirty and had children, Annie Flynn continued to work as a seamstress when she could find child care. Elizabeth Gurley Flynn followed in her mother's footsteps by becoming a financial supporter of her family.

In the 1870s and 1880s, the labor of recent immigrants like the Gurleys drove the expansion of the American economy. However, many of these workers felt shut out of the blessings of prosperity enjoyed by a rising middle class. Annie and her brothers and sisters joined the Knights of Labor, a rapidly expanding national organization that sought to organize all "producers" in order to fight the power of big business in politics and demand basic rights for workers, such as the eight-hour workday. In Concord, New Hampshire, the Knights advertised their meetings with "chalked signs on the sidewalks," fearing that more lasting evidence of their organization could be used to prosecute them for conspiracy. Local chapters of the Knights functioned as labor unions, staging strikes and boycotts in order to win better working conditions, higher pay, and shorter hours. Unlike more traditional craft unions, which focused on skilled male workers, the Knights reached out to women, immigrants, and unskilled workers. They supported votes for women and equal pay for equal work.[4]

Annie Gurley's strong sense of herself as a worker and supporter of her family fed her "rebellion against male supremacy." She saved her earnings to buy tickets to hear the suffrage advocates Susan B. Anthony and Elizabeth Cady Stanton speak at White's Opera House in Concord.[5] Furthermore, she insisted on using female physicians to deliver her four children. She named Elizabeth, who was born in 1890, after one of these doctors. As Elizabeth later recalled, "Mother admired intelligent women who did 'worthwhile things.'"[6] Annie

Flynn did not consider becoming a housewife to be a suitable career: "To be self-reliant and self-supporting, a person in one's own rights was her ideal."[7] This sentiment inspired Elizabeth, the first of four children, to make her mark in the world. Elizabeth's two sisters, Kathie and Bina, also pursued careers. Kathie became a teacher and Bina an actress. Their quiet brother, Tom, who became an optician, lacked his sisters' drive and often seemed overshadowed by the strong women in his family.

Elizabeth's father shared his wife's radical sensibilities. Born in 1859, Tom Flynn grew up in Maine, the son of Irish immigrants. At age ten, he followed his father and his two brothers into the granite quarries, and in 1875, he joined his fellow workers in forming a chapter of the Knights of Labor to protest low wages, substandard housing, and dangerous working conditions.[8] Tom lost sight in one eye after he was hit by a shard of stone at the quarry. Having watched all but one of his male relatives die from lung disease caused by granite dust, he decided to pursue the education he needed to get out of the quarries, entering the Thayer School of Engineering at Dartmouth College. When Tom's older brother died, Tom had no choice but to leave school to help support his mother and his three sisters. Although Tom did not graduate from Dartmouth, he had learned enough to find work as a civil engineer. He turned to mapmaking, a growing field in the urbanizing, industrializing United States.[9] Despite his upward mobility, Tom continued to sympathize with working people. Elizabeth absorbed this attitude: because of her father's working-class roots, she always felt at home around miners and other men who performed hard physical labor under dangerous conditions.

Tom Flynn and Annie Gurley were married in Concord, New Hampshire, in 1889, and Elizabeth was born a year later. Tom seemed to have bright prospects as a mapmaker.[10] His work took him to growing towns and cities throughout New England and the Midwest, and his family followed. Although her father was fairly well paid for his work, Elizabeth soon encountered children in desperate economic circumstances. In New England towns such as Adams and Manchester, she saw gray cotton mills that "stretched like prisons along the banks of the Merrimac River." Half of the workers in these mills were women earning a dollar per day. Children had to leave school early to bring their parents lunch. One day, Elizabeth and her classmates heard "piercing screams from the mill across the street." A young woman was "literally scalped" when her hair became caught in a machine without any safety devices.[11] This exposure to the difficult lives of textile workers and their families may have inspired Elizabeth's leadership in strikes in the textile mill towns of Lawrence, Massachusetts, and Paterson, New Jersey, in 1912 and 1913.

The Flynn family's comfortable circumstances changed dramatically in 1900 after Tom Flynn's employer failed to pay him for two summers' worth of work. The family "suffered from misery and crushing but . . . revolutionizing poverty," Elizabeth Gurley Flynn explained in 1907.[12] They moved to the Bronx, where her Aunt Mary, her mother's sister, a widow who worked as a dressmaker, lived with her five children. The Flynn family's first Bronx apartment was infested by "mice, rats, cockroaches, and bedbugs," Flynn recalled. They could barely afford heat, soap, or clothing. "On cold winter days," she remembered, she and the rest of the family would "huddle in the kitchen and shut off the rest of the house." The Flynn children did their homework by the light of "a kerosene lamp when the gas was shut off for non-payment." Their only real entertainment was reading. They walked across the bridge to borrow books from the public library on East 125th Street. After about a year, they managed to move to a slightly better apartment about a block away, at 511 East 134th Street, but it, too, was small and lacked central heating.[13] They decorated their home with pictures of men and women who "defied the existing order of society," including the English novelist George Eliot, the French revolutionary Jean-Paul Marat, and the Russian playwright Maxim Gorky.[14] Despite their material deprivation, the Flynn family enjoyed a rich intellectual life.

In the Bronx, Elizabeth Gurley Flynn and her family experienced the problems of poverty firsthand. Most of their neighbors were Irish and German immigrants. Many of the men worked for the railroad; they would throw scraps of coal off the cars to neighborhood children to help them heat their apartments. As in the textile mills, in railway work there were few safety precautions, and workers frequently suffered accidents and even death. The Flynn children enrolled in the local public school, but many of the other neighborhood children went out to work at age fourteen or even younger. They "made paper boxes, pencils, shirts, handkerchiefs (at three dollars a week and bring your own thread)." Lack of day care meant that many mothers who had no choice but to go out to work had to leave their children home alone, where accidents often occurred.[15] Flynn's childhood in factory towns and in the Bronx demonstrated the brutality of turn-of-the-century capitalism: workers were regularly endangered on the job, women were paid even less than men, and children were forced out of school and into the labor force because their working parents could not support them.

Surrounded by poverty, and informed by the ideals of Irish freedom and the Knights of Labor, the Flynns questioned the justice of capitalism. As Flynn later explained, "we were conditioned in my family to accept socialist thinking long before we came into contact with socialism as an organized movement." They first encountered socialism around 1902 at a free Sunday-evening program presented by German socialists at the Metropolis Theater on East 142nd Street and Third Avenue. At the turn of the century, German Americans constituted a considerable presence in the socialist movement in New York and in other cities, such as Milwaukee and Chicago. Excited by what they heard at the meeting, Flynn recalled, her family brought home a socialist newspaper "and as many pamphlets as we could afford." The lectures and the literature explained how capitalism led to poverty for working people and proposed an alternative system of organizing society. As Flynn later remembered it, "socialism was a great discovery" for her, "a hope, a purpose, a flame within me."[16] In a sense, socialism became her religion, linking her to a community, explaining the challenges of daily life, and supplying a vision for a brighter future.

Her father, Tom, became an ardent socialist, dragging the children to many long meetings. Elizabeth was old enough to understand what went on at the meetings, but her younger siblings often fell asleep. Later in life, she agreed with her sister Kathie that Tom Flynn could have helped his family more by finding stable work than by sitting at the kitchen table reading Marx. Tom was employed only sporadically as an engineer and mapmaker. He became "irritable and explosive" when he was out of work and at home for long periods of time.[17] The marriage was rocky, and the children sympathized with their mother. She was an excellent cook and made all of her family's clothes, although, Elizabeth later admitted, "she was no model housekeeper." Annie read widely and encouraged her children's love of literature. She "was interesting and different," Elizabeth recalled, "and we loved her dearly."[18]

Elizabeth Gurley Flynn excelled at school, earning straight A's and winning a medal for excellence in debate.[19] When she was about fourteen, an impacted tooth that became infected forced her to take a six-month break from school. But she spent the time reading, pondering questions she would wrestle with for the rest of her life: What justified revolution? How could women become free individuals? What was the balance between individual self-expression and collective strategies for social change? She surveyed revolutionary thinkers such as Thomas Paine, whose writings had helped spark the American Revolution, and Karl Marx, whose work had inspired European socialists in their attempted revolutions of 1848. She also dipped into Henry David Thoreau's treatise on civil disobedience and copied passages from Ralph Waldo Emerson's thoughts on self-reliance into her scrapbook. She turned to plays by Henrik Ibsen and the writings of George Bernard Shaw to explore women's struggles to become independent.[20] She studied Victoria Wollstonecraft's classic *Vindication of the Rights of Woman* as well as August Bebel's *Women and Socialism*.[21] All of these works informed Flynn's thinking in the years to come.

Flynn remained an avid reader throughout her life. Just after she turned fifteen, her mother gave her Edward Bellamy's utopian novel *Looking Backward*. The book made a "profound impression" on Flynn. Written in the late nineteenth century, it projected a future socialist America. Bellamy described a world from the imagined vantage point of the year 2000 in which social class had disappeared, housework had been abolished, and production and consumption were managed by the state to assure the well-being of all. To Flynn, the book seemed to be "a convincing explanation of how peaceful, prosperous and happy America could be under a socialist system of society."[22]

Flynn's understanding of social problems also developed through her tracking of current events. She followed the anthracite coal strike of 1902, led by the United Mine Workers of Pennsylvania. New York City streetcars ran on coal and nearly stopped operating, but the city's workers still sympathized with the miners. Flynn wrote a school essay arguing in favor of public ownership of the mines. Outside of school, she studied and debated social problems as a member of the Hamilton Literary Society, which included students from all over the city.[23] In January 1906, Flynn joined a parade of nearly 6,000 people who marched from Lower Manhattan to Union Square to commemorate the one-year anniversary of Russia's "Bloody Sunday," when Cossacks had killed thousands of peaceful protesters in St. Petersburg who had marched to the Winter Palace to deliver a petition to the czar. Most of the participants in the New York City parade were Jewish refugees. They waved red flags and carried banners calling for working people of all countries to unite.[24] Flynn's childhood in New York City, a city full of immigrants, exposed her to transnational currents of social protest.

The Lower East Side seemed to be bursting with revolution. Flynn was soon taking the train downtown from the Bronx to attend "crowded meetings" in "long and narrow" halls decorated with red socialist banners and charters of the "landsmen" clubs of Jewish socialists. The rooms were cold and poorly lit, "with sawdust on the floors to protect it for the dancing" that took place at weddings. Fresh from Russia, these Jewish socialists made "the South Bronx Irish railroad workers" and German workers who made pianos ("drinking their beer in corner saloons") seem "sedate and dull." Flynn admired the way these Yiddish-speaking socialists combined the culture and politics of protest. Music, art, stories, and dancing engaged the homesick, overworked crowd as much as the lectures.[25]

Flynn transformed from observer to actor when she took the stage on January 31, 1906, to present her first public speech. About seventy-five people gathered in the small hall of the Harlem Socialist Club on West 125th Street, up two flights of stairs, to hear this "slender, serious girl, not yet 16," discuss "What Socialism Will Do for Women." She "wore a long full skirt" down to her ankles along

with "a white shirtwaist and a red tie." Her long black hair was tied
back with a ribbon. Invited to speak because of her reputation as an
excellent debater, Flynn had worked hard to prepare for the event,
resisting her father's efforts to tell her what to say. Facing "an adult audience for the first time," she "began to quake inwardly at the start."
But the audience was sympathetic, and Flynn was soon sailing along
"serenely." She outlined women's oppression under capitalism, which
included denial of the right to vote as well as denial of "all legal rights
over their children, homes, or property." Women who went out to
work were paid less than men, ignored by unions, and stuck in dead-
end jobs. Most women spent their lives doing housework for their
families, which Flynn characterized as "drudgery and monotony." Socialism would free women from this endless round of labor, Flynn
announced, by "industrializing" tasks such as cooking, laundry, and
child care. The weekly socialist paper described Flynn as "very bright"
and remarked at her "surprising grasp of the subject." This speech
launched Flynn's career as a speaker and began her lifelong campaign
for women's equality.[26]

Speaking on stages and street-corners throughout New York City,
Flynn quickly earned notice from the daily papers as "an East Side
Joan of Arc." She seemed like a Lower East Side revolutionary even
though she lived in the Bronx. The struggling writer Theodore Dreiser, who later became a leading realist novelist, heard Flynn speak and
became fascinated by her. Dreiser described Flynn as "a typical Irish
beauty" who "electrified her audience with her eloquence." Like nearly
all of the journalists who reported on Flynn during the early years
of her career, Dreiser remarked on Flynn's "youth and loveliness." In
an era of muckraking journalism built on contrasts between rich and
poor, virtue and vice, Flynn's youthful beauty created the perfect foil
for revolutionary statements that one hardly expected to hear coming
"from the lips of a girl."[27] Flynn put this shock value to good use by
drawing public attention to radical causes that the mainstream press
generally ignored, and that many people of the time associated with
dangerous immigrant men.

Flynn "plunged into street speaking . . . and loved it."[28] Her early
speeches, which can be traced in the many clippings she collected

and saved in scrapbooks, drew together her belief in socialism and her concern with women's oppression. Traveling with her father, who took pride in her growing reputation, Flynn soon expanded her reach beyond New York City to include working-class neighborhoods in Philadelphia and textile towns in New Jersey. On a Philadelphia street-corner, she argued that "capitalists have had their day." Armed with an understanding of socialism, working people would soon overthrow capitalism and enact "a just distribution of the fruits of labor." Socialism promised women "equality and freedom."[29] It would provide mothers with financial support to raise their children so they would not have to depend on their husbands. Communal "laundreys [*sic*], cooking places, cleaning rooms, kitchens and nurseries" would end women's enslavement to housework. Flynn found a receptive audience, especially among working-class women, who greeted her proposals with applause.[30]

Emma Goldman, a Jewish anarchist from Russia, who first heard Flynn speak at an open-air meeting in 1906, was struck by Flynn's "beautiful face and figure" and her "voice vibrant with earnestness." Goldman rejected the authority of the state and the church and advocated free love. When Flynn attended her lectures, Goldman recalled, "I often found it hard to take my eyes off her."[31] In those days, anarchists and socialists mingled freely, and the terms, according to Flynn, "were loosely interchanged." Flynn's parents were wary of the anarchists because of their advocacy of free love.[32] Nevertheless, Flynn, like Goldman, began to think critically about sexuality and marriage. In an early speech, Flynn described marriage under the capitalist system as little better than "legalized prostitution."[33] Married women turned control of their bodies over to their husbands, who expected sexual subservience in exchange for economic support. Lacking birth control, women had more children than they and their husbands could afford to feed. Unmarried working girls, whose wages rarely covered the costs of food, clothing, and rent, sometimes had no choice but to turn to prostitution.

Flynn agreed in theory that women needed the right to vote. However, she viewed women's economic dependence on men as a far more pressing and fundamental problem. This conviction stemmed from her socialist analysis of women's secondary position in all walks of life. She had read the work of Charlotte Perkins Gilman, an author suggested by her mother, but disagreed with Gilman's conclusions.[34] Gilman urged women to free themselves from lives constrained by domesticity by taking jobs outside the home. Flynn objected to this method of emancipation because she believed that by going out to work in a capitalist economy, women became "wage slaves" just like their husbands. Gilman's plan might work for upper-class or even middle-class women, but it had no relevance for working-class women. Gilman envisioned women of different classes working together to bring about economic and social improvement. But Flynn rejected Gilman's vision of feminist solidarity across class lines. She believed that working women and working men needed to pull together to fight capitalism and establish socialism.[35]

Although Flynn believed strongly in women's equality, she objected to pursuing it through separate women's organizations. Young leftist women in Europe shared this rejection of all-female organizations. Clara Zetkin, for example, an outspoken German socialist whom Flynn admired, dismissed cooperation with "bourgeois feminists" in favor of working-class solidarity. This view represented a new, seemingly more modern approach to achieving social change. However, women who rejected cross-class organizations in favor of working-class solidarity often found that organizations run by men paid little attention to the particular problems that female workers faced, including low pay, sexual harassment, and the double burden of wage labor and domestic work.[36] Flynn's childhood experiences and her mother's feminism made her acutely aware of these problems. But in 1906, Flynn was young and eager to find new solutions to familiar problems. Inspired, in part, by reading the Russian anarchist Peter Kropotkin's *Appeal to the Young*, she sought a new, more radical version of socialism in a new organization, the Industrial Workers of the World.

2

Wobbly Agitator—
Fights for Free Speech

On a cold winter morning in 1909, Elizabeth Gurley Flynn woke up in a Spokane, Washington, jail cell to the unwelcome feeling of a strange man's hand on her cheek. She sat up and told him she was not there to be insulted. He backed off, leaving Flynn her breakfast: weak coffee and stale bread. She had spent the night in jail after being arrested on conspiracy charges. Pregnant, she had been thrown into the single women's cell with two prostitutes. Flynn's cellmates had tried to make her comfortable, sharing some food and lending her a pillow. Having been arrested several times before, Flynn was relieved that she was not alone, "at the mercy of men you do not trust a moment, day or night, unable to defend yourself or call for help." Despite the company the women offered, the heavy door to the cell had opened and closed all night as the jailers brought the women downstairs to visit "sweet-hearts." Flynn found the women and the jailers to be on terms of "disgusting familiarity." Later that day, Flynn was out on bail. Awaiting trial, she reflected, "This all in the name of law and order! Oh Liberty, what crimes are committed in thy name."[1]

Flynn grew up fast. Within a few years, she went from being a socialist child prodigy to a fearless agitator for the Industrial Workers of the World (IWW) at the center of a brewing battle over free speech. The best-known female leader of the Wobblies (as members of the IWW were known), Flynn helped draw national attention to local conflicts, publicizing the existence of the IWW and exposing abusive police practices and a biased justice system. Flynn's youth, beauty, and skill as a speaker attracted attention to her cause: building a new, egalitarian society. Her status as a woman protected her from some of the worst abuses that male members of the IWW suffered, such as being beaten up by the police, but it made it difficult for her to form and maintain the female friendships she enjoyed at other points in her life.

Flynn had mounted soapboxes and stages to speak on behalf of socialism since she was fifteen. She soon grew impatient, however, with the moderation of the Socialist Party, which fielded candidates for office and attracted intellectuals and professionals as well as workers. Flynn wanted to be part of something "more militant, more progressive and more youthful." The fact that her parents and their friends belonged to the Socialist Party made it seem "stodgy" and "middle-aged."[2] Inspired by her reading of Marx, Flynn believed that workers needed to form their own movement, without the help of "professors, lawyers, doctors, ministers," and other middle-class types. Like Marx, Flynn was not a wage worker herself, but she embraced the empowerment of the working class as the key to social transformation.

Inspired by the Russian Revolution (which began in 1905 and culminated in the Bolshevik Revolution of 1917), Flynn believed that socialism was just around the corner. To hasten its arrival, she gravitated to the IWW, a new organization, founded in 1905. Flynn joined in 1906 and earned a position as an organizer within a year. Rather than seeking change through the political system, the IWW sought to mobilize the working class through "direct action," a combination of organizing techniques that included strikes and slowdowns on the job as well as "picketing, parades, demonstrations," and public speeches.[3] Its members advocated industrial unions, which would include all workers in a particular industry. Ultimately, these industrial unions would form "One Big Union," which would become the basis of a new, socialist society.[4] In industrial societies around the world, the

On the road as an IWW agitator (1908).
NP18-7, EGF Photographs, Tamiment Library, NYU

term "syndicalism" gained currency to describe socialism rooted in workers' organizations and achieved through direct action.

The IWW began in Chicago with labor leader Bill Haywood at its helm. Big, tall, and missing an eye owing to a childhood accident, Haywood personified the scrappy but militant spirit of the IWW. Born in 1869 and raised in Utah, Haywood received little formal education. He became a miner at age fifteen. He joined the Western Federation of Miners (WFM), one of the most confrontational unions in the United States, in 1896. Charismatic and direct, he rose quickly to a leadership position in the WFM. Several other veterans of labor and radical movements joined Haywood in launching the IWW. They included Eugene V. Debs, the former leader of the American Railway Union, who ran five times for president of the United States on the Socialist Party ticket between 1900 and 1920, and Lucy Parsons, the African American widow of one of the Chicago anarchists executed during the Haymarket Affair, the campaign against radicals that had erupted in Chicago at the peak of the movement for an eight-hour workday in 1886. Unions of miners and brewers interested in creating stronger organizations in their industries joined, too. About 60,000 workers were represented at the founding convention of the IWW, which included a volatile mix of socialists, syndicalists, anarchists, and industrial unionists.[5]

Despite the youthful appeal of the IWW, the organization harked back to the Knights of Labor, where Elizabeth Gurley Flynn's parents, Annie Gurley and Tom Flynn, had formed their political consciousness in the 1870s and 1880s. The Knights had sought to organize all "producers," regardless of whether they were skilled or unskilled, male or female. Likewise, the IWW sought to organize all workers into "One Big Union." The IWW also resembled syndicalist movements in Italy, France, Great Britain, and Scandinavia, which sought to abolish the state except as an extension of workers' organizations.[6] The IWW shared anarchists' hostility to the state as an agent of capitalist power. By calling themselves the Industrial Workers of the World, the group's members indicated their sense of common struggle with radical workers of other nations. Haywood and several other IWW leaders visited Europe to learn more about syndicalism, and branches of the IWW appeared in Australia, New Zealand, Mexico, and Canada.[7]

Taking the American Revolution as their model, the organizers of the IWW issued a statement explaining their aims. Reprinted many times in IWW pamphlets and newspapers, the preamble of the IWW set out a bold challenge to the status quo: "The working class and the employing class have nothing in common. There can be no peace so long as hunger and want are found among millions of working people and the few, who make up the employing class, have all the good things of life." This protest statement echoed the analysis of social inequality found in political economist Henry George's *Progress and Poverty* (1879) as well as the 1892 platform of the Populist Party. Asserting a fundamental conflict between capital and labor, the IWW insisted that all of the workers in each industry must organize in order to form the basis for a new society.[8]

The Knights of Labor had faded in the 1890s to be replaced by the American Federation of Labor (AFL), which took a much more limited, but to some degree more effective, approach to organizing workers. The AFL focused on the "labor aristocracy" of skilled white men, who seemed to be in the best position to negotiate their terms of employment. Samuel Gompers, a German Jewish immigrant and former cigar maker who directed the AFL, made it his priority to get the best possible deal for his members in terms of wages, hours, and control over working conditions. The IWW rejected this strategy as dividing the working class. Instead, they insisted on organizing all workers and embraced a broader vision for social change that some, but by no means all, workers found appealing.[9]

Given their differing philosophies, the AFL and the IWW quickly became bitter enemies. When strikes erupted among workers, the AFL and the IWW often competed for members. Flynn characterized Gompers as a "labor fakir" who believed, mistakenly, that capital and labor shared many of the same interests and could therefore form lasting agreements.[10] Like other IWW leaders, Flynn believed that the labor contracts sought by the AFL made workers complacent and killed their revolutionary spirit.[11] Gompers dismissed the IWW's leaders, in turn, as "rainbow chasers" whose radical politics threatened to undermine the respectability and effectiveness of the American labor movement.[12]

The IWW focused on organizing the large mass of unskilled workers that the AFL ignored. Given her idealistic upbringing and her exposure to poverty, Flynn appreciated the fact that the IWW championed "the poorest, the most exploited, the most oppressed workers." She described IWW members as "foreign-born workers in the mass production industries of the East and the unorganized migratory workers of the West." In her hometown of New York City, IWW locals formed among workers who made cigars, textiles, and pianos; workers who labored in hotels joined, too. Many of these workers were recent immigrants. In the western United States, the IWW appealed to American-born and immigrant men from poor families who put their muscle into jobs as miners, lumberjacks, farmworkers, and shipbuilders.[13] Flynn managed to reach both eastern and western members of the IWW. In the East, she focused on female factory workers, applying her reading on women and socialism. In the West, she drew on her father's stories of work in the Maine granite quarries to relate to migrant workers.

As an IWW "jawsmith" (as Wobblies called their speakers), Flynn charmed audiences with her wit and impressed them with her logic. She hammered away at the flaws of capitalism, and she described the potential of socialism to transform American society. Flynn gained her first experience as an IWW strike organizer in the summer of 1907, when she helped organize 1,200 workers who made steel tubes in Bridgeport, Connecticut. Flynn "participated in strike committee meetings, mass picketing and daily meetings in two languages," English and Hungarian. Many of the workers brought their violins along to the meetings. The IWW respected ethnic traditions of solidarity and sought to build on them, often enlivening their meetings with music. Flynn helped to build public support for the strike by organizing street meetings, where she explained the workers' grievances to the public. The strike was defeated, however, in part by the AFL, which encouraged skilled workers to return to the job in order to defeat the IWW.[14]

Despite a mixed record of success, early IWW strikes—like the one Flynn joined in Bridgeport—helped to pioneer new techniques of protest. In some instances, rather than walking off the job, workers stayed at their machines and refused to work. This tactic illustrated the power that workers had to stop production and prevented them from being locked out by their employers. It also kept employers from breaking the strike by hiring scabs. The Congress of Industrial Organizations (CIO) emulated this technique in the 1930s, using sit-down strikes to unionize the automobile industry.

In the fall of 1907, the members of Flynn's IWW local in New York City elected her to represent them at the national IWW convention in Chicago. Having just turned seventeen, Flynn brushed aside her parents' concerns and traveled alone by train. She scraped together the $18 fare from contributions and rode in the coach car, where she tried to sleep sitting up. Wealthy passengers purchased comfortable places to sleep in the Pullman car, which provided beds.[15] Flynn found the IWW convention itself uneventful. Tensions surfaced between members of the Socialist Party, who endorsed political action by electing socialist candidates to office, and the industrial unionists, who rejected political change as impossible to accomplish within a capitalist society. Led by Bill Haywood, the industrial unionists won control over the IWW, and more moderate figures, such as Eugene V. Debs, drifted away (although he grew to admire Flynn's talent as a speaker and an organizer).[16] Vincent St. John, a former miner and a legendary labor organizer, who had been shot in the hand while leading a strike in Colorado, became the leader of the IWW from 1908 to 1915.[17] The revolutionary direction of the IWW suited Flynn just fine.

Flynn "loved Chicago." She found it to be "a big sprawly town— dirty, dingy, alive, [and] real." The city teemed with immigrants, many of whom were employed in mass-production industries such as the stockyards. Visiting Chicago around the same time that the novelist and muckraking journalist Upton Sinclair published *The Jungle*, Flynn shared Sinclair's socialist critique of production organized for profit. Seeing rats running through streets near the stockyards and hearing the cries of animals as they were being slaughtered confirmed her earlier decision to become a vegetarian. Capitalism, she concluded, subordinated both people and animals to the profit motive. She covered her costs by selling IWW newspapers and buttons at nightly speeches on the corner of Halsted and O'Brien streets, an immigrant neighborhood with large numbers of Russian Jews. News of Flynn's magnetism spread quickly. A reporter who showed up to hear her speak found Chicago's "ghetto audience" deeply moved by her radical socialist message.[18]

On her way back home from Chicago, Flynn crisscrossed Ohio and Pennsylvania, which were then the center of American manufacturing. Traveling from town to town by train, she gave speeches and tried to learn more about workers' lives. In Elyria, Ohio, she visited a glass factory, where she "saw workers blow electric bulbs at the end of long glass tubes." She toured the Homestead Steel Works, the scene of a "grim battle" fifteen years earlier between Andrew Carnegie and his workers. After signing a release, Flynn entered "an inferno" with "crashing noises" and incredible heat. She saw "sweating toilers, some stripped to the waist attending great furnaces and cauldrons." At the Heinz factory, she watched "girl packers" churning out jars of ketchup and pickles. Their fingers "moved so fast . . . along the belt-line, you could hardly see them." Flynn contrasted the cleanliness and efficiency of the Heinz factory with the miserable hotels where the workers lived. The company's delivery horses seemed to be fed and housed more carefully than its workers. Observed firsthand, these details helped Flynn relate the conditions of American workers to the social theories she had been studying since she had come of age.[19]

Flynn returned home to the Bronx with a new sense of independence. To her surprise, the IWW paid her two weeks' salary, which amounted to $36—$20 of which went to pay her family's rent. After traveling out west by herself, she found life back home "singularly dull." Flynn agreed to "agitate" for the IWW on the Mesabi Range in Minnesota, iron-ore country controlled by US Steel. Against the advice of her parents and teachers, she dropped out of high school—a decision she later regretted. Speaking in mining towns on the range, clad in a red dress, Flynn encountered "basic industry in the raw, in a rough and wild country." "Socialistic fervor" seemed to emanate from her "expressive eyes," according to one reporter.[20] Flynn became more intimately acquainted with the details of workers' lives by staying in their homes while she traveled. When she met Jack Jones, a dashing blue-eyed miner in his early thirties who was also working as an organizer for the IWW, romance ensued. Vincent St. John, who became a close friend, joked, "Elizabeth fell in love with the west and the miners and she married the first one she met." In retrospect, Flynn considered her hasty marriage a mistake.

Flynn, who retained her maiden name, returned home from the Mesabi Range, broke, with her new husband in tow. The couple arrived at her family's apartment in the Bronx with "suitcases full of dirty clothes." Elizabeth's mother was furious that Jones had married her teenage daughter without first consulting her parents. She feared that Elizabeth would become the mother of a large, poor family. The atmosphere in the Flynn family apartment grew even more tense when Elizabeth admitted she was pregnant. Her father, who was working as an engineer, helped Jack find a job, but both men were fired for agitating for the IWW. Elizabeth recalled that "it was bad enough" for her mother "to have one man around the house out of work, spouting ideas and reading books, while she toiled to keep our small crowded quarters clean and make ends meet—but to have two of them was just too much."[21]

Elizabeth and Jack headed back out to Chicago, where Jones found a job shoveling coal. Money was tight. They moved into a tenement apartment shared by a group of male IWW organizers living on the North Side. Vincent St. John and his wife lived nearby. Jack spent his free time painting enormous, brightly colored diagrams outlining how the industrial unionism of the IWW would reorganize society. Elizabeth's housemates managed to get her a glass of milk to drink and an egg to eat each day. Jack's father had been an alcoholic, and Jack refused to touch the stuff, but Flynn's friends took her along with them for the free lunch offered at the local saloon. Despite this camaraderie, she must have missed her family when tragedy struck. She gave birth prematurely to a baby boy who did not survive the night. Flynn's housemates blamed her early labor on Jack: the smell of paint and turpentine permeated the apartment. The baby's death drove a wedge between the couple. Depressed and in debt to the "the landlady, the doctor, and the undertaker," Elizabeth was relieved when Vincent St. John booked her on a western speaking tour for the IWW.[22]

Flynn attempted to repair her relationship with Jones by meeting him in Missoula, Montana, where St. John had sent Jones to drum up support for the IWW.[23] However, events in Missoula soon overshadowed Flynn's concerns about her personal life. Arriving in September 1909, she led the first of at least twenty-five fights that the Wobblies waged in defense of their right to free speech.[24] The Wobblies needed to be able to speak freely on city streets in order to pursue their goal of "direct action," an organizing technique built around public protest. In Missoula, Jones, Flynn, and other agitators drew crowds of lumberjacks and miners by criticizing the practices of local labor contractors, who collected fees from transient workers without providing them with steady jobs. The contractors complained to city authorities, as did local shopkeepers, who feared that the Wobblies were driving away business. The city invoked an ordinance preventing the disturbance of the "peace and quiet of any street." When the Wobblies refused to stop speaking in public, they were arrested and put in jail.

Drawing on her debate-team drilling in the Constitution and the Bill of Rights, Flynn charged the City of Missoula with violating the Wobblies' right to free speech. After the first wave of arrests, which included Jones, along with Frank Little, an impassioned IWW organizer of Native American and white descent, Flynn sent a telegram to IWW headquarters in Spokane, Washington, calling for reinforcements.[25] The Spokane IWW urged members to "go to Missoula and, if necessary, be arrested for the crime of speaking on the street."[26] Wobblies streamed into town, and "as soon as one speaker was arrested, another took his place." Flynn spearheaded a protest that spread beyond its local origins and took root in Spokane.

The conflict between the IWW and the Missoula authorities heated up as the population of "foot-loose rebels" grew and the jails filled to capacity. About one hundred men were arrested, and seventy at a time were jailed. The IWW used songs as a form of protest. Prisoners sang "revolutionary airs" day and night, keeping the guests at the city's main hotel across the street awake and disturbing the proceedings in the nearby courthouse. The hubbub only increased when the fire chief turned the hose on the protesters, who refused to disperse. Several people were injured in the melee, and college professors from the University of Montana began joining the fight. Flynn spread the IWW gatherings throughout the city. She was savvy enough to time the protests so that the men who were arrested had to be fed dinner in jail. Men released in the morning refused to leave without first eating breakfast. They demanded jury trials, which prolonged the proceedings and added to the city's expense.[27]

On Sunday evening, October 3, Missoula police arrested Elizabeth Gurley Flynn while she was leading an open-air meeting. Everyone in town knew that she was the force behind the fight, but police had been reluctant to go after this innocent-looking nineteen-year-old girl. One local reporter described Flynn as "a woman of considerable power as a speaker and of unquestioned courage when engaged in the work of her organization." Yet another characterized her as an "arch disturber, organizer, and leader of the Industrial Workers of the World," who had incited chaos in Missoula.[28] The sheriff treated Flynn "with kid gloves," even though he had beaten up her husband while he was in jail and treated the other men roughly. After Flynn's arrest, the Butte Miner's Union passed a resolution describing Missoula's crackdown on the Wobblies as "un-American and un-just." Flynn's case was quietly dismissed.[29]

After several weeks of disorder, mounting costs, and negative publicity, the town of Missoula got tired of fighting Flynn and the Wobblies. They released all the prisoners, dropped the pending cases, and accepted the right of the Wobblies to make speeches and recruit members on city streets. Ironically, lack of censure sapped some of the interest in what the IWW had to say. Nonetheless, Flynn and the IWW regarded the free-speech fight in Missoula as a victory. It affirmed their right to protest and drew attention to the organization. Over the next few years, the IWW used similar tactics in more than two dozen different battles in places such as Spokane, Denver, San Diego, and Kansas City, Missouri.[30] The strategy of using peaceful protest to provoke arrest anticipated the civil rights struggles of the 1950s and 1960s. However, these early victories may have given the IWW's leaders a false confidence in their ability to triumph over the forces of law and order. During World War I, Flynn and other IWW organizers learned that it was one thing to overwhelm the authorities in a small town like Missoula, and quite another to set their improvisational organization against the juggernaut of the federal government.

Fresh from leading the IWW to victory in Missoula, Flynn set out for Spokane, the central city in an inland empire of logging, mining, and agricultural work, where transient workers gathered to find jobs. Flynn arrived in December 1909, visibly pregnant, much to the dismay of the all-male committee coordinating the protest. In those days, pregnant women generally tried not to appear in public. Flynn viewed the shame associated with sex and pregnancy for women as silly and old-fashioned, but she respected the feelings of the more traditional men with whom she worked. She agreed not to speak at open-air street meetings, where she was most exposed and most likely to be arrested. Instead, she limited her appearances to the IWW hall, which was "situated in the heart of skid row, surrounded by cheap flop houses and employment agencies." The Spokane IWW had about 3,000 members (just half of whom paid dues), and the IWW hall served as a social center as well as an organizing hub for migrant workers.[31]

In Spokane, as in Missoula, the IWW targeted employment agencies, known as "sharks," that charged workers high fees without offering them steady jobs. The "sharks" struck back by winning a city ordinance prohibiting street meetings. As in Missoula, the IWW protesters insisted on their right to free speech. Wobblies poured into town to join the fight. Trying to remain useful while avoiding too many public appearances in Spokane, Flynn traveled to Seattle and to mining towns in Idaho and Montana to raise money to defend arrested workers. In later years, she would continue to defend workers who were arrested because of their political beliefs. As Flynn's pregnancy advanced, and it became more difficult for her to travel, she took over as editor for the local IWW paper, the *Industrial Worker*, which reached a broad working-class readership in Spokane and the surrounding area. The previous five editors had been put in jail.

Despite Flynn's caution, she was arrested as Spokane city authorities tried desperately to deaden the protest. The police charged her and six other IWW leaders with "conspiracy to incite men to violate the law." Conspiracy charges were far more serious than violating a city ordinance: conspiracy was a state felony punishable by a minimum of two years in the state penitentiary. The use of conspiracy in this case foreshadowed state and federal use of the charges to crush the IWW during World War I. Pending her trial, Flynn was jailed for just a night, as described at the start of this chapter. Free on bail, she wrote an account of the incident for the *Industrial Worker* that shamed the city. Flynn's sensational story was reprinted in newspapers across the country, and letters of protest poured into Spokane. The local women's club demanded that a woman be hired to oversee the female prisoners in Spokane. Equally important, Flynn's story of her arrest and imprisonment drew public attention to the official use of violence to thwart the IWW.

The circus-like atmosphere of mass arrest in Missoula took on a much darker cast in Spokane. From November 1909 until March 1910, more than four hundred men were charged with violating the city ordinance against public speaking. Flynn found her time in jail insulting, but male Wobblies were subject to much more serious abuse. A judge who was often drunk sentenced nearly all of the men to thirty days in prison and a $100 fine. Once in the hands of the law, treatment of the men verged on torture. Police who arrested Wobblies often beat them, threatened to kill them, and stole whatever money they were carrying. Jailers then packed as many prisoners as they could fit into a "sweat box," a room of about six by eight feet fed by a steam pipe. The heat was so intense that men would take off their clothes. After about fifteen hours, they would dump the men into "an ice-cold cell" without beds or blankets. The next day, the prisoners were brought out to a country schoolhouse that had been repurposed as a prison and assigned to chain gangs. They were fed on bread and water. Some would be repeatedly awakened during the night and beaten in the darkness. IWW prisoners suffered head injuries and broken limbs. After a month, most were nearly starving, and some broke down mentally under the strain.[32] As brutally as they were treated, IWW prisoners followed their own code of conduct and looked out for each other. Wobblies who had been in prison together felt a sense of kinship that strengthened their commitment to the IWW.[33]

Bearing witness to Spokane's sadistic treatment of the men who were arrested for speaking on the streets taught Flynn to view the state as an enemy rather than an ally to workers in a capitalist society.[34] When intimidation failed, police raided the offices of the *Industrial Worker*, seized copies of the paper, and arrested everyone who sold it, even newsboys.[35] These experiences strengthened Flynn's belief in the necessity for socialist revolution. Even though she appreciated the support of progressive reformers, who rallied behind the IWW in its fight for free speech in Missoula and in Spokane, Flynn fundamentally disagreed with their belief that state power could be used to press employers to treat their workers more humanely. In Spokane, the ugly truth seemed to be that local authorities supported the rights of businessmen and property owners at the expense of migrant workers, who possessed only as much power as they could muster collectively. The ballot meant little to these transient workers, since they seldom stayed anyplace long enough to vote.

Even though male leaders of the IWW in Spokane tried to keep Flynn out of the spotlight, she quickly became a cause célèbre. The press followed her activities, and her presence in Spokane drew national attention. After Flynn's arrest, a local lawyer advised the prosecutor to release Flynn because she seemed likely to mount such a devastating defense. "Hell, no!" the prosecutor replied. "She's the one we are after. . . . She puts the fight into the men."[36] As the city's resources wore thin, authorities dismissed all of the cases save two: Flynn's and that of an Italian-born organizer named Charley Filigno.[37] At this time, native-born white Americans directed considerable prejudice against Italian immigrants. Many Italians carried anarchist and syndicalist beliefs with them from Italy to the United States, and Italians made up an important part of the IWW.[38]

Flynn had spent weeks raising money for labor defense. Now some of those funds went to hire a defense lawyer for her and Filigno. In Missoula, Flynn had insisted that Wobblies defend themselves by invoking their constitutional right to free speech rather than hiring a lawyer to defend them. As Flynn explained, "it is only the exceptional lawyer that doesn't apologize for revolutionists and attempt to explain away all the vital issues they represent."[39] However, the seriousness of the charges leveled against her and Filigno led Flynn to relent and hire a professional. She let her attorney give the opening statement, but she then grew impatient during the two-week trial. She took the stand to defend Filigno, fearing that her coconspirator—a male immigrant—would take the blame for a battle that she in fact had led. Flynn's fears came to pass when she was acquitted and Filigno was found guilty. Incensed with the all-male jury's verdict, the prosecutor followed the foreman out of the courtroom and into the hallway. "What in the hell do you fellows mean by acquitting the most guilty, and convicting the man, far less guilty?" the prosecutor asked. The foreman's answer spoke volumes to Flynn's charm and to popular ideas about the innocence of white womanhood: "If you think this jury, or any jury, is goin' to send that pretty Irish girl to jail merely for bein' big-hearted and idealistic, to mix with all those whores and crooks down at the pen, you've got another guess comin'."[40]

Flynn's acquittal marked the end of the IWW's free-speech battle in Spokane. As in Missoula, officials in Spokane buckled under the pressure of negative publicity and unwelcome taxpayer expense. The mayor agreed to stop enforcing the city ordinance against speeches on the street if the IWW would stop calling in outside agitators. Broke and exhausted, IWW leaders complied. They had won a "practical victory." The mayor agreed to "allow the IWW to open up their hall and hold street meetings." To Flynn's relief, "all prisoners," including Filigno, "were released and pending cases dropped."[41] According to IWW leader Bill Haywood, the free-speech fight that began in Missoula and Spokane contributed greatly to the growth of the IWW by exciting "the imagination of the working class throughout the country."[42]

The conclusion to the IWW's battle for free speech in Spokane in April 1910 came just in time for Flynn. Her baby was due in a few weeks, and she had to decide whether to return to her husband, Jack Jones, who had not visited her while she was working in Spokane. Jones wanted Flynn to move to Butte, Montana, where he could work in the mines and she could settle down and become a conventional wife and mother. He assumed that she would give up her work as an IWW agitator once the baby was born. His plans had absolutely no appeal to Flynn. As she recalled, "I wanted to speak and write, to travel, to meet people, to see places, to organize for the IWW." The victories Flynn had helped to win in Missoula and Spokane had shown her that she could make a meaningful contribution to the labor movement. True to her feminist beliefs, she "saw no reason" why she, "as a woman, should give up [her] work for his." Flynn decided to go home to her mother, who had encouraged her to "be somebody." During her five-day trip, Flynn switched trains in Chicago, where Vincent St. John came to meet her for a brief visit. St. John seemed unsurprised by Flynn's decision to leave Jones—but he was concerned that she make it home before she went into labor.[43]

Flynn's entire family showed up to greet her at Grand Central Station in New York City. She never regretted her decision to return home. Although it would not be easy to be a single mother, she had the support of her family, all of whom admired her growing reputation as a Wobbly leader. Elizabeth's mother and her sister Kathie would care for her son, Fred Flynn, who was born on May 19, 1910. With her family's support, Elizabeth was able to continue her work in the labor movement, but she had to make compromises. As her friend Mary Heaton Vorse later remarked, Flynn's marriage to Jack Jones did not change her, but motherhood did. As married men like Haywood and St. John traveled to Europe to learn more about syndicalism firsthand, Flynn settled into a new life in which she had to balance care for her son with her ambition to ignite a socialist revolution in the United States.

3

Building Solidarity with the IWW— Landmark Strikes

After giving birth to her son, Fred, Elizabeth Gurley Flynn escaped the oppressive heat of her Bronx apartment to spend an idyllic summer on Caritas Island, the summer retreat of the Stokes family off the coast of Connecticut. The invitation to Caritas came from Flynn's friend Rose Pastor Stokes, a working-class Jewish immigrant, who was married to James Phelps Stokes, a wealthy socialist. Flynn spent her days reading "outdoors in the sun" and nursing her son. Visitors to Caritas included socialists, writers, poets, Flynn's mother, and her sister Kathie, who came to help with the baby. Once Elizabeth returned to New York City, she decided to wean Fred so that she could return to work. Her father was unemployed and her family was desperate for cash. By October, Vincent St. John had found her a part-time job helping to lead a strike of Brooklyn shoe workers. Before long, she was traveling to speak on behalf of the IWW, leaving her son in her mother and sister's care.

Flynn had rejected her husband's suggestion that she settle down and become a conventional wife and mother. Instead, she stayed true to her dream of serving the labor movement and working to bring

Shortly after the birth of her son, Fred (nicknamed "Buster"), Flynn took a vacation on Caritas Island with her sister Kathie and their mother, Annie (1910).

NP18-80, EGF Photographs, Tamiment Library, NYU

socialism to America. In groundbreaking strikes in Lawrence, Massachusetts, and Paterson, New Jersey, Flynn inspired thousands of workers with her vision of solidarity. In both conflicts, she gave voice to the aspirations of immigrant workers who sought a better life for themselves and their families in the United States, but found harsh conditions, low pay, and lack of respect.

As the leading female IWW agitator, Flynn sought to build on an upsurge of interest in labor organization among wage-earning women that followed the "Uprising of the 20,000," a massive strike of female shirtwaist makers in New York City from November 1909 to February 1910. The immigrant Jewish women who made up most of the strikers displayed remarkable militancy and commitment to becoming union members. However, the AFL remained lukewarm toward organizing women. Frustrated by the sexism of the AFL, many of the working-class women who led the Uprising of the 20,000 went to work for the Women's Trade Union League (WTUL), a cross-class group of women dedicated to increasing women's representation in the labor movement. The WTUL became the most significant women's labor organization in the nation in the early twentieth century, establishing branches in New York, Boston, Chicago, and several other cities. However, immigrant Italian workers had less affinity for the WTUL than Jewish or US-born female workers; their experience with direct action in Italy made them more receptive to the IWW.[1]

Flynn had no interest in the WTUL. It drew on cross-class alliances and tried to affiliate the women it organized with the AFL. Flynn insisted that workers must organize as a class. Sex differences should be overcome through organization rather than institutionalized within a separate women's labor movement.[2] Aiming directly at the female reformers who supported the WTUL, Flynn pronounced "the sisterhood of woman, like the brotherhood of capitalism and labor," to be "a hollow sham."[3] This statement fit within the IWW strategy of heightening class conflict in order to bring about revolution. However, this rhetoric also obscured the cross-class friendships that Flynn developed in the 1910s, and it discounted the value of allies whose funds and political support helped the IWW achieve some important victories.

In 1910, Flynn sensed an opportunity to bring female factory workers into the IWW, which focused on groups of workers that the AFL had either ignored or disappointed. In speech after speech, she painted the struggles of wage-earning women in radical, socialist terms. Flynn went beyond "bread-and-butter" issues such as wages and hours to include more sweeping proposals to foster women's freedom. Flouting prohibitions against public discussion of sexuality, Flynn insisted that women needed access to birth control in order to time the arrival of their children and limit the size of their families. She insisted on women's "right to <u>choose</u> motherhood."[4] The amorphous nature of the IWW made room for a host of radical proposals. Vincent St. John and other IWW leaders gave Flynn free rein to articulate the IWW's position on women's issues. Bill Haywood, who remained one of the most important figures in the IWW, echoed Flynn's support for birth control.

The IWW's dream of overcoming the divisions of sex, skill, and nationality to build working-class solidarity came closest to fulfillment in the famous "bread-and-roses" strike in Lawrence, Massachusetts, a center of wool cloth production. On January 1, 1912, a new law went into effect in Massachusetts reducing women's working hours from fifty-six to fifty-four a week. This legislation seemed to be a victory for reformers, who advocated shorter working hours for women in industry, but employers cut women's pay in proportion to their reduced hours. In one Lawrence factory, Polish women who ripped open their pay envelopes shouted, "Short pay!" In another, Italian women led a massive walkout. Within days, 10,000 workers were on strike, nearly all of them immigrants. Italians made up the largest portion of an incredibly diverse group that included Syrians, Russians, Armenians, Turks, Belgians, Austrians, Irish, and English workers.

Italian workers in Lawrence had established a small IWW local in 1910. When the strike began, the national organization sent one of the IWW's most talented organizers, Joe Ettor, who had been one of Flynn's housemates when she had lived in Chicago. He had also worked with Flynn on the Brooklyn shoemaker's strike. Ettor crafted an innovative and effective strike committee composed of workers of at least twenty-five different nationalities. Arturo Giovannitti, an Italian syndicalist editor and poet known for his powerful voice and "mystical intensity," soon joined Ettor.[5] Their efforts built on local networks of mutual aid among immigrant communities.[6] The size of the crowds and their status as immigrants antagonized the local authorities. Police met strikers waving American flags with bayonets. The mayor called in the state militia, and the militiamen arrived on horseback, injuring and intimidating many of the demonstrators. Almost from day one, the strikers found themselves engaged in constant clashes with the authorities. When a young female striker named Anna Lo Pizzo was killed during a demonstration, the police arrested Ettor and Giovannitti and charged them with inciting violence. The action outraged the workers, who clamored for justice from their employers and their new country.

Elizabeth Gurley Flynn and Big Bill Haywood took over the leadership of the strike after Ettor and Giovannitti's arrest. Twenty-one-year-old Flynn felt intimidated at first by Haywood, whom she considered a "heroic giant of the American working class." He had helped establish the IWW and had recently returned from Europe, where he had attended the Second International Socialist Congress. However, Haywood's experience had been almost exclusively in the western United States among working men. Flynn wondered if he would be able to reach the workers in Lawrence, at least half of whom were women. He succeeded splendidly. Flynn and Haywood became a force to be reckoned with. Flynn recalled, "We talked Marxism as we understood it—the class struggle, the exploitation of labor, the use of the state and armed forces of government against the workers. It was all there in Lawrence. . . . [W]e did not need to go far for the lessons."[7]

Haywood's powerful speaking style impressed Flynn; it was "like a sledge-hammer blow, simple and direct."[8] She admired how Haywood spoke to the workers in simple English, using words they knew from their children. Explaining the difference between the AFL and the IWW, he illustrated with his hand: spreading his fingers apart, he declared, "The AFL organizes like this!" showing the separation of the various groups of workers. "Weavers, loom-fixers, dyers, spinners." He then showed the IWW's approach to organization by clenching his big hand into a fist and shaking it: together, all workers had the power to fight their bosses.[9] Shedding the persona of the precocious schoolgirl, Flynn followed Haywood's example and began "to use short words and short sentences."[10] She continued to punctuate her presentations with dramatic hand gestures and to establish an almost electric link with her audience.

Flynn credited Haywood with teaching her how to speak to workers, but those who saw Flynn speak in Lawrence considered her a strong force in her own right. She remained slim and beautiful. Although she dressed more maturely now, in a dark dress or a white blouse and dark skirt, with her hair pinned up, her appearance was little changed from the "girl socialist" who first gained public attention in 1906. Mary Heaton Vorse, a popular journalist, described Flynn as "the picture of a youthful revolutionary girl leader." Vorse found Flynn's ability to inspire workers remarkable. Sitting in on a strike meeting, Vorse felt as though "something beautiful and strong had swept through the people and welded them together."[11] Vorse was one of many outside observers radicalized by what she saw in Lawrence.[12] Although Vorse came from a privileged background, she developed a radical consciousness, and she and Flynn became good friends.

Flynn and Haywood built solidarity in Lawrence by organizing special meetings for women. Haywood had cut his teeth with the Western Federation of Miners, a union that won tough strikes in isolated areas by building strong networks of family and community support. Flynn worked to keep women in sympathy with the strike by articulating the special challenges they faced as workers. Many became pregnant while working in the mills. They stood at their looms until their labor pains began, miscarried from the strain, or sought dangerous illegal abortions. They had little time to rest once their children were born. Eager to get back to work in order to feed their families, they left their undernourished infants in day nurseries. Nearly one-third of the babies born to female factory workers died during the first month. To Flynn, these cold facts of life spoke to "the ruthless invasion of family life by capitalism." In the socialist future projected by the IWW, women who became mothers could choose to remain at work or to stay home and care for their children. "The free choice of work is the IWW ideal," Flynn explained, for women as well as men.[13]

Flynn focused her speeches on the gap between immigrant women's dreams of finding prosperity in the United States and their actual conditions, which entailed long hours at the factory with barely enough money to afford food and clothing. They hoped for a better life for their children, but had little choice but to yank them out of school by the age of fourteen—or even younger—so that they could earn wages to help support their families. Working families paid high rent for shabby, cramped apartments. Although they worked in factories that churned out endless yards of fine wool, the women could not afford to buy coats for themselves or their children. Workers, not mill owners, supported local businesses, Flynn argued. If workers were paid more, they would spend more. Flynn urged female strikers to bring this message to local merchants in order to build broader community support for the strike.

Living among the Lawrence strikers, Flynn watched women face off against employers, the police, and even male relatives who did not want them "going to meetings and marching on the picket line."[14] Flynn became convinced that women could be either the most radical or the most conservative force in a strike depending on what they felt their families had to gain or lose. She watched as women moved to the front of parades, speeches, and demonstrations. Reflecting on her experiences in Lawrence, Flynn remarked, "The IWW has been accused of putting women in the front. The truth is rather that the IWW does not keep them to the back <u>and they go to the front</u>."[15]

Because of the duration of the strike, Flynn's mother joined her in Lawrence with two-year-old Fred, now nicknamed Buster. As Flynn recalled, her mother would take the boy to the park, "while a few blocks away a violent fracas occurred." However, Buster "was fat and healthy and did not seem to mind." Flynn, who had been traveling almost constantly since a few months after her son's birth, "was happy to see him daily."[16] As a mother, she gained insight into the difficult struggles that working-class mothers in Lawrence faced as they attempted to participate in labor actions, care for their children, and feed their families on very limited budgets.

Flynn became instrumental in the "Children's Crusade," a brilliant strategy of sending strikers' children out of Lawrence to be cared for by sympathetic families in other cities. The IWW adapted this tactic from European strikes. Flynn organized the convoys of children and vetted the host families with the help of Margaret Sanger, a socialist nurse practitioner who became a leader of the birth-control movement. On February 17, 1912, the first group of 150 children arrived in New York City. Their arrival generated intense publicity. Nearly 5,000 people turned up to meet their train at Grand Central Station. The malnourished, poorly dressed children created a sensation when they paraded up Fifth Avenue holding signs that read, "A Little Child Shall Lead Them," and "Someday We Will Remember this Exile." Host families rushed to buy the children hair ribbons, suits, new shoes, and toys to bring home.[17]

Nationwide sympathy for the children taken out of Lawrence outraged town officials. On February 22, the town passed an ordinance forbidding the removal of any more children, and two days later, the police pounced on a group of fifty children waiting with their mothers at the train station to travel to Philadelphia. Women were shoved and clubbed and bayonets extended to prevent children from boarding the train.[18] According to Flynn, the incident "shook America," and public opinion began to swing decisively behind the strikers. By humanizing the conflict through the Children's Crusade, Flynn helped the strikers win a moral victory. Despite her revolutionary rhetoric, Flynn learned to recognize the practical value of building cross-class alliances. Broad public support for the strike helped generate funds and put pressure on the manufacturers to settle with the workers.

Working in tandem with Haywood, Flynn helped the striking workers to remain united through two months of bitter conflict. On March 12, 1912, the American Woolen Company, the largest of Lawrence's wool manufacturers, agreed to the demands of the strikers: an across-the-board raise of 5 to 25 percent, with the lowest-paid workers receiving the largest increase. The company also agreed to pay workers time and a quarter for overtime and promised not to fire anyone who had joined the strike. Other companies soon followed. In his victory speech, Haywood told the Lawrence workers, "You have demonstrated, as has been shown nowhere else, the common interest of the working class in bringing all nationalities together."[19] Historians consider the Lawrence strike to be the IWW's finest moment. However, they also note that immigrant workers in Lawrence may have appreciated the IWW's help in winning their strike without accepting its revolutionary socialist message.[20]

In Lawrence, the IWW showed that it could organize a remarkably diverse group of workers. It had less success, however, with keeping those workers as dues-paying members. As Flynn later admitted, "Most of us were wonderful agitators but poor union organizers." This failure to establish a lasting organization was due in part to the principles of the IWW itself: the organization insisted on leadership from the bottom up and refused to squash the free expression of any of its members. Thus, when someone unfurled an anarchist banner at a parade in defense of Ettor and Giovannitti, who both remained in prison awaiting trial after the strike ended, neither Flynn nor any of the other IWW leaders had the authority to pull it. Most Americans associated anarchism with violence, and the incident unleashed a backlash against the IWW in Lawrence.[21] On a national level, the IWW suffered from infighting and struggled to maintain stability and remain solvent.[22] The history of the IWW demonstrates some of the organizational challenges that can be inherent in balancing grassroots activism with effective leadership.

Flynn remained in Lawrence through the summer of 1912 to work for the acquittals of Ettor and Giovannitti. A strong community of radical Italian immigrants rallied to their defense, bringing Flynn into a fateful meeting with Carlo Tresca.[23] Born in 1879 to an aristocratic family in Central Italy that had lost its money, Tresca became a radical newspaper editor in his twenties. At various points in his career, he described himself as a socialist, a syndicalist, and an anarchist, but he never fit neatly into any single category. Tresca migrated to the United States in 1904 to escape prosecution for libel after he published stories critical of local politicians in his hometown of Sulmona. Living first in Philadelphia, then in Pittsburgh, Tresca

Carlo Tresca around the time that Flynn fell in love with him (c. 1912).

NP18-120, EGF Photographs, Tamiment Library, NYU

gravitated to the IWW and became an important leader among radical Italian workers.[24]

Flynn remembered Tresca in 1912 as "a tall, slender handsome man in his mid-thirties" with blue eyes and light brown hair. He attacked tyranny of all types in his Italian-language newspaper, *L'Avvenire* (The Future), from the *padrone* system of labor contracting to the abuses of the Roman Catholic Church. Tresca made enemies as easily as friends. A beard covered a scar on his cheek from being knifed. Tresca did not yet speak much English, but Flynn found him "very resourceful, a good strategist," and "an eloquent and dynamic speaker." Defying a police ban, Tresca organized a funeral march for Anna Lo Pizzo. He brought 10,000 workers onto the Lawrence common to pledge to strike again if Ettor and Giovannitti were convicted. The two men were acquitted in November 1912 and released from prison, completing the IWW's victory in Lawrence.[25]

Flynn and Tresca fell madly in love while working together in Lawrence and they were soon inseparable. Tresca presented Flynn with a copy of his favorite novel, writing in the front of the book, "One heart has the same flame for you alone." Beneath it, Flynn later wrote, "I always remember. And you? Carlo? How soon you forgot."[26] Tresca's appeal to women was legendary, and Flynn turned out to be just one of his many lovers.[27] She had her share of romantic liaisons, too, but she seems to have been faithful to Tresca while they were a couple. Tresca held a special place in Flynn's heart even after they parted. In her small diary, Flynn scribbled, "I wonder if I can ever infuse another love with the same blind, passionate devotion. . . . I hope not."[28]

Tresca moved in with Flynn and her family toward the end of 1912. Despite their cramped quarters in the Bronx, Tresca charmed the Flynn family with his gregarious personality and his excellent cooking skills. He became like a father to Buster.[29] Flynn had created an unconventional but loving family. Both she and Tresca remained legally married to other people, but they lived and worked together until 1925. As Flynn later explained, "This was according to our code at the time—not to remain with someone you did not love, but to honestly and openly avow a real attachment."[30] Flynn's personal choices reflected her political views: women and men should not be bound by marriage, which trapped couples in deadening relationships. True to her feminist views, Flynn never relied on Tresca financially.[31]

Flynn and Tresca soon charged into their next battle: the organization of hotel and restaurant workers in New York City. In the winter of 1913, 6,000 culinary workers went on strike as part of a decades-long battle to establish a union that would include all of the workers in their industry. The workers were an ethnically varied group, hailing from Italy, France, Germany, and Greece. Ettor and Giovannitti stepped in, as did Haywood, Tresca, and Flynn. Thus, the principal leaders of Lawrence reunited in January 1913 to organize service workers seeking shorter hours and higher pay. Chefs, waiters, and kitchen workers held their strike meetings downstairs in Bryant Hall on Sixth Avenue and 42nd Street. "Upstairs," Flynn recalled, "rehearsals were going on of Broadway shows . . . with choruses of beautiful singing and dancing girls." Flynn found it "a lively atmosphere, quite different from austere New England."[32]

Flynn's celebrity status increased during the strike. The *New York Times* described her as "the power behind the hotel workers," and the *New York World* dubbed her "the girl captain" leading a host of men.[33] Flynn did, in fact, run the strike for the IWW, articulating concrete demands, such as an abolition of tips in favor of higher weekly wages and an eight-hour day.[34] To Flynn's embarrassment, her affair with Tresca became public. During a scuffle with police, an inscribed book of poems that Flynn had given Tresca dropped out of his vest pocket. The next day, the papers were filled with pictures of the attractive couple and tales of this "IWW romance." Flynn was mortified, "but the mighty chefs and cosmopolitan waiters thought nothing of it" and considered it good publicity for their cause.

Flynn and Tresca helped the striking workers generate further publicity through creative techniques characteristic of the IWW. Picket lines of cooks wearing top hats and carrying canes encircled the city's most elegant hotels. Well-dressed sympathizers went out for dinner, then blew their whistles at an appointed time, signaling the cooks and waiters to walk out.[35] Flynn gathered testimony from restaurant workers on common but unappetizing practices such as reusing napkins and serving soup that had been simmering for weeks.[36] However, the strike lost public support when it became violent. When the Knickerbocker Hotel on Broadway and 42nd Street dismissed striking workers, Tresca led a procession of 2,000 strikers, and some of them broke the hotel's windows with rocks and umbrellas.[37] Hotels hired private security forces to protect their guests and intimidate the strikers. The strike collapsed, and the AFL jockeyed to take control of the union.[38] The magic of Lawrence would be difficult to re-create even with a glamorous couple like Flynn and Tresca at the helm.

In February 1913, workers who made silk cloth in Paterson, New Jersey, launched a protest that quickly became the IWW's next major battle. Flynn described the dramatic work stoppage: "Knotted color-stained hands came out of the dye boxes, women's slender hands turned away from the looms, children's little hands ceased to wind silk, and the mills were dead." An estimated 25,000 workers joined the strike. They rejected manufacturers' attempts to increase the number of looms they tended and demanded an eight-hour day. As in Lawrence, a diverse group of immigrant workers, many of them women, suffered from low pay, poor housing, and an inability to purchase any of the beautiful goods they produced. Again, Flynn and Haywood held special meetings of women focusing on their roles as workers, mothers, and consumers. They sought to translate the workers' material concerns into the IWW's vision for socialist revolution.[39]

In a popular pamphlet, Flynn advocated "sabotage" as a tool for workers to use in their ongoing struggle with employers. She defined sabotage as "the conscious withdrawal of the workers' industrial efficiency." Workers could slow down, produce poor work, or reveal shoddy practices by manufacturers themselves, who often cut corners to save money.[40] The word had dangerous connotations, but Flynn described sabotage as nonviolent resistance used by disgruntled employees when they could not get their demands met through strikes. Far more violence was directed at the IWW than was perpetrated by members of the organization.[41] However, Flynn's use of the term "sabotage" was controversial and would later be invoked to prosecute the IWW.

Flynn speaking to strikers in Paterson, New Jersey (1913).
NP18-124, EGF Photographs, Tamiment Library, NYU

Flynn and Haywood found allies for their fight in Paterson among the bohemians who congregated in Greenwich Village. This group of writers, artists, and other creative types challenged the mores of middle-class American culture and sought more authentic forms of experience. Many considered themselves socialists. They began to take the train out to Paterson to see the Wobblies in action. Mabel Dodge, an heiress who held a weekly salon in her Lower Fifth Avenue apartment, found battle-scarred Wobblies thrilling. Flynn never liked Dodge, but Haywood became a fixture at her soirées. When Haywood complained about the difficulty the IWW had generating publicity for the strike, Dodge's lover, the journalist Jack Reed, came up with a novel idea: stage the story of the strike as a theatrical production at

Madison Square Garden to show the world what was happening in Paterson. Reed and other Greenwich Village radicals donated their time and talent hoping that the June 7 pageant would build public support for the strike and help the IWW raise badly needed funds.[42]

The Paterson Strike Pageant was a bold artistic experiment. Reed masterminded an epic production in which more than 1,000 workers reenacted the most dramatic moments of the strike against a huge hand-painted silk backdrop. Flynn, Tresca, and Haywood all delivered actual speeches they had given to the strikers. The evening concluded with the entire crowd singing "The Internationale," the socialist anthem of revolution. According to Flynn, the production "moved the great audience tremendously" and was hailed as "a new form of art." Unfortunately, the show diverted energy from the strike itself. In retrospect, Flynn considered it "detrimental to our real picket lines and meetings." More damaging still, the pageant proved to be a financial failure. The expenses of staging the one-night show were enormous and barely recouped through ticket sales. In hindsight, Flynn judged the pageant to be "disastrous to solidarity in the last days of a losing strike."[43]

The IWW leaders admitted defeat in Paterson in July 1913. Why had they failed to duplicate the victory they had won in Lawrence the year before? First, the town of Paterson had responded even more aggressively than Lawrence had to the IWW leaders, whom it characterized as "outside agitators." The police had arrested Flynn, Tresca, Haywood, and other strike leaders repeatedly and had also arrested at least 1,000 striking workers. The IWW had to spend a considerable amount of time and money bailing members out of jail and defending them in court. Second, many small firms produced silk in Paterson, making it more complicated for the IWW to negotiate a settlement on behalf of the workers. Third, sharper divisions existed in Paterson than in Lawrence between skilled, native-born workers and unskilled immigrants. After seven months, the skilled, native-born workers, most of whom worked making ribbon, decided to settle with their employers. They cut the unskilled workers out of the deal, leaving most of the strikers out of work or forced to return to work under the same conditions.[44]

Workers in Paterson would stage future strikes, winning an eight-hour day in 1919, but in 1913 the leaders of the IWW felt the sting of defeat. Haywood developed stomach ulcers and lost eighty pounds. He traveled to Europe to recover. Despite suffering from severe bronchitis, Flynn continued to visit Paterson and surrounding towns to speak on behalf of the IWW and the workers who remained in jail after the strike ended. She felt that it had been an error for the IWW leaders to leave Lawrence once the strike had ended, and she tried not to repeat the mistake. But she remained under indictment for inciting violence (a tactic frequently used to silence strike leaders) and often found herself blocked from speaking by local authorities. In the fall of 1915, she was finally tried on charges related to the strike. Greenwich Village radicals who supported the right to free speech rallied to her defense, demonstrating, in this case, the utility of cross-class allies.[45] To Flynn's relief, she was acquitted, and city authorities began allowing IWW meetings. Flynn considered this a small but significant victory in an otherwise depressing landscape of defeat.[46]

When the ordeal ended, Flynn and Tresca traveled by boat to Tampa, Florida, at the invitation of Ybor City cigar workers, a mixed group of Italian- and Spanish-speaking workers who wanted to meet the leaders of the Paterson strike. Although the struggle had been lost, the example of a broad-based group of workers pressing for economic justice inspired these radical workers. Flynn and Tresca spoke in the town square of Tampa on May Day. A picnic and a dance followed. Although Tampa cigar workers organized unions that included Cuban men and women of African descent, public spaces were segregated. Looking out beyond a fence encircling the park, Flynn "saw dark faces, lit with interest and eagerness to hear 'the IWW from the North.'" Flynn and Tresca went out to speak to the African American workers "and told them of the hundreds of Negro longshoremen who belonged to the IWW in Philadelphia and of the militant Negro dye workers we knew in the Paterson strike." Flynn was shocked by her first experience with segregation.[47] Although the IWW had an unwavering commitment to workers' equality regardless of sex, race, nationality, or skill, those factors could still divide workers. Flynn hated racism and she intensified her battle against it when she became a communist.

During the course of the Paterson strike and the free-speech battle that followed, Flynn got to know some of the radicals from Greenwich Village. She was especially impressed with the women, who, like her, were seeking to forge new, more modern identities. These women were the first Americans to call themselves feminists.[48] Henrietta Rodman, a schoolteacher, for example, protested against women being fired once they had children and led a campaign for teachers to receive equal pay for equal work. Rodman dressed unconventionally, wearing a loose shift dress rather than a restrictive shirtwaist. When Rodman married, she refused to change her name. In a similar vein, Mary Heaton Vorse, a journalist, and Crystal Eastman, an attorney, established professional identities and sought egalitarian relationships with men.

These women supported suffrage as part of a broader set of social changes designed to end women's dependence on men and give them a voice in public affairs. In 1913, Flynn found suffrage theoretically right, but practically wrong: it emphasized political action (which the IWW rejected), and she feared it would divide working-class women from working-class men. Once women gained the vote in 1920, however, Flynn recognized its importance in raising women's political consciousness.

After the Paterson strike, Flynn joined "Heterodoxy," an all-female club that met twice a month in the Village. As the club's name implied, the group demanded no single position, but encouraged frank discussion of women's status. After years spent working with men, Flynn found her time spent at Heterodoxy to be "a broadening experience." Plus, her inclusion in this group of illustrious women pleased her mother.[49] At Heterodoxy, Flynn pondered the differential in power between men and women. The ideas of "a brilliant woman" received a less-serious hearing than those of a "common-place man." Women earned less than men. Most women depended on their husbands for support and took sole responsibility for housework and child care. Regardless of their achievements, women's lives seemed to be defined by marriage, children, and home. Men seemed able to enjoy all of these things, yet could also stand apart from them as individuals. Conversations at Heterodoxy confirmed Flynn's beliefs that women deserved the right to control their own bodies, an idea that entailed sexual freedom and birth control. She also believed that women needed economic independence in order to become fully formed individuals.[50]

Flynn's vision of women's freedom differed, however, from that of most of her feminist contemporaries. Flynn insisted on the primacy of social class, and she saw capitalism as the central force in women's oppression. Thus, Flynn characterized feminists' calls for women to become economically independent by earning wages as misguided. Working-class women had no choice but to go out to work and they were miserably underpaid. In Flynn's eyes, their work amounted to slavery rather than freedom. Only the end of "wage slavery" and the establishment of socialism would create the potential for women, like men, to become free and independent. With the help of birth control and public support for bearing and raising children, women would be able to choose whatever occupation suited them. The full-time work of motherhood would become a choice rather than a vocation for all women.[51]

Flynn chose to work for her feminist goals through class-based organizations, an unconventional choice that has led some scholars to question her commitment to feminism.[52] However, she viewed women's emancipation as a central project of socialism. She envisioned socialism as producing "a free woman socially and sexually, a woman who thinks as she pleases, does as she pleases, works as she pleases, speaks as she pleases, and belongs to herself alone."[53] Flynn tried to live by this ideal. She imagined a future in which men and women would work together as equals and forge relationships based on mutual attraction rather than economic need. Together, men and women would create a new society free from the oppression of both sexism and capitalism. In 1914, however, the world lurched in a very different direction. World War I not only destroyed millions of lives, but also crushed the organization to which Flynn had devoted her youth.

4

The Question of Violence

On Saturday, September 29, 1917, a knock came at the door of Flynn's Bronx apartment. Her mother, Annie, opened it to find the neighborhood cop there, accompanied by two federal agents. The policeman knew the Flynns well. They proceeded to arrest Elizabeth, but the local officer apologized, assuring Annie that he had "nothing to do with it." As Elizabeth left the building, she passed her seven-year-old son, Buster, playing on the street. Alarmed at seeing his mother with the strange men, he ran up to her. Flynn must have felt panicked, but she told him calmly, "It's all right, dear, I have to go to a meeting. You go upstairs to Mama." The federal agents nabbed Flynn's lover, Carlo Tresca, on the platform of the elevated train station at 134th Street. The agents took Flynn and Tresca to the Lower Manhattan offices of the US Department of Justice. Both Flynn and Tresca had been arrested before, and they refused to answer questions without a lawyer. They were transferred to the New York City House of Detention known as the Tombs, a "massive structure" that "looked like a dungeon." Flynn spent the weekend on the women's side of the jail, "a damp, evil-smelling place" with "unspeakably awful food" and an "atmosphere dreary and full of human sorrow."[1]

Despite the general misery of the Tombs, Flynn hit it off with the Irish American matron, who appreciated Flynn's connection to Irish radicals and gave her copies of the Sunday papers. Flynn learned that she was the sole woman named in a federal indictment of 168 IWW leaders for "seditious conspiracy, a crime ranking next to treason." The assistant US attorney general described the IWW as "a degenerate organization" and promised that the nationwide arrests would help "to rid the country of traitors." The federal government accused IWW leaders of violating at least twenty-four laws and government acts, including President Woodrow Wilson's declaration of war, the Espionage Act, and "the registration and draft acts." Since entering the Great War (later known as World War I) in the spring of 1917, the federal government had acted aggressively to curb any group that might hinder the war effort. With the encouragement of employers in war-related industries, the government had identified the IWW as public enemy number one.[2]

To Flynn, the federal government's crackdown on the IWW proved once again that the state was in league with capitalists, who sought to stop the IWW from representing workers in their struggles for shorter hours, better wages, and decent working conditions. Flynn continued to believe that socialism was the only true solution to workers' demands for equitable treatment. But her relationship with the IWW had frayed since the beginning of the war. She struggled to come to terms with a rising tide of violence directed against the labor movement by employers and police and perpetrated, in some cases, by labor radicals who fought back. She found herself increasingly at odds with her friend Big Bill Haywood, who had become the head of the IWW in 1916, replacing Vincent St. John. Under the pressure of wartime repression, IWW leaders became divided over tactics: Should they continue to mix labor organization with socialism, or should they become a straight industrial union? Should they accept violence as a legitimate tool of class struggle, or should they repudiate it in order to separate themselves from anarchists, including some who "embraced violence as a tool for social transformation"?[3]

Even before war broke out in Europe, Flynn imagined herself as part of an epic battle between capital and labor. By 1914, she "had been in daily contact with workers and their struggles for eight years." She had seen "their honesty, modesty, decency, their devotion to their families and their unions." As a result, she "hated those who exploited them, patronized them, lied to them, cheated them and betrayed them." She felt as though she had "lived through a long period of ruthless, brutal force, of terror and violence against workers." Police, militia, judges, and armed guards all seemed to be at the beck and call of employers. Thus, she considered herself, like Karl Marx, to be "a mortal enemy of capitalism."[4] Seen from the distance of nearly a century, however, conflicts within the labor movement over how to respond to violence are equally clear.

Flynn's sense of an irreconcilable conflict between capital and labor was sharpened by the IWW's campaign among the unemployed. During the winter of 1913–1914, the economy suffered one of its frequent downturns. In this era before welfare or unemployment insurance, the government had no comprehensive plan to provide for unemployed workers or their families. Continuing its commitment to organize the most marginalized, the national IWW urged the creation of an "army of the unemployed" to support their search for jobs, food, and shelter. The IWW advocated a six-hour day to distribute jobs more evenly. Its leaders urged those who were out of work not to allow employers to use them to lower the wages and labor standards of existing workers. They hoped that the IWW's responsiveness to workers' material problems would reveal the failure of capitalism and further the cause of a revolution that would abolish capitalism and the government that supported it.

Flynn's brilliant campaign to remove the children from Lawrence had generated widespread public sympathy and support for the IWW. But many members of the general public felt threatened by large groups of unemployed men calling for "Bread or Revolution" in cities throughout the United States and Canada. Police in Los Angeles, Sacramento, and San Francisco broke up IWW-led protests of unemployed workers with billy clubs and arrested their leaders. In Detroit, where workers flocked, hoping to get jobs working for Ford at $5.00 a day, 8,000 unemployed men who gathered for a protest in front of an employment office in subzero weather on Lincoln's birthday were greeted by police "with drawn revolvers, wielding their clubs right and left." The IWW was one of the few secular organizations that gave hope to workers who felt they had been shut out of the blessings of prosperity.[5] The depressed economy threw women out of work, too, but they were less likely to leave their families in search of a job, or to join street protests, which often became violent. Thus, men became the most visible of the unemployed as they staked a public claim to their right to fulfill their traditional responsibilities as breadwinners.

In New York City, Flynn joined a group of IWW members who tried to help some 300,000 unemployed men during a bitterly cold winter in which "the snow never stopped falling." City employment bureaus found jobs shoveling snow for 3,646 men, but did little more. Men slept in doorways, and breadlines wound around city blocks. The IWW distributed coats and warm clothing to the needy. Echoing some of the theatrical tactics that IWW organizers had used in a waiters' strike the year before, they handed out tickets that promised the bearer a free meal charged to the Mayor's Committee on Unemployment. Hundreds dined for free at restaurants across the city before the prank was discovered.[6]

Flynn supported Frank Tannenbaum, a twenty-year-old bus boy and IWW member who staged marches of homeless men to city churches to demand shelter. At one church, the priest called the police, who arrested Tannenbaum and 190 homeless men who had hoped to sleep in his church for the night. The *New York Sun* argued that it was "better to club and shoot rioters" than to allow the IWW to continue to rile up "bands of idle men—some of them honest dupes, most of them vicious outcasts." Tannenbaum was sentenced to a year in prison for inciting a riot, although bystanders testified that he had asked his men to leave the church peacefully.[7]

When Tannenbaum and his "army" were arrested, Flynn jumped in to help coordinate their legal defense and to seek "truthful representation" of their cause in the press. Flynn was joined by a diverse group of radicals operating out of labor journalist Mary Heaton Vorse's brick house at 13 West 11th Street. Flynn and Vorse had met during the 1912 strike in Lawrence and had become good friends. Several other veterans of the IWW's battles in Lawrence and Paterson also signed on, including Bill Haywood, Arturo Giovannitti, and Carlo Tresca. The IWW members proved to be the moderates of the group. To the left stood anarchists such as Emma Goldman and her former lover,

Alexander Berkman, who was known for his botched assassination attempt on Henry Frick, the manager of Andrew Carnegie's Homestead Steel mill during the bitter strike of 1892. To the right stood the muckraking journalist Lincoln Steffens, who sought to expose social problems as the first step toward solving them. As Vorse recalled, the movement that formed around the unemployed "drew people to it as an arc light draws moths."[8] Anarchists, socialists, syndicalists, and liberals mingled together during this period in ways that would soon become impossible.

Neither Flynn nor Haywood felt "eager" to associate with the anarchists, however. Philosophically, syndicalists such as Flynn and Haywood shared with the anarchists a hatred of capitalism, an emphasis on direct action, and a distrust of centralized authority. But some anarchists, including Berkman, endorsed violent retribution against employers and political figures as "the inevitable reply to the much greater violence" these authority figures perpetrated against workers. Berkman believed that symbolic acts of violence could provoke a revolution.[9] From 1880 to 1914, anarchists in Russia, Spain, Italy, France, and the United States carried out more than 150 assassinations. Goldman seemed less inclined than Berkman to resort to violence, but she defended politically motivated crimes as warranted in certain circumstances.[10]

In an era marked by industrial accidents and by strikes that often escalated into bloody standoffs, it was hard to find labor leaders who renounced violence completely. But Flynn viewed violence as counterproductive and argued that it was more likely to flare up in strikes run by the AFL than in those organized by the IWW.[11] Haywood told the workers that the most powerful thing that they could do in a strike was to fold their arms and refuse to work. But he also played off his masculine image as a roughneck and his history as a confrontational union leader. In speeches, he described himself as a "two gun man," then whipped out his membership cards for the Socialist Party and the IWW.[12]

Neither Flynn nor Haywood advocated violence as an IWW tactic, but if workers were attacked, should they turn the other cheek or fight back? This question echoed through labor and radical circles in the spring of 1914. Flynn and the activists who gathered at Vorse's house sought to come to terms with the Ludlow Massacre in Colorado, which had been "the scene of intense labor struggle" since the 1890s.[13] By 1910, the United Mine Workers of America had organized nearly one-third of all coal miners. Mine owners fought back fiercely. John D. Rockefeller, Jr., one of the richest men in the United States, led an open-shop drive, insisting that employers had the right to hire workers who did not belong to the union. A violent strike ensued. Rockefeller's company, Colorado Fuel & Iron, evicted striking workers from company housing, who then moved into tents. Yet the strike continued, and the company called in the state militia. On Easter night, the militia shot and killed three strike leaders at close range, then set fire to the tent colony, killing two women (one of them pregnant) and eleven children. The ten-day battle that followed left more than thirty people dead.[14]

Among the dead in Ludlow lay Carlo Costa, a friend of Carlo Tresca's. Costa was shot at least twenty times, and his wife and two children, ages six and four, were burned to death in their tent.[15] As the editor of an Italian-language newspaper and a popular speaker and strike leader, Tresca had contacts among radical Italian workers that stretched to industrial and mining towns throughout the United States. At a May Day memorial in New York City, his eyes filled with tears as he asked his audience to call out the name of the murderer of Costa and his family. Shouts of "Rockefeller!" and "Vendetta" rang out through Union Square.[16]

Tresca's notion of justice reflected Italian traditions of community action in order to remedy a wrong as well as anarchist convictions that violence against workers must be met with equal force.[17] Tresca accepted—and advocated—violence when other methods of justice failed. During the Paterson strike, he had disagreed with "the IWW's policy of passive resistance in the face of police brutality" and called for "blood for blood." Now he declared himself an "anarcho-syndicalist," tying together two strains of socialist protest that Flynn and Haywood preferred to keep separate.[18] Charges of anarchism had been used to discredit and prosecute labor organizations since the Haymarket Affair in the 1880s. By associating the IWW with violent anarchism, Tresca threatened to alienate the liberal allies and Green-wich Village bohemians whom Haywood valued as opinion-makers and potential contributors to labor defense.

Rockefeller's callous response to the victims of the Ludlow Massacre fueled the flames of radical discontent. Testifying before Congress after the incident, the financier declared himself willing to lose "millions" of dollars and to see the violence in Colorado continue rather than sacrifice the great American principle of the open shop. In New York City, picketers dressed in mourning led a silent protest in front of the Rockefeller Offices at 26 Broadway. Tresca led louder demonstrations outside the gates of Rockefeller's Pocantico Hills estate north of New York City in Westchester County. The police arrested a dozen protesters and charged them with disorderly conduct.

On July 4, 1914, three of the men due to stand trial were killed when a bomb they had made exploded in their apartment house on Lexington Avenue near 103rd Street.[19] Most people assumed that the bomb had been intended for Rockefeller. Rushing to get a scoop on the sensational story, reporters questioned Tresca, who admitted that he had known one of the would-be bombers, Arthur Caron, and that Caron had wanted to kill Rockefeller. Haywood quickly denied any connection between Caron and the IWW. Flynn found herself in the difficult position of mediating between Tresca and Haywood, and of reconciling her own rejection of violence with Tresca's acceptance of it. As Flynn wrote in a letter to Vorse, who was spending the summer in Provincetown, Massachusetts, "It is all very terrible and everybody is busy here repudiating the poor boys although no connection was actually established between them and the bomb or dynamite." Tresca was "a nervous wreck" and had been suffering from stomach trouble since the incident. Flynn described him as "hot headed" and added that he needed her to keep him steady.[20]

Flynn tread a fine line between honoring the dead and disavowing violence at a memorial meeting in Union Square organized by Berkman (who had secretly masterminded the bomb plot).[21] She focused on Tresca's friend Arthur Caron. A weaver from Fall River, Massachusetts, of French and Native American ancestry, Caron had fallen on hard times when he lost his job and his wife and baby died.

"Grief and loneliness" had driven him to New York City, where he had hoped to make a new start. Instead, he found himself one of the hundreds of thousands of unemployed men, with little choice but "to tramp the streets hungry and cold." Searching for some way to improve his life, he stumbled into Tannenbaum's "army," as the homeless men who gathered around the charismatic IWW leader were known. Caron was arrested twice: first in the church raid and then after a meeting at Cooper Union. With the second arrest, the police took him into an automobile and beat him brutally.[22] He staggered back to Vorse's house with his shirt splattered with blood, the right side of his nose crushed.[23] After the assault, Caron became depressed. He brooded over news of the Ludlow Massacre. When he tried to speak in front of Rockefeller's mansion, "he was pelted with rocks and mud by the law-and-order element," who wanted to drive the radicals out of town.

Flynn summed up Caron's state of mind in a few powerful words: "He asked for bread. He received the blackjack. He asked to be heard. He received a volley of stones." Admitting the fatal mistake Caron had made by attempting to solve his problems with violence, Flynn asked, "*Who is responsible? Who taught it to him?*" She rejected some anarchists' resort to violence, but she called for "sympathy" for Caron's "intense suffering that found an outlet only in this desperate futile way." She reiterated her own creed of nonviolence: attacking Rockefeller would not "change conditions" or bring back to life the babies killed in Ludlow. Only systemic change could make a difference. In the meantime, she counseled, "we should fix our condemnation on the brutality that produced such a psychology."[24]

Privately, Flynn vowed "never to speak with the anarchists again." In a letter to Vorse, she described the meeting as poorly managed. The speakers and the audience were left standing in the blazing sun for hours. What should have been "a dignified memorial meeting" gave way instead to calls for more dynamite and "hysterical proclamations of personal opinion." She found Berkman dictatorial and his young followers sycophantic.[25] Given their shared rejection of anarchism, Haywood may have doubted Flynn's decision to appear at the meeting. Having worked closely with Flynn and Tresca for the past few years, Haywood may have worried that Flynn's intense love for Tresca could lead her to put her own principles aside. Flynn's letters to Vorse, written on Tresca's stationery, reflected a merging of the two lovers' identities that would later prove painful to disentangle.

Flynn judged 1914 to be "a barbarous and bloody year in the class struggle in America." Although the United States did not enter the war until 1917, federal officials began a campaign of "preparedness" that centered on stoking patriotism to prepare for possible battle. As fighting engulfed Europe, demand for American oil, steel, coal, lumber, and weapons increased. Profits soared, pulling the US economy out of its slump. This temporarily solved the problem of unemployment. But Flynn, like most other socialists, viewed mobilization for war negatively. "No War Except Revolution is Workers' War," she proclaimed. She predicted that workers would pay for the conflict with their taxes and their lives. Appeals to nationalism, Flynn believed, cloaked a capitalist fight to divide the spoils of imperialism. She urged workers to stay true to socialist ideals and maintain international solidarity.[26] She joined trade unionists in New York City who called for price controls as wartime inflation raised the costs of food, fuel, and housing.[27]

In 1915, now twenty-five years old, Flynn embarked on her first cross-country speaking trip since Buster's birth. Despite being a mother, she was a restless soul, and she craved adventure and disliked staying in any one place for too long. She took her first tour of California, stopping off in Denver, and visiting Los Angeles and San Francisco. She spoke on "Violence and Preparedness," framing both as threats to the IWW. At this point, the IWW counted only about 15,000 members, down from a high of 18,387 in 1912.[28] Wartime organizing would soon lift membership figures dramatically. The IWW would have an estimated 40,000 members in 1916 and nearly 100,000 a year later.[29]

The most memorable stop on Flynn's trip was in Salt Lake City, "with its windswept wide streets and long blocks," to visit Joe Hill, "a troubadour of the IWW," who was lodged in the county jail. A Swedish immigrant who had traveled the country taking odd jobs, Hill had written catchy songs that were heard at IWW meetings and "on picket lines and in jails from coast to coast." Some of his tunes were original; others consisted of new words to popular songs and religious hymns. His most famous numbers included "Casey Jones" and "There Is Power in a Union." Hill was being held for the murder of a Salt Lake City grocer that occurred during an armed robbery. Flynn and other labor radicals viewed the affair as "a crude frame-up." The prosecution found no motive for the crime, produced no physical evidence, and failed to find a witness placing Hill at the scene. Legend has it that Hill refused to give an alibi for his whereabouts the night of the murder because he was having an affair with a married woman.[30]

Prosecution of Wobblies had increased during the war, and Flynn counted Hill among several imprisoned IWW members she met on her trip. Entering the jail, she was struck by the contrast between the "green shimmer, high altitude, and clear pure air" of Salt Lake City and "the familiar fetid jail odor," cut only by "the sickening smell of disinfectants." Given the flimsiness of the case against Hill, Flynn felt optimistic about his future. But Hill doubted he would be freed and announced his readiness to die, leaving Flynn with a deep feeling of "foreboding." Flynn took a leading role in the campaign to free him. Working her connections with some of the liberals she knew from the free-speech movement, Flynn managed to get an audience with President Woodrow Wilson to plead on Hill's behalf. Wilson "listened attentively" and later sent a message to the governor of Utah urging him to reconsider the case. But the governor refused. Hill was executed by a firing squad on November 19, 1915.[31] To Flynn, and to many other Wobblies, Hill's violent death provided more evidence that workers had little chance of receiving justice in a capitalist system.

Hill left behind a song dedicated to Flynn, "The Rebel Girl." The IWW sold it as sheet music. The cover featured a heroic image of Flynn, wearing a white shirt and black skirt, striding forward with a huge red flag bearing the IWW slogan, "One Big Union." "The Rebel Girl" celebrated Flynn's fierce commitment to the working class, describing her as "a precious pearl" who brought "courage, pride and joy, to the fighting Rebel Boy." In his last letter to Flynn, Hill urged her to locate "more Rebel Girls like yourself, because they are needed and needed badly." Flynn continued to reach out to female workers and to the wives of working men as members and supporters of the IWW, but she remained one of the few female leaders of the Wobblies. Throughout her life, she took tremendous pride in the tribute Joe Hill paid to her, entitling her autobiography "The Rebel Girl."

Flynn's trip across the country and her meeting with Hill may have inspired her to return to strike leadership. In the spring of 1916, she traveled to the Mesabi Range in Minnesota, iron-ore country, where Carlo Tresca, Joe Ettor, and Frank Little were leading a strike for the IWW. Ettor had been one of the original leaders of the Lawrence strike; Little had worked with Flynn on free-speech fights in Missoula and Spokane. More than 16,000 strikers were locked in a brutal battle with their employers for an eight-hour day and an end to a contracting system rife with abuse, including demands for sexual favors from miners' wives and daughters.[32] Mining companies hired "plug uglies" to back up the police. "Armed with clubs and Winchesters," the vigilantes swarmed over the range, breaking up IWW meetings and intimidating the strikers. At the funeral of a murdered IWW member, Tresca called for "an eye for an eye, a tooth for a tooth." Shortly afterward, a deputy sheriff and an innocent bystander were shot. The police arrested Tresca and several other strike leaders on charges of inciting violence. Afraid of being arrested herself, or becoming a victim of vigilante violence, Flynn shuffled between strikers' homes, getting barely any sleep for weeks.

The arrests of the leaders crippled the strike. Flynn called for reinforcements. Vorse traveled to the range in August to report on the strike for several magazines. To Flynn's frustration, Haywood, who had recently taken over the leadership of the IWW and moved to Chicago, declined to visit the range, or to disburse enough money to defend the arrested men. Flynn visited Haywood twice, but she could not convince him to provide more support. She began raising funds for the men's defense herself, traveling as far as New York City.[33] Dorothy Day, a young reporter for the *New York Call*, who became the leader of the Catholic worker movement, recalled a meeting in Brooklyn where Flynn "moved the large audience to tears." When Flynn took up a collection, Day gave all the money she had in her wallet, including the money for her fare home.[34] Flynn did not mind traveling

Flynn photographed in the sheriff's office on the Mesabi Range (1916).

NP18-19, EGF Photographs, Tamiment Library, NYU

to New York City, because it gave her a chance to see her son, but she resented Haywood for leaving her high and dry. The four-month strike ended with the mining companies agreeing to raise wages and improve conditions. But Haywood condemned both Flynn and Ettor for negotiating a plea deal that freed Tresca and the IWW organizers but left three miners in prison for three years each.[35] Ettor left the labor movement and Tresca returned to editing his newspaper.

Flynn herself regretted the decision and later wondered if her passion for Tresca had clouded her judgment. Visiting the range twenty-five years later, she described her younger self as "divided and disarmed." She "suffered so from love" that she lived for her weekly visits to Tresca. When the guards turned away, he held her hand and kissed her on the throat. "The pain and joy of those hot fleeting caresses" lasted all week. Tresca relished the role of romantic revolutionary. After Flynn helped get him out of jail, he gave her a photo of himself inscribed with his thanks to her for devoting "her time, her energy, her youth to rescue me from the capitalist bastille."[36] Flynn and Tresca seemed equally in love with each other and with the cause of revolution.

Haywood refused to give Flynn any further assignments, but she resisted his efforts to push her out of the organization. She made her last trip west on behalf of the IWW in January 1917, traveling to Seattle to help raise funds for IWW prisoners who had been arrested in the so-called Everett Massacre. On November 5, 1916, about three hundred IWW members sailed from Seattle to Everett to challenge the town's ban on public speaking. A large group of armed vigilantes and policemen met the Wobblies at the dock and shot at their boats. Five protesters and two vigilantes were killed, seven people went missing (most likely drowned), and fifty more were injured. Seventy-four Wobblies were charged with murder.[37]

Tresca was outraged that Flynn would even consider leaving him so soon after his release from prison. He punished her by refusing to write to her for six weeks. But Flynn's mother and her sister Kathie "sympathized" with her need to live up to her revolutionary ideals. They sent her news of her son, Buster, whom she missed badly. In Seattle, Flynn joined an energetic group of radicals who were seeking

justice for the imprisoned IWW members. Flynn met Charles Ashleigh, a talented British writer, who fired off press releases. She joined
Dr. Marie Equi, a radical physician from Portland, in visiting the men
behind bars to raise their spirits and to be sure they were receiving
adequate medical care. Heading back east in May 1917, Flynn was
gratified when she received a cable on the train informing her that the
cases against the IWW prisoners had been dismissed. The conductor
who delivered the message could not believe Flynn was an IWW organizer, "since they always rode the rods, not the cushions."[38] Flynn's
gender, youth, and beauty continued to have shock value in connection with her radical politics.

On her way back home, Flynn stopped off in Chicago for one last
visit to IWW headquarters, a three-story building at 1001 West Madison Street, where Haywood had centralized the organization's opera-
tions and printing. Although there was some bad blood between Flynn
and Haywood, she still "loved and respected him," and she thought
"the new orientation of the IWW toward job organization and mass
action" was "correct." With the help of wartime labor shortages, the
IWW was making impressive gains among agricultural and industrial
workers. Scaling back their calls for revolution, the IWW leaders advocated basic labor rights, such as the eight-hour day. However, Haywood, in Flynn's opinion, had displayed dictatorial tendencies since
taking over the leadership of the IWW in 1916. He dominated every
aspect of the organization, and he replaced "the flamboyant agitators,
strike leaders and propagandists" of the past, such as Flynn and Tresca,
with more conventional labor organizers. Even Haywood's friend
Ralph Chaplin described him as "a revolutionary tycoon."[39]

Flynn and Haywood, whose deep connection had been forged in
numerous labor battles, had one last debate. In an informal meeting,
Flynn urged Haywood and the IWW editors to rethink their publishing strategy. She was alarmed that her 1914 pamphlet, *Sabotage*, had
been introduced as evidence of the Wobblies' violent intentions in the
Everett trials. "Why put ammunition in the hands of the enemy?" she
asked. Haywood countered with a hostile question, "What's the matter,
Gurley? Are you losing your nerve?"[40] The comment distanced Flynn
from the all-male leadership of the IWW and left her "completely at

odds" with Haywood. Flynn continued to believe in Wobbly ideals, but she gave up on the IWW as a vehicle for further activism.

Flynn was relieved to get home to her crowded family apartment in the Bronx. She realized that her extended absences had taken a toll on her family. She worried about Buster's health. He was "a frail child" with a tendency toward asthma. Flynn felt guilty about the burden of caring for him that she had imposed on her aging mother and her sister Kathie. Tresca had shown signs of stress since his imprisonment, aggravated by the "hectic pace he had kept up since his release." Flynn herself felt exhausted from the "nervous strain" of her ten years as a Wobbly agitator. Flynn and Tresca decided to "rest, relax, and recuperate" by spending the summer at South Beach, Staten Island. Bringing Buster with them, they rented a small cottage overlooking the water in a neighborhood of Italian workers. The local Italians "feasted on spaghetti and wine out under the trees"; Flynn found Italian food hard to resist and began to put on weight, a problem that would plague her for the rest of her life. However, she was gratified to see Buster begin "to flourish." He became "an excellent swimmer."

Even in this idyllic setting, however, Flynn could not escape the specter of violence. Looking down to the harbor, she could see ships loading men and supplies bound for the war in Europe. One weekend, her brother, Tom, took the ferry to visit. He spent the day at the beach with a neighbor from the Bronx, a German American teenager who had just been drafted. With the United States at war with Germany, people of German descent came under suspicion; the federal government sponsored campaigns for "100% Americanism" and tried in vain to find links between the IWW and German subversion. Flynn was at the stove cooking dinner when Tresca, who had gone to town to get the newspapers, walked in with shocking news: Frank Little, an IWW organizer whom Flynn had known for eight years, had been lynched in Butte, Montana. Flynn sat down and began to cry. Tom's friend asked sadly, "So that's what I'm going to fight for?"[41]

The lynching of Frank Little seemed to be the culmination of the violence and hatred directed toward the IWW since the beginning of the war. In western states, governors and business owners accused the Wobblies of being enemy agents. The Committee on Public

Information picked up and amplified this message, planting stories in the press associating IWW membership with treason. Western senators and governors lobbied Washington for federal troops to put down strikes in the lumber and mining industries, where IWW organizing surged. When federal aid was not forthcoming, they encouraged vigilante violence, which continued even after federal troops arrived. During the spring and summer of 1917, vigilantes raided IWW offices in Kansas City and tarred and feathered IWW organizers in the Midwest. Little seemed to be the perfect target: he spoke out against the war and had a loyal following among western miners. His status as part Native American, and the fact that he had a broken leg, added to his vulnerability. On July 31, six masked men broke into his room, "dragged him from his bed," and threw him into an automobile. They tortured him on the ride out of town, and taking him to a railroad trestle, they hung him. Lest the meaning of their actions be lost, they pinned a sign to Little's body with the names of other strike leaders that read "First and Last Warning." Thousands of people attended Little's funeral, the largest ever held in Montana until that time.[42]

Little's "dreadful, violent death" demonstrated the forces that were arrayed against the IWW. By September, the Labor, War, and Justice Departments were all cooperating to crush the IWW. Responding to pressure from western politicians and employers, these federal agencies decided that something must be done to prevent the Wobblies from undermining the war effort. They were not deterred by the fact that no links were ever discovered between the IWW and the Germans. On September 5, 1917, as Haywood recalled, "the secret agents of the Department of Justice swooped down on the IWW like a cloud of vultures." They raided IWW offices from coast to coast. In the Chicago headquarters, federal agents seized organizational records, books, and pamphlets along with "furniture, typewriters, mimeograph machines, pictures from the wall and spittoons from the floor." All of this was to be used as "evidence" against the IWW.[43] But in fact, a US attorney who directed the raid in Philadelphia admitted that their purpose was "very largely to put the I.W.W. out of business."[44]

Flynn was arrested a couple of weeks later in the indictment, which named 168 IWW leaders plus "Frank Little, now deceased."

"Even in death," Flynn remarked bitterly, "they could not let him rest in peace." Out on bail, Flynn acted quickly to formulate her legal strategy. She advocated severing the cases, calling for individual trials in order "to tie this dragnet case up in legal knots."[45] Labor lawyers advocated separate trials in conspiracy cases, since prosecutors lumped activists together and charged them with multiple crimes when they did not have enough evidence to convict any one of them individually.[46] Flynn had pursued this strategy when faced with mass arrests of IWW members during the free-speech fights in Missoula and Spokane. Now she went further, denying that she, Ettor, Tresca, and Giovannitti had been members of the IWW during the period covered by the indictment. Indeed, she and Ettor had both fallen out with Haywood after the strike on the Mesabi Range, and neither Tresca nor Giovannitti ever formally belonged to the IWW, although both had worked for the organization on numerous occasions.[47] The federal government severed the cases of Flynn and her friends but kept them pending until 1919 in order to facilitate future prosecution.[48] Tresca and Giovannitti, who had both been born in Italy, faced possible deportation.

Flynn and her friends drew fire for refusing to follow Haywood's directive that every IWW member named in the indictment voluntarily surrender to federal authorities. Given Flynn's falling out with Haywood, however, it is hardly surprising that she refused to follow his directions. Wobblies who obeyed Haywood would be deeply disillusioned in 1921, when he "jumped bail and fled to the Soviet Union" to avoid a twenty-year prison term. Haywood had planned to use the cases against the IWW leaders to make an example of the abuse of federal power during wartime. Instead, his strategy contributed to many of the indicted men languishing in federal prisons until 1923. Many of the immigrants in the group were deported.[49] "It was a tragedy," Flynn reflected, "and an avoidable one—that all of these splendid working men should have been sewed up in this manner in one case, without even a fight."[50] In response to those who questioned her solidarity and her loyalty, Flynn spent the next six years working to free the imprisoned and to secure humane conditions for those who faced deportation.

5

Defending Workers
During the Red Scare

In November 1917, the Bolsheviks took control of Russia. Announcing the birth of a new, socialist republic, they withdrew from the Great War and abolished private ownership of land and natural resources. Many of Flynn's friends traveled to Russia to see this "great historical experiment now unfolding."[1] Jack Reed, a writer who had been radicalized by the strike at Paterson, narrated the Bolshevik Revolution in his dramatic firsthand account *Ten Days That Shook the World*. Journalist Lincoln Steffens, who had worked with Flynn on the IWW campaigns to organize the unemployed, announced, "I have seen the future and it works." Flynn read all she could about the Soviet workers' cooperatives, which seemed as though they might fulfill the syndicalist dream of a new society based on workers' organizations. "Everything that we of the left-wing movement heard from [Soviet Russia] through the press fired us with enthusiasm," Flynn recalled.[2] However, she did not rush to join the communists, who pledged support to extend the revolution in Russia. Instead, she built a broad coalition to fight the reaction against it, known as the Red Scare.

The indictment of Flynn and 168 other IWW leaders in September 1917 kicked off a federal campaign against radicalism. Shortly after the Bolshevik Revolution, Justice Department agents raided

IWW offices in Omaha, Sacramento, and Spokane. As a result, several hundred more IWW leaders went to prison. The roundup extended to leaders of the Socialist Party, who had been considered legitimate participants in American politics since the 1880s. Eugene V. Debs, the elder statesman of socialism, was imprisoned for speaking against the war; so, too, was Kate Richards O'Hare, the nation's most prominent female socialist. Native-born radicals faced sentences of five to twenty years in prison, but the foreign-born faced even harsher consequences. Regardless of how long they had been in the United States, immigrants who uttered thoughts deemed dangerous or joined organizations judged subversive were deported. Flynn's friend Emma Goldman was sent back to Russia, as were many other immigrant radicals. The Red Scare found its final victims in Nicola Sacco and Bartolomeo Vanzetti, two Italian anarchists who were executed in 1927. By the time the Red Scare subsided, the IWW, the Socialist Party, and the anarchist movement lay in ruins.

Flynn remembered the decade from 1917 to 1927 as a "hideous nightmare." She found it "hard to convey the human suffering, the mental torture, the loss of liberty, the broken homes, the cost in dollars for defense, inflicted upon militant American workers." Having managed to escape jail herself, she worked day and night on behalf of labor activists who had been imprisoned for their political beliefs. The war ended in November 1918. Flynn toiled until Christmas of 1923 to free approximately 1,500 people who had been convicted on charges relating to activities or affiliations judged threatening to national security. Their crimes ranged from refusing to enroll in the military to leading strikes in war industries, belonging to the IWW, or participating in organizations that supported the Bolshevik Revolution. At the same time, Flynn sought to limit the scope of deportations and to secure decent treatment for those still in federal detention. Flynn's long hours, which often extended through evenings, weekends, and holidays, made her feel cut off from her family, her son, and her partner, Carlo Tresca.[3]

Flynn forged connections with a wide range of people alarmed by the wartime prosecution of workers, including "liberals, pacifists, church leaders, professionals and many conservative labor leaders." Through her sheer force of personality and her excellent organizing skills, Flynn bridged differences among these groups. She emerged as an important leader of the free-speech coalition that formed in the 1920s, working closely with Roger Baldwin, the founder of the American Civil Liberties Union (ACLU).[4] Baldwin's commitment to free expression drew from an American libertarian tradition developed in the work of Henry David Thoreau. Baldwin also drew from anarchist philosophy, which he began reading after hearing Emma Goldman speak in 1909.[5] He rejected state coercion, and he spent a year in jail for refusing to serve in the military during World War I. Flynn served on the board of the ACLU, and she borrowed $250 from Baldwin to launch the Workers' Defense Union (WDU), an organization devoted to defending members of the labor movement who had been jailed or slated for deportation for political reasons.[6]

As the general organizer of the WDU, Flynn adopted a more mature and moderate public persona than she had as an IWW "agitator." Aware that she, like other radicals, could easily be jailed for "seditious conspiracy," an event that would impede her work and leave her seven-year-old son without a mother—and her family without a breadwinner—she stopped calling for revolution.[7] Instead, she crafted commonsense pleas for acceptance of dissenting ideas as central to the American political tradition. This new approach enabled her to skirt prosecution and to assemble a broad base of support. The founding conference of the WDU at Forward Hall at 175 East Broadway included delegates from 163 labor and socialist organizations throughout New York City. Each of these groups pledged funds to support the WDU's fight to secure the release of political prisoners, end deportations, and defend the right to free speech. The WDU enjoyed a "close and friendly" relationship with the ACLU.

Flynn found an office for the WDU in a back room at the Rand School, a center for workers' education run by the Socialist Party at 7 East 15th Street, just off Union Square, where Flynn had delivered many speeches. The dark, cramped quarters of the WDU felt far removed from the open-air lecture platform and the adoring crowds that had hung on Flynn's every word before the war. Flynn compared her office to a prison: "There were bars on the windows, it was dark and gloomy, facing a small closed airshaft." Fumes from nearby factories wafted through the windows. She kept the "electric lights" on all day to combat the gloom. Flynn "often felt" that she, "too, was in jail," and would not be freed until "the others came out."[8] Indeed, it seems that Flynn imprisoned herself voluntarily to prove that she had not been selfish or cowardly in severing her case from the mass indictment of IWW leaders and avoiding a lengthy prison term.

Flynn breathed life into her grim surroundings. Eugene Lyons, a young journalist, whom Flynn hired as a press secretary for the WDU, found Flynn, at age thirty, "attractive" and "winsomely Irish in her wit and savor of life." He discovered "a remarkably cool intelligence behind her fiery oratory and personality." Tresca, whose newspaper offices were close by, appeared "big, bearded, boastful, life-loving," and "as unlike" the stereotype of the "the embittered anarchist . . . as possible." Vincent St. John, who hung out at the WDU office while out on bail for indictment as an IWW leader, shared his "mature class-war wisdom, tales of prospecting for gold, and off-color stories." Scores of other people stopped by to see Flynn, including IWW members, "anarchists, socialists, American lumber jacks, Jewish clothing workers, Russian intellectuals," and Irish and Hindu nationalists. Ella Reeve Bloor, a socialist agitator who became a communist, worked as a field organizer for the WDU.[9]

Flynn developed a distinctive strategy to seek freedom for those who had been incarcerated due to their political beliefs. She publicized the facts of each case, highlighting biographical details in order to humanize the prisoners and build public awareness of the scope of government prosecutions. She sent out letters describing previously unknown workers. Members of the WDU learned that Emile Peltman, held for deportation to Germany in Prescott, Arizona, for his work as an IWW organizer, had served in the Spanish-American War. He had lived in the United States since he was a baby and did not speak German. William Nye Doty, a railroad worker imprisoned in Fort Douglas, Utah, for refusing to report for the draft, was a *Mayflower* descendant. His ancestors had come to America seeking "the right of spiritual, political and economic freedom." Why should it be denied now, asked Flynn. Charles Ashleigh, languishing in Leaven-worth federal prison, was a talented British poet and journalist. His sole crime had been to work for the acquittal of the IWW members charged in the Everett Massacre.[10] These details made the prisoners and detainees seem like innocent people caught in an unjust federal dragnet who desperately needed help.

Flynn rallied members of the WDU to write letters of protest to the president of the United States and to the secretaries of labor and immigration and to donate money to help pay for legal fees. Lyons composed press releases to be sent to radical newspapers, such as the *New York Call*, the daily paper published by the Socialist Party. The *Call* fought federal efforts to push radical publications out of business by banning them from using the postal service. Flynn worked closely with Harry Weinberger, a defense attorney specializing in civil liber-ties cases who had grown up on the Lower East Side and was the son of Hungarian Jewish immigrants. Weinberger frequently traveled to Washington to lobby on behalf of the prisoners. He kept up a steady stream of correspondence with federal officials, making appeals for clemency and faster processing of cases. Weinberger found the attack on socialists and others who dared to question the US government "galling." He confided to Flynn, "These damn cases get under my skin."[11] The WDU also hired local lawyers to manage cases through-out the country. Flynn worked in tandem with defense organizations that sprang up in Boston, Detroit, and Oakland. Cities that had been centers of radical activity prior to the war became key sites in the gov-ernment's fight against labor organizations deemed dangerous to na-tional security during and after the war.[12]

Flynn kept in touch with prisoners by writing letters and vis-iting when she could. She responded to requests for items such as clothes, shoes, soap, underwear, writing paper, and tobacco. She sent each prisoner $5.00 in Christmas money, and she worked with fe-male volunteers who made sure each prisoner received mail. These small actions were calculated to reduce the psychic and physical toll of prison. After all, Flynn reflected, prisons were designed "not to as-sert but to destroy human dignity." Prisoners reported many stories of abuse in their letters to Flynn, from being strung up by their wrists to witnessing or becoming the victims of racial violence that was encouraged by prison wardens. In Leavenworth, imprisoned IWW leaders organized a strike of 3,700 inmates to protest the lack of decent food and to demand humane treatment. These prisoners joined an international strike wave in 1919 that drew in 4 million workers in the United States alone.

Once released, many of these prisoners bore scars that never healed. Some were relatively minor, such as an aversion to parsnips, a root vegetable served at nearly every meal at Leavenworth. Others were more serious. Men and women who had been held in solitary confinement struggled to maintain their sanity. Several prisoners contracted tuberculosis or some other contagious disease and died soon after being released. Furthermore, each prisoner left behind family members who had to cope with anxiety about their loved one's fate, shame at the incarceration of a family member, and the material strain of losing a wage earner.

Flynn's brief arrest during World War I had traumatized her son, Buster, whose teacher told him that his mother must be a criminal, because "only people who lie and steal and kill are put in jail." As a result, Flynn moved Buster to Friends Seminary, a Quaker school on Stuyvesant Square, where many people who opposed the war sent their children.[13] She or Tresca rode the train downtown with Buster in the morning. Buster often stopped by the WDU offices after school to finish his homework. Although Flynn sometimes felt imprisoned by her job, she must have appreciated her good fortune compared to an actual prisoner: even if she worked long hours, she could see her son every day and go home at night.

Flynn paid particular attention to women who became the victims of mob violence and government repression during the war. After Flynn's arrest in September 1917, a group of women, many of them friends from Heterodoxy, the Greenwich Village feminist club, formed a committee to post bail for her and hire a lawyer. Flynn joined a women's committee to free Kate Richards O'Hare. The attractive and well-coiffed mother of four was a well-known socialist from Kansas. As a US-born white woman, O'Hare was nearly exempt from the popular prejudice often expressed toward immigrant or anarchist working-class men. But O'Hare's wholesome image did not stop the Bureau of Investigation (a precursor to the FBI) from sending a spy to report on Flynn's speech at an open-air meeting and fundraiser on behalf of O'Hare in Harlem in July 1919. Recently acquitted of the charges that had been pending against her since 1917, Flynn issued a "scathing indictment" of the "Justice meted out by the Government." She presented the details of O'Hare's case and argued that the government ought to make a distinction between common criminals and political prisoners.[14] The women's committee helped reduce O'Hare's sentence from five years to two.

Like the IWW leaders held in Leavenworth, O'Hare continued to organize and agitate from behind bars in Jefferson City, Missouri. (O'Hare also made sure that her son continued to practice his violin; he often came to play outside the prison walls.) O'Hare served her sentence with Emma Goldman, who had been imprisoned for speaking against the draft. Meeting Goldman around 1906, Flynn had marveled "at the force, eloquence and fire that poured from this mild-mannered, motherly sort of woman."[15] The straitlaced O'Hare and the bohemian Goldman formed an unlikely alliance. Goldman remarked, "Had we met on the outside, we should have probably argued furiously." In prison, they overcame their "theoretical differences" and "found common ground." They started a library and tried to improve the food and medical care the female prisoners received.[16] O'Hare's letters describing prison conditions prompted a government investigation. After her release, O'Hare wrote a book, *In Prison*, critiquing the class inequalities institutionalized in a penal system designed to serve "a social system based on the sacredness of profits."[17]

Flynn joined with O'Hare to free the remaining political prisoners. They focused public attention on the prisoners' children. They worked with the wives of tenant farmers from Oklahoma and Arkansas whose husbands had been jailed for resisting the draft. Reprising her tactics from the Lawrence strike, Flynn led a parade of children and mothers in Grand Central Station; they marched through the terminal carrying signs that read, "Is the Constitution Dead?" Tapping old friends among New York City's culinary workers, Flynn made sure the protesters dined well before continuing on to Washington, DC.

The group of gaunt mothers and shabbily dressed children visited Congress and picketed in front of the White House. Their presence brought the human costs of the Red Scare into view and helped build pressure to free the remaining political prisoners.[18]

As head of the WDU, Flynn fought wave after wave of antiradicalism. In October 1918, Congress passed an Immigration Act ordering the expulsion of all "alien anarchists" and other immigrants who advocated the overthrow of the US government. Flynn sharply criticized the policy of deporting foreign-born workers for their "political opinions." America, Flynn insisted, should be "a haven of refuge for the persecuted in all lands." On behalf of the WDU, she argued that the new policy violated the principles of individual liberty upon which the nation was founded and introduced a double standard of justice for the native- and foreign-born. Furthermore, it placed arbitrary power in the hands of the immigration inspector, who acted as prosecutor, judge, and jury.[19] At a meeting of a defense committee organized by the deportees (and attended by a Bureau of Investigation spy), Flynn decried the fact that the new law empowered the government "to deport men and women for their membership in an organization." Agreeing with "an idea" or "a set of principles," she argued, should not be grounds for deportation.[20]

By the summer of 1919, hundreds of foreign-born workers had been shipped to Ellis Island to await forced transport back to Europe. These immigrants found themselves imprisoned on "Hell's Island," as they called it, within view of the Statue of Liberty, a beacon for exiles "yearning to breathe free." Flynn kept in contact with detainees at Ellis Island through letters (all of which were read by federal agents) and weekly visits via ferry. She discovered "abominable housing" in "ill-ventilated rooms," "scanty food," and "inconsiderate treatment." The WDU scraped together funds to provide extra food and adequate clothing. A daily menu forwarded to Flynn from one of the prisoners included the handwritten comment, "A lot of swell names for swill." The detainee remarked on the irony of serving "Liberty Pudding" for dessert—"Can you beat it. On a par with the Liberty Statue, surrounded by various kinds of jails."[21] Indeed, new federal policies that allowed expulsion of "alien radicals," spying on suspected subversives, and censoring of the federal mail seriously undermined American liberty.

However, a series of bombings and bomb scares in the spring of 1919, combined with worldwide labor unrest, fanned fears that the existing order in the United States was imperiled by anarchists, communists, and other labor radicals. In April, thirty packages containing explosives were sent to politicians, industrialists, and bankers. Most went unmailed due to lack of postage, but one bomb, directed to a Georgia senator, blew off the hands of the maid who opened the package. In June, bombs exploded in seven US cities. Targets included the US attorney general, Mitchell A. Palmer, whose home in Washington, DC, was severely damaged. A night watchman guarding the home of a judge in New York was killed.[22] The violence helped to justify aggressive federal, state, and local prosecution of radicals as being necessary to preserve public safety.

In June 1919, the Lusk Committee, a group of New York State legislators, ordered police to raid the Rand School. Flynn and her coworker Ella Reeve Bloor hid their most important documents in the cellar. Luckily, WDU offices were not searched, as the seizure of records would have seriously undermined their work.[23] In November, Palmer unleashed raids in eleven cities timed to coincide with the second anniversary of the Bolshevik Revolution. The targets included the Union of Russian Workers, an immigrant organization that supported the Bolsheviks. The raid in New York City was typical: at 8:45 p.m., police barged into the Russian People's House at 133 East 15th Street. Most of the people in the building were workers attending night school. A teacher who asked what was happening was answered "with blows that smashed the spectacles he wore and wounded his face severely." Tons of books and pamphlets were carted away as "evidence," and nearly 100 people were arrested. Additional raids bore down on recently formed communist groups in thirty-three towns and cities across the nation, resulting in 2,500 more arrests. The raids were "terrifying" to those who experienced them, but they revealed no clues about the bombings.[24]

One of the most chilling episodes of the Red Scare occurred on December 21, 1919. The *Buford*, an old leaky ship, packed with 249 "alien radicals" who were being deported, set sail from Ellis Island "in the blackness of early morning" at 4:20 a.m. The deportees were given just a few hours' notice and denied the chance to say good-bye to family or friends or to notify their lawyers. Their destination, Soviet Russia, was not revealed until the ship had been at sea for twenty days. One hundred and eighty-four of the 249 passengers had been charged with no crime except membership in the Union of Russian Workers. The secretary of immigration later admitted that the proceedings resembled "vicious kidnappings."[25]

Flynn's friend Emma Goldman, who had been released from prison only to be deported, was one of three women aboard the *Buford*. The women were given a separate cabin and the dubious honor of eating in the captain's dining room. Goldman found the treatment of the men, including her friend Alexander Berkman, "simply harrowing." Waves swept the decks, flooding the cabins and soaking the men, who slept in "wet bunks covered with dripping blankets." The food was nearly inedible, and many of the men became sick. Their pathetic lack of preparation for the voyage was revealed by the fact that there were only thirty-seven trunks total, the vast majority of deportees having been "rushed out of the country without even a change of clothing." Many lacked basic documents, such as a passport. All of them had left their hard-won savings behind, a total of more than $45,000.[26]

Goldman and Berkman sent an open letter to Flynn at the WDU, hoping that she could somehow help, or at least let people know what had happened. "You can not, you must not, permit" the deportees "to be torn out of their adopted land, root and branch, kidnapped from their families, robbed of their loved ones, and sent away in tatters on the open ocean," they pleaded. Believing more strongly than ever in the necessity of free speech, Goldman and Berkman warned, "Remember, dear friends, silence is next to consent."[27] Flynn had distanced herself from the anarchists in 1914, but she found their treatment by the federal government disgraceful.

Flynn and Lyons worked through Christmas Day of 1919 drafting a letter to labor leaders and progressive intellectuals around the country alerting them to the deportations. They described the distraught wives of the deported men aboard the *Buford*, who had been left "behind to weep and starve." Letters came back to the WDU commenting on the "public hysteria" created by "politicians and the press" and questioning why the United States did not give those suspected of a crime "a chance to defend themselves in open court." Many expressed concern that a few officials had been granted a dangerous amount of power, worrying that it could "very easily be used as a club to terrorize foreign-born workmen." One correspondent lamented the "all too common assumption that once we rid the country of agitators, we can sleep in peace."[28] Concerns about national security seemed to be undermining the very foundation of America, which was built on respect for the Constitution and the Bill of Rights.

Flynn focused on the families that had been left behind. Robbed of their husbands, who had served as their families' primary wage earners, most of the women wanted desperately to return to Russia with their children, but they were completely broke. The WDU helped foot the bill for a delegation of American women to travel to Washington to lobby on behalf of the wives of the Russian deportees, arguing that the federal government owed them support and tickets to travel to Russia. But the federal government refused to help. Most of the children of these couples had been born in the United States—so the federal government had no authority to deport them.[29] Ultimately, Flynn and the WDU raised funds to send the wives and children of the deportees back to Russia.

As head of the WDU, Flynn was also sensitive to the role of women as family supporters. She started a trust fund to help the family of Mollie Steimer, a twenty-year-old Jewish seamstress from Russia who had been imprisoned and then deported for handing out pamphlets criticizing the United States for sending troops to fight the Bolsheviks. Steimer left behind her widowed mother and four younger siblings, who had depended on her earnings for support.[30] Privately, Flynn remarked to Steimer's lawyer, Henry Weinberger, "If we all had her courage and spirit of no compromise the workers might get somewhere but jail."[31]

Despite the pain of being torn away from family and friends, Steimer and Goldman put a brave face on their deportation. Writing from aboard the *Buford* in concert with Berkman, Goldman described Soviet Russia as "the incarnation of a flaming ideal, the inspiration of the New Day." Once Goldman and her fellow deportees arrived, however, they would be bitterly disappointed by limits on free speech, repression of dissent, the militarization of daily life, and widespread hunger and deprivation.[32] After witnessing the brutal suppression of an uprising in Kronstadt and a government campaign against anarchists, Goldman and Berkman fled. Goldman became an exile in a string of cities, including London, Paris, Berlin, Toronto, and St. Tropez, where she wrote her memoirs. Berkman moved to France. Steimer was crushed by the brutal reality of the "Dictatorship of the Proletariat." The secret police infiltrated all dissident groups and tolerated "NO freedom of opinion," she despaired. Thousands of workers languished in prison for daring to disagree with government policies or organizing to demand better working conditions. Steimer was imprisoned in Russia, then deported in September 1923. She moved to Paris and Berlin before joining a community of Russian political exiles in Mexico City in 1940.[33]

Given Flynn's admiration and support for Goldman and Steimer, it seems likely that she followed their travails once they arrived in the Soviet Union. V. I. Lenin described suspension of free speech as a temporary measure necessary to ensure the future of the revolution. But Flynn supported "the movement on behalf of political prisoners in Soviet Russia," a stance that may have kept her apart from the American Communist Party, which formed in 1919.[34] Flynn clipped a newspaper article reporting Bill Haywood's death in Moscow in the summer of 1928. The reporter described Russia as being "as far from Revolution as it is from Utopia." Indeed, the socialist revolution in which Flynn and Haywood had placed their hopes in the 1910s seemed "to be going in the opposite direction." Before long, the reporter predicted, Russia would revert to the rule of the czars.[35] From the Great War through the 1920s, both the United States and the Soviet Union seemed to illustrate the anarchist contention that all governments are inherently coercive and destructive to individual liberty.

Flynn was not an anarchist. However, she did keep in touch with the Italian anarchist community through Carlo Tresca. She sympathized with the anarchist goal of creating a society free from government coercion, even if she, like the many nonviolent anarchists, rejected bombings and assassinations as tools of social struggle. Anarchists remained under suspicion for the actual and attempted bombings of 1919. A horse-drawn wagon filled with dynamite exploded on Wall Street in September 1920, killing thirty-nine people and wounding hundreds more. These terrorist acts set the nation on edge and intensified the Red Scare.

On a trip to Boston to speak on behalf of several hundred deportees held on Deer Island, Tresca asked Flynn to look in on "two Italian comrades in big trouble in Massachusetts," Nicola Sacco and Bartolomeo Vanzetti, who had been charged with murder. Threading her way through "the turbulent but colorful over-crowded slums" of Boston's North End, with its "crooked streets and narrow houses," Flynn made contact with the Sacco-Vanzetti Defense Committee. They were suspicious of outsiders, but they accepted Flynn because of her work as a strike leader in Lawrence and her connections to Italian radicals. Flynn and Tresca both became devoted to saving Sacco and Vanzetti, but Flynn eventually became more active than Tresca as a result of rivalries among Italian anarchists.[36]

Based on her experience in the WDU, Flynn helped shape the story of Sacco and Vanzetti in ways that appealed to a wide audience and eventually made them an international cause célèbre.[37] She emphasized their humble backgrounds. Both men had migrated to the United States in 1908. Sacco, who was married and had two children, worked as an edge-trimmer in a shoe factory. Vanzetti, who remained single, worked as a fish peddler. Known as anarchists by the local police, Sacco and Vanzetti became prime suspects in a payroll robbery and murder that occurred at a shoe factory in South Braintree, Massachusetts, on April 15, 1920.[38] Flynn believed passionately that the two men were innocent of the crime.

Flynn hired Art Shields, a Seattle labor journalist, to produce a dramatic thirty-two-page pamphlet, *Are They Doomed?* Linking the prosecution of Sacco and Vanzetti to the recent, widespread repression of radical workers, Shields argued that "the attack" upon Sacco and Vanzetti was "obviously an attack upon all workers who dare to think out loud."[39] The WDU printed 50,000 copies of the pamphlet and distributed them to workers around the country to raise funds and build awareness of the case.[40]

Historians debate the guilt or innocence of Sacco and Vanzetti, but they agree that their identities were considerably more complicated than the simple image that Flynn helped to create. Flynn knew that Sacco and Vanzetti belonged to a group of militant anarchists directed by Luigi Galleani, who had been deported in 1919, but she saw them as idealists, people who might commit violence for a cause, but would never engage in what Sacco called "a gunman job." Historians believe that the Galleanisti orchestrated the bombings that took place in cities across America in April and June 1919 and on Wall Street in September 1920 (although they remain unsure of Sacco and Vanzetti's exact role).[41] Flynn's idealism and her desire to create symbols of labor repression may have prevented her from asking more probing questions about Sacco and Vanzetti.

Shields recalled that "Flynn threw all her splendid organizing talents into this freedom campaign for Sacco and Vanzetti. She made scores of speeches, wrote hundreds of letters and stirred many key figures in the labor movement to act."[42] Despite her efforts, Sacco and Vanzetti were convicted of murder on July 14, 1921, and sentenced to death. Their trial focused more on their identity as Italian anarchists than on the evidence in the case. Flynn spent the next six years agitating for a retrial. She raised money to cover legal fees and the costs of "publicity, literature [and] meetings.[43] She conducted a special outreach to union members, who staged huge demonstrations.[44] Last, but not least, she toured the country to spread the story of Sacco and Vanzetti.[45]

By 1925, most of the political prisoners who had been arrested during and immediately after World War I had been freed, and the "deportations delirium" had run its course. The WDU merged with the Chicago-based organization International Labor Defense (ILD). Flynn became the secretary of the Garland Fund, a million-dollar trust established by a young Harvard graduate to fund radical causes. She now found herself in the enviable position of writing checks of from $500 to $50,000 each "to bail out strikers, or to provide a good defense to workers." But, as she assured a newspaper reporter, she still identified with the working class, and she enjoyed going out to talk to longshoremen as much as she ever had.[46]

Flynn's friends and coworkers organized a party for her on Valentine's Day of 1926 to honor her twenty years in the labor movement. Roger Baldwin, the head of the ACLU, presided. About three hundred anarchists, communists, socialists, and Wobblies joined to celebrate Flynn, whose enemies called her "the most brilliant female agitator in the US."[47] Daily papers featured stories about her. No relic of the old days, photos showed an attractive woman with dark hair, wearing make-up and speaking on the telephone.

News coverage of the party provided a snapshot of Flynn's pragmatic political views in the 1920s. She commented on the changes she had seen since her early days of organizing. Women now had the right to vote. As a result, they displayed more spirit and more interest in political affairs than they ever had before. Most women, however, still saw themselves as temporary workers, and were therefore reluctant to join unions. Concerned with the well-being of working-class families, Flynn supported recent laws mandating an eight-hour day for female industrial workers, even if these laws violated the principle of equal rights, putting her, like most labor figures, at odds with feminists in the National Women's Party. In principle, the severe restriction of European immigration in 1924 had been wrong, Flynn thought. In practice, however, she hoped that it would facilitate organization, because it would reduce the availability of cheap labor and increase the number of workers who spoke English. (In fact, employers found enough workers from the American countryside, Mexico, and Canada to avoid having to raise wages.) Flynn continued to believe in the IWW principle of industrial organization as the basis for socialist revolution, but she thought that Americans must work out their own labor program: "It must be home-grown, and not a rehash of Karl Marx [or] the Russians."[48]

Telegrams and letters came in from around the world congratulating Flynn. Eugene V. Debs celebrated her for her "proud and enviable position in the American labor movement." Despite her accomplishments, she remained "one of the humblest and most unpretentious of

*Flynn around the time of the twentieth anniversary
of her career in the labor movement (c. 1926).*

NP18-21, EGF Photographs, Tamiment Library, NYU

its members." Since the beginning of her career, she had "championed the cause of the weakest, lowliest, most despised and persecuted." She had "never weakened or wavered" even "when she stood almost alone."[49] Sidney Hillman, the leader of the Amalgamated Clothing Workers of America, lauded Flynn for her "wholehearted devotion" to the labor movement "during stormy years." He, too, commented on her "unselfish interest and energy in the struggles of the working class." Mike Gold, a Jewish communist author and editor, sent a more personal note, describing Flynn as "a real friend to half the world, the mother of every bum, the sister to every ham poet, and one person who will surely be getting another dinner from the red radicals twenty years from today—for Elizabeth will never haul down the red flag." Goldman sent greetings from Paris. Vanzetti sent a letter from prison in his characteristically imperfect English. He wished that he could be there to celebrate Flynn's "faithfulness to and perseverance for the triumph of more and more true freedom and justice." He promised that he had not yet lost hope. From his prison cell, he lifted his "tin-cup of water to drink and to toast."[50]

The party at the Yorkville Casino began at 7:00 p.m. and lasted until after midnight. Since World War I and the Bolshevik Revolution, the American Left had been decimated by wartime repression and divided over whether to sign on to the Soviet program or maintain their own independent movement. Now, they seemed to enjoy a rare moment of unity. One attendee doubted whether such an illustrious "united front" could be assembled for anyone but Flynn. At the end of the evening, Flynn must have felt loved, appreciated, and admired for all that she had done on behalf of the American working class, much of it behind the scenes in recent years. This glowing picture was only part of the story, however. Flynn's private life was in turmoil, and her personal anguish would soon lead her to reject nearly all the connections she had worked so hard to build.

6

"No Present Prospects of Returning East"— Oregon Years

Elizabeth Gurley Flynn lived her life according to her political ideals. She rejected marriage as an intolerable compromise of freedom, advocated the use of birth control, and insisted on women's equality. She found a partner in love and social struggle in Carlo Tresca. Since their fateful meeting in Lawrence in 1912, the dashing pair could be found on the forefront of labor struggles and battles for free speech around the country. Although they were not legally married, they were well known as a couple and widely regarded as husband and wife. However, their relationship was "tempestuous," according to Flynn, owing to their "strong personalities with separate and often divided interests." As the years passed, differences in their political priorities and their ideas about gender became more apparent. After World War I, Flynn devoted her energies to labor defense while Tresca remained immersed in Italian anarchism and his newspaper, *Il Martello* (The Hammer). Flynn valued her work and expected her family to support it. Tresca felt that he should come first. Devoted to the idea of smashing the established social order, Tresca nevertheless clung to old-fashioned ideas about women while giving himself free rein to pursue numerous love affairs.

By the mid-1920s these differences had worn away at least part of the bond between Flynn and Tresca. They remained linked by their sense of family and by their shared work to secure a new trial for the Italian anarchists Sacco and Vanzetti, but their initial passion for each other had cooled. Tresca continued to live in the Flynn family apartment in the Bronx and to act as a father to Flynn's son, Buster, who loved him dearly. Although Flynn and Tresca both worked long hours, they often met for dinner at John's, an Italian restaurant on East 12th Street, where they remained part of a lively scene of downtown radicals.[1]

A dark secret lurked within the Flynn family, however. Carlo and Bina, Elizabeth's youngest sister, had an affair. Although Bina lacked Elizabeth's fire, she was by all accounts "a dreamy Irish beauty." She had found some success as an actress and aspired to be a poet. Bina was eight years younger than Elizabeth and nearly twenty years younger than Carlo, who continued to be considered handsome in his forties, although he had put on quite a bit of weight since Elizabeth had first met him. Bina became pregnant with Carlo's child in March 1922. Seeking to cover up the affair, she quickly married a friend, James "Slim" Martin, and divorced him soon after the birth of her son, Peter Martin, on January 6, 1923.[2] Ironically, Tresca would be indicted the following year for advertising birth control in the pages of *Il Martello*.

Tresca's indictment suggests how federal agencies continued to prosecute "reds" throughout the 1920s on the slimmest of charges. The Federal Bureau of Investigation closely monitored Tresca's activities, sending spies to report on his speeches in hopes that he would say something inflammatory enough that he could be classified as an anarchist and deported. A translator for the US Postal Service studied each issue of *Il Martello* looking for evidence that could be used against Tresca. After Tresca printed insulting comments in *Il Martello* about the Italian monarchy and the new fascist leader of Italy, Benito Mussolini, the Italian ambassador urged the US secretary of state to prosecute Tresca and shut down his newspaper. In the end, advertising birth control was the only crime that would stick.[3] Flynn took charge of Tresca's defense and managed to get his sentence reduced to four months. Although she did not yet know about Tresca's affair with her sister, Flynn felt "great unhappiness" as her work on behalf of Tresca concluded. She sensed they would be parting ways "when this ordeal was finished."[4]

On January 6, 1925, Flynn said goodbye to Tresca at Grand Central Station, where he took the train to Atlanta to enter a federal prison. He now corresponded more actively with Bina than he did with Elizabeth. Unable to take the strain of living at home, Bina moved to her own apartment and sent her two-year-old son, Peter, to live with a Spanish anarchist couple in Newark. Bina visited Peter every weekend and kept Carlo informed about the boy's health and his progress in learning to talk. She became the editor of *Ranch Romances*, a popular magazine with short stories set in the American West featuring feisty female heroines who fought off bad guys and came to each other's aid. In her letters to Carlo, Bina insisted that they must come clean about the affair and start a new life together once he got out of prison. "In all this terrible situation, Carlo dear, none of us are bad or cruel," Bina assured him. She believed that "things would take on a different aspect entirely when the strain of secrecy is removed."[5] Carlo seems to have agreed, at least in part. He sent Elizabeth a letter proposing a separation. When he was released from prison in the spring of 1925, however, he broke off his relationships with both of the Flynn sisters. Sometime after that, Elizabeth learned that Carlo had fathered Bina's son. Elizabeth and Bina stopped speaking to each other, and the formerly close-knit Flynn family fractured. Buster continued to live with Elizabeth's parents and her older sister, Kathie, and brother, Tom, but Elizabeth, unwilling to remain in the apartment where the affair had occurred, moved out.[6]

Devastated by the betrayal, Flynn threw herself into her work. She joined a strike of 15,000 woolen workers in Passaic, New Jersey— the first strike in the United States to be led by communists. Flynn had visited Passaic in 1913 as a leader of an IWW strike in nearby Paterson. In March 1926, Flynn began visiting Passaic daily, making speeches and distributing supplies sent to aid strikers' families. Using money from the Garland Fund, she enlisted her friend Mary Heaton Vorse, a journalist, to direct a creative publicity committee. Vorse emphasized the high toll that low wages took on working families. Mothers had no choice but to work at night, and teenage daughters had to leave school to enter the mills. Families could barely afford to buy milk for their children, much less participate in the expanding consumer economy of the 1920s. As in previous strikes, police cracked down hard on the protesters, turning fire hoses against picket lines and making mass arrests. The violence escalated to the point that New York City newspapers began using armored cars when they sent their reporters to Passaic. Photographs of the strike included Flynn demonstrating how to use a gas mask developed during World War I, a measure she recommended the strikers use to protect themselves after police started throwing gas bombs at strikers.[7]

Nostalgic, perhaps, for the Paterson strike, where Tresca had been by her side, Flynn became romantically involved with the twenty-five-year-old leader of the Passaic strike, Albert Weisbord, who appeared "resourceful, inventive, [and] courageous."[8] The son of working-class Jewish immigrants from Russia, Weisbord had won a scholarship to Harvard Law School. He became a communist shortly after his graduation in 1924.

At this point, the American communist movement consisted of a small group of people who were united in their admiration for Soviet Russia, but divided over how the principles of the Bolshevik Revolution should be applied in the United States. Weisbord belonged to a faction that hoped to take control of the American Federation of Labor. However, the AFL, which had long opposed socialism, rejected communism and criticized the Bolsheviks for subordinating workers' organizations to the Soviet state.[9] Former IWW members had mixed opinions about the Soviet Union. Some, including Flynn's friends Ella Reeve Bloor, an organizer for the WDU, and Vincent St. John, a former leader of the IWW, saw the communists as bringing the war against capitalism into a more militant phase. Others, however, disliked the Bolsheviks' emphasis on central state control and their suppression of dissent. Many people found the communists cold, if not boring, compared with the eclectic figures who had populated the

IWW. Privately, in a letter to Flynn, Vorse characterized the communists as "clapping, empty jaws," more interested in talking about revolution than in the real struggles of working people.[10]

Given Flynn's legendary status as a leader of prewar fights for free speech and labor rights, Weisbord was one of many communists eager to convert Flynn to his cause.[11] After busy days of strike meetings in Passaic, Weisbord often took Elizabeth out to dinner in Manhattan. They would return to her basement apartment in the East Village for a glass of wine. In a letter to Vorse, Flynn described Weisbord as "the sweetest and most satisfying lover one could have."[12] At thirty-eight, Flynn's personality continued to sparkle with warmth and vitality. To younger people, however, Flynn appeared "motherly," with "the figure of an old-fashioned opera singer."[13] The stress of her breakup with Tresca and the punishing schedule she set for herself may have made Flynn appear older than she was. Popular culture now associated youth with beauty, and aging became an awkward proposition for a woman best known as the "rebel girl." Few models for revolutionary womanhood existed between the "girl revolutionary" and the maternal but sexless figures, such as Mary Harris "Mother" Jones (1837–1930), a fiery advocate for workers and their families, who continued to work for many of the same causes as Flynn. Middle age seemed to be an awkward time for Flynn, whereas male revolutionaries, like Tresca, remained attractive and self-confident.

Flynn's relationship with Weisbord proved to be short-lived. In September 1926, Flynn and Weisbord traveled together to Chicago to attend a meeting of International Labor Defense, which had merged with the WDU. The ILD elected Flynn chairman and featured her as a speaker. Weisbord, who expected to be applauded for his leadership in Passaic, was generally ignored. Furthermore, he was left out of meetings and parties held by communists in Chicago who were eager to win Flynn's allegiance. He became "jealous and possessive." Flynn and Weisbord fought on the train ride back to New York City. He questioned her loyalty to him, and she questioned his loyalty to her—knowing that he had been seeing another woman, Vera Burch. He ended the argument by cabling Burch and asking her to meet their train when it arrived at Grand Central Station.

Writing to Vorse, Flynn admitted, "I really do love him a lot, yet I see all his faults and realize he probably will never love anyone but himself." As the heat of sexual attraction subsided, Flynn's cool intelligence prevailed, but she felt humiliated by being caught, yet again, in a romantic triangle.[14]

In the summer of 1926, the communists in charge of the Passaic strike decided to abandon the nearly yearlong effort and hand over the workers they had organized to the United Textile Workers, an affiliate of the AFL. Their decision reflected a policy of working within existing trade unions rather than forming competing organizations. However, it underscored Flynn's sense of failure. Flynn's old animosity toward the AFL died hard, and she doubted the commitment of trade unions to the unskilled, immigrant workers in Passaic, many of them women. Flynn delivered her final speech in Passaic just before Labor Day of 1926. She promised that she would travel across the country in order to raise money to defend workers who remained in prison after being arrested during the strike. Groups of female workers from Poland and Hungary presented Flynn with bouquets of flowers and thanked her for being "the soul of the strike."[15]

In Passaic, as in Lawrence and Paterson, Flynn felt responsible for the workers she had led, regardless of the outcome of the strike. However, Vorse worried about Flynn's fitness for a cross-country trip. Visiting Flynn before she left, Vorse was alarmed to see "Elizabeth for the first time in all the years I have known her destroyed." Flynn seemed exhausted and unhinged, "talking like a girl of her lost love." Vorse, who had just been through her own miserable breakup with a younger man, returned home to Provincetown, Massachusetts, with "a grim sense of death."[16]

As Flynn's train hurtled west from Chicago toward the Rocky Mountains, Vorse's premonition seemed to be coming true. Elizabeth felt breathless, with stabbing pains in her back and a "heavy feeling around her heart." Determined to fulfill her promises, she gave speeches on behalf of the Passaic strikers and Sacco and Vanzetti in Denver, Salt Lake City, and Los Angeles. Once she reached San Francisco, however, she collapsed. Ella Reeve Bloor, who was also in San Francisco, checked Flynn into a hotel and made her rest. Writing back

Flynn (second from left) and Marie Equi (third from left)
in an unidentified photo, taken, most likely, in Seattle in 1917,
when they worked together to defend imprisoned IWW members.

Library of Congress, LC-USZ62-55896

(b&w film copy negative)

to Vorse, Flynn admitted the trip did not "thrill" her as she had hoped it would. Flynn had experienced "too many emotional shocks in the last few years." They had left her feeling "tired and empty way inside of myself." Yet Flynn refused to give up and return home. Joe Ettor, who had worked with Flynn in Lawrence and on the Mesabi Range before leaving the labor movement to become a successful wine merchant on the West Coast, drove Flynn to her next destination, Portland, Oregon.[17] Flynn planned to stay with Dr. Marie Equi, a friend since the 1910s who was known for her advocacy of free speech and birth control.

Flynn arrived at Equi's home at 1423 Southwest Hall Street sometime around Christmas of 1926. Flynn had always returned home for the holidays, but now she found herself in new surroundings: a large quiet house on a hill overlooking a verdant city. Alarmed by Flynn's failing health, Equi insisted that Flynn stay until her medical problems could be diagnosed and she could make a full recovery. The doctor ordered a series of tests, which revealed heart strain and a strep infection caused by an impacted tooth. Prior to the development of antibiotics, these problems could be treated only with rest, which Equi facilitated by dosing Flynn with whiskey smuggled in from Japan. Flynn hovered between life and death for several weeks, hearing "the rush of angel's wings." Equi called a bishop to perform last rites, a ritual that Flynn, an atheist, surely would have refused had she been conscious. Flynn credited Equi with saving her life.

Back in New York City, Flynn's family reacted to news of her illness with alarm. Tresca sent a telegram to Equi that read, "ELIZABETH SHOULD GIVE UP IMMEDIATELY AND STAY UNDER YOUR CARE." He promised, "I WILL TAKE CARE OF BUSTER PAYING WEEKLY ALLOWANCE AND RENT." He added, "MAMA AGREE."[18] Tresca must have known that his affair with Bina had contributed to Flynn's breakdown. He tried to make amends by helping Flynn's family, but it was too little, too late. A heart specialist warned that Flynn risked developing a heart lesion if she experienced any further strain. A strep specialist predicted that it would take Flynn at least five years to recover from her illness. She remained in Portland, separated from her family and nearly all of her friends for twice that length of time. She may have needed a decade to grieve over her losses, which included Tresca, her youth, and the vivid prewar labor movement in which she had been such a central figure.[19]

Flynn described Equi as a "stormy petrel of the Northwest." The petrel is a dramatic seabird whose appearance foreshadows a storm. In 1927, Equi had dark but graying hair and light gray eyes. Tall, dignified, and usually dressed in well-tailored suits, she cut a striking figure. Equi's politics aligned closely with Flynn's, even though her personality was considerably more volatile. Equi's biography forms a counterpoint to Flynn's, illustrating the development of radicalism in the Pacific Northwest.

Born in 1872 in New Bedford, Massachusetts, to an Irish mother and an Italian father, Equi had dropped out of high school to work in a textile mill to help support her family. In 1893, she seized the chance to head west with Bess Holcomb, a graduate of Wellesley College, who took a teaching position in The Dalles, a town in Oregon on the Columbia River. Holcomb claimed a homestead nearby. When Holcomb's boss paid her $100 less than she was owed for her first year of teaching, Equi confronted him in his downtown office with a horsewhip. Delighted by this example of frontier justice, town residents auctioned off the whip and gave Equi and Holcomb the proceeds. A few years later, the couple moved to San Francisco, where Holcomb taught school and Equi entered college. Determined to become a doctor, Equi then moved to Portland, where she earned her medical degree in 1903.[20]

Equi took advantage of the relative openness of the West to transcend her working-class upbringing and become a respected professional. She established a successful medical practice in Portland and began a long-term relationship with Harriet Speckart, an heiress to the Olympia Brewing fortune. Having watched her mother suffer under the burden of many unwanted pregnancies, Equi became one of two female doctors in Portland willing to perform abortions, serving women of all classes. The illegality of abortion led her to form alliances with city police, who granted her various favors, such as supplying her with alcohol during Prohibition. In 1915, Equi and Speckart adopted a daughter, "Mary, Jr.," who later became a well-known female aviator. Mary called Harriet "Ma" and Marie "Da." Harriet briefly married a male IWW organizer around the same time, which may have been related to the adoption.[21]

Equi's political activism began with progressive causes. She joined the battle for women's suffrage—won in Oregon in 1912. Like many female professionals of her era, she focused on the health of working-class women and children. In 1913, she joined a cannery strike led by the IWW. She was radicalized by the experience. Canneries were exempt from most of Oregon's labor laws. At harvest time, they employed women and children for long hours as temporary low-wage workers. The strike convinced Equi of the need for "direct action" as the best means for workers to control their conditions. Equi joined IWW campaigns among the unemployed and investigated health conditions in lumber camps throughout the Pacific Northwest. Meanwhile, she intensified her advocacy of birth control, helping Margaret Sanger rewrite her pamphlets so that they would be more accurate. Sanger described Equi as "a rebellious soul, generous, kind, brave, but so radical in her thinking that she is almost an outcast." Flynn modulated her public persona as the "rebel girl" in order to be loved by multitudes of workers and admired by many liberals. Equi, however, pushed beyond the boundaries of acceptable feminine behavior.

US entry into World War I made Equi even more confrontational. At an antiwar demonstration in downtown Portland, she unfurled a banner that read, "Prepare to Die, Workingmen, J. P. Morgan & co. Want Preparedness for Profit." Mary, Jr., remembered people spitting on her and her "da" after the incident. But most Portland IWW members shared Equi's antiwar views, and trade unionists knew her as a staunch defender of working people. Neither group cared much about Equi's romantic relationships with women, which extended beyond Speckart to include visiting female radicals such as the Irish nationalist Kathleen O'Brennan.

Government officials, however, soon made an issue of Equi's lesbianism. The US attorney for Portland classified Equi as "degenerate" due to her sexual preferences and deemed her "the most dangerous person at large in Oregon." The head of the Federal Bureau of Investigation in Portland launched an obsessive campaign to "get" Equi, hiring spies and paying informants to claim she had disparaged the military in a public speech. The agent assaulted Equi and called her an "unsexed woman" as she emerged from a federal courtroom, where she was sentenced to three years in prison under the Espionage Act. Organized labor joined western feminists to fund Equi's appeal and demand the agent's resignation. News of the case spread east. From the offices of the Workers' Defense Union in New York City, Flynn cabled Equi as she headed to San Quentin Prison in October 1920, saying, "Just received the bad news that you must go. Words cannot express amazement and sorrow. I have supreme faith in your courage and spirit."[22]

In prison, Equi became troubled by her sexuality. By 1920, popular ideas about women who formed romantic partnerships with other women had shifted from late nineteenth-century acceptance of "Boston marriages" toward a stigmatization of same-sex relationships between women as "unnatural." (In contrast, sex between men was illegal, and domestic partnerships between them had never gained wide acceptance in the United States.) But female prisons were working-class spaces given to frank discussion—and pursuit— of sex and love between women.[23] These cross-cutting currents led Equi to question the validity of her sexual preference for women. In a letter to a friend confessing a crush on another prisoner, Equi revealed her fear that she was "queer." Equi's friend assured her, "It is a fact you have dared to do the unestablished thing, and therefore the unapproved, that you are looked upon as queer. . . . [Y]ou are perfectly sane, though." While in prison, Equi kept in close touch with Speckart, expressing concern for their daughter. The couple separated, however, after Equi's release. Mary, Jr., went to live with her "ma" (Speckart) in Seaside, Oregon.

As radical movements crumbled under the pressure of wartime repression and postwar red scares, Equi and Flynn both struggled to find a place for themselves in public life. The Wobblies were decimated. The communists spent most of their time squabbling among themselves. The AFL shrank under the pressure of an open-shop drive known as the "American Plan." Sacco and Vanzetti lost their appeal and were executed in August 1927. Feminists fought with each other over how far to extend the principle of equal rights. Advocates for birth control shifted from radical calls for women's emancipation toward arguments about the need to produce a racially healthy population. Popular culture glamorized the flapper, celebrating youth and heterosexual fun, with little political content to the rebellion. Equi and Flynn turned to each other for companionship in a landscape that both found barren of political possibility. There is no proof that Flynn and Equi became sexual partners; nor does such proof exist for many romantic relationships, regardless of sexual orientation. But "it is certain" that Flynn and Equi "had an intense, emotionally involved and occasionally stormy relationship."[24]

As the Roaring Twenties gave way to the Great Depression, and Flynn's absence from New York stretched from months to years, her possibilities for self-support dwindled. In 1928, the Garland Fund found a new secretary, having concluded that Flynn's "absence from New York will probably be indefinite." Flynn resigned as the chairman of International Labor Defense in 1929, urging the board of directors to give the position "to some active and useful person." She refused to stay on as a figurehead, concluding, "No present prospects of returning East. Decision final."[25] While in Portland, Flynn did undertake some limited political activities, appearing at rallies in support of Tom Mooney, a political prisoner who had been charged with detonating a bomb at a Preparedness Day parade in San Francisco in 1916.

On a visit home for several months starting in 1929 but extending into 1930, Flynn felt like a burden to her family, which was trying to survive on Kathie's earnings as a schoolteacher. Straining family finances further, Kathie was paying for Flynn's son, Buster, to attend the University of Michigan, where he was an indifferent student. Writing to Vorse, Flynn complained that she found New York to be "a nerve-wracking place." The labor movement was "a mess torn by factionalism and scandal and led by self-seekers." Flynn felt relieved when Equi, whom she always called "Doc," urged her to come back to Portland.[26] Back in Equi's comfortable home, Flynn spent her days reading, plowing through the classics, history, science, and even the Bible, which she considered an example of great storytelling.[27]

Flynn admitted that Equi "was not the easiest person to get along with" and "had a high temper." However, she thought Equi had "a brilliant mind and a progressive spirit." Furthermore, she appreciated the comfortable lifestyle the doctor provided. In exchange for Equi's economic support, Flynn took care of Mary, Jr., who came to live with them in 1927 when she was about twelve years old, after Harriet Speckart's death. Flynn, who had never spent much time with Buster, grew very attached to Mary. Furthermore, Flynn agreed to

Fred "Buster" Flynn's photo of his mother, Elizabeth,
while visiting Crater Lake in Oregon (1927).

NP18-20, EGF Photographs,
Tamiment Library, NYU

"keep the books" for Equi's medical practice and "help in the household." Flynn's job was not too demanding, as they also hired help "to do the cleaning, laundry and other household chores" and ate out frequently.[28] However, Flynn took on a more domestic role than she had ever assumed before. Flynn and Equi's relationship became more complicated after 1930, when Equi suffered a heart attack and became bedridden. Flynn, who now became Equi's caretaker, felt increasingly isolated and depressed. In a letter to Vorse, Flynn admitted, "I am so lonely at times for my past activities, my old friends, and the places where life was so full."[29]

Flynn's family remained concerned about her. Her father, Tom, seemed mystified by his daughter's decision to move to Portland and withdraw from public life. Kathie worried that Elizabeth would damage her reputation by living with a lesbian. But Bina became most alarmed. The sisters reconciled in the early 1930s. In the summer of 1934, Elizabeth visited Bina and her family in Miami, Arizona, where they had moved to ride out the Depression. Bina thought that Elizabeth seemed unhappy with Equi, yet unable to pull away. Soon afterward, Mary, Jr., flew her plane down to Miami. She landed in an open field and spent her visit "talking about the sick relationship between her mother and Elizabeth."[30] It is impossible to know whether Mary's characterization of the relationship included judgments about her mother's lesbianism, but it seems clear that Flynn felt trapped in her relationship with Equi. Flynn seemed almost immobilized, in contrast to her earlier life, when she could never stay in one place for very long. Flynn's inactivity showed on her body: she gained seventy pounds, and the extra weight made her look very unlike the slim girl who had captured public attention for her bravado and her beauty in her teens and twenties. Statuesque in her thirties, Flynn was overweight in her forties and remained heavy for the rest of her life. In a letter to a friend in 1934, Flynn described herself as "too stout, probably from a rather inactive, indoor life."[31] Flynn felt bad about her weight, and it became another factor separating her from her former life.

In contrast, Bina seemed to be a whirlwind of activity. Shortly after her relationship with Tresca fell apart, Bina had married Romolo Bobba, a former IWW organizer and political prisoner. Bina and Bobba had met in 1921 at the offices of the WDU. Like Tresca, Bobba was tall, good-looking, and Italian. But Bobba was far more conventional than Tresca. By the mid-1920s, he had a successful business selling novelties to carnivals. He agreed to raise Bina's son, Peter, as his own, although Peter's resemblance to his father, Carlo Tresca, became unmistakable as Peter got older. Bina and Bobba had two more children, Jane and Roberta. When Bobba's business went bankrupt during the Depression, he moved his family out to Miami, Arizona, where he worked first for the Department of Highways and later as a union organizer. When he lost his job, the family had to go on relief in order to survive.

Miami, Arizona, a grim former mining town, was a far cry from Greenwich Village, where Bina had hoped to make her mark on the literary scene. In a letter to Carlo Tresca, asking if he could send some money to help get Peter's teeth fixed, and buy him some books and clothes, Bina remarked, "The standard of living [here] is low and the standard of thought is lower."[32] Fed up, Bina and her family moved to San Francisco in 1935. She found a job for the city inspecting dance halls. Romolo began selling Italian food products. If Bina felt any lingering guilt over her affair with Carlo, she may have expiated it by rescuing Elizabeth from a relationship in which she had become strangely passive and subservient to Equi.

In a story that might have been ripped from the pages of *Ranch Romances*, Bina and Romolo Bobba drove up to Portland in April 1936, determined to save Elizabeth. Bobba banged on Equi's door. Once inside the house, he shouted that he was not leaving unless Elizabeth came with him. Stunned or relieved, Elizabeth complied. She packed her bags quickly and left with the Bobbas. Afraid that Equi would use her police connections to stop them, Romolo drove back to San Francisco at top speed.[33] Elizabeth remained with Bina and her family for three months before getting up her nerve to go back to

New York City and restart her life. In August, the prodigal daughter returned. As always, Flynn's mother welcomed her home.

The Flynn family remembered the personal elements in this story: Elizabeth's depression, Bina and Romolo's dramatic rescue, Marie Equi's domineering personality. But politics were at play, too. Radicalism was reviving in the mid-1930s. Flynn felt like she had to get back in the game. Six months after her return home, Flynn began her "second life" as a key figure in the American Communist Party.

7

"My Second Life"— The Communist Party

By the mid-1930s, revolution was in the air, and Flynn could no longer sit on the sidelines.[1] As the Great Depression dragged on, people questioned the viability of capitalism. The Communist Party (CP) launched a broad range of programs to mobilize workers, housewives, and the unemployed. Unions began to thrive, bolstered by the New Deal and by the creation of the Congress of Industrial Organizations (CIO). From Marie Equi's home in Portland, Flynn had followed the news in 1934 as massive strikes broke out among West Coast longshoremen, Toledo autoworkers, and Minneapolis truck drivers. Textile workers from Maine to Alabama walked off their jobs.[2] To Flynn, the workers who were organizing industry-wide unions were reaping the harvest of the seeds sown by IWW members "who were mobbed, jailed, and [had] died" for the cause.[3] In 1935, Flynn felt "electrified" when she read about the Popular Front, a communist initiative to build progressive alliances to fight fascism, which had emerged in the form of authoritarian political parties that had taken over Italy and Germany and were fighting to overthrow the elected government in Spain. Watching labor and radical movements mobilize made Flynn "ashamed to be idle." She decided that she "must go home" and "get back to work."

To Flynn, returning home to New York City and resuming her life as an activist felt like coming "out of darkness, into the light again." Flynn arrived at her family's Brooklyn apartment on her forty-sixth birthday, August 7, 1936. She was happy to be reunited with her parents and her sister Kathie, but she mourned the death of her forty-two-year-old brother, Tom, who had committed suicide in January. He had become an optician and had opened a store that failed during the Great Depression. Kathie, a schoolteacher in the Bronx, remained the family's sole wage earner. She now had a four-year-old daughter, Frances, the product of a relationship that had ended. Like Buster, Frances took her mother's last name. Flynn's mother, Annie, by then in her late seventies, seemed increasingly fragile. Flynn's father, Tom, Sr., remained robust, but he and Annie did not get along well. Tom spent much of his time living in a small cottage in rural Connecticut on land that Bina and Romolo Bobba had purchased in the 1920s. Buster had found a job in Washington, DC, crunching numbers for a federal agency. Happy to be back home with her "dear" family who "loved and tolerated her," Flynn felt "frightened" and confused about "how to pick up the scattered pieces" of her work.[4]

Flynn's "great anxiety" in the summer and fall of 1936 that she would seem like a "ghost" passed quickly.[5] Old friends and associates welcomed her back. They invited her to dinners and cocktail parties. Flynn ran into Carlo Tresca at John's, a restaurant they had once frequented together. Their meeting must have been painful for Flynn, but they renewed their friendship. Tresca had married Margaret De Silver, the wealthy widow of Albert De Silver, a founder of the American Civil Liberties Union (ACLU). Tresca and De Silver lived in a gracious home in Brooklyn Heights and spent their summers on Cape Cod. In contrast, Flynn's life remained Spartan. She and her family lived in a working-class neighborhood in Brooklyn, and Flynn could not afford to leave the city during the summer to escape the stifling heat. Her first romantic partner now that she was back in New York City was a young redheaded sailor from New Orleans who worked as a communist organizer. He shared Flynn's room for a few months before he shipped out.[6]

Flynn picked up "the broken thread" of her work. She renewed her associations with Heterodoxy, International Labor Defense, and the ACLU. Prior to her move to Portland, she had reached the public primarily as a speaker, and her writing had seemed wordy and fragmented. After a decade spent reading, however, Flynn demonstrated new facility as a writer. She contributed chatty but pointed articles to publications such as the *Woman Shopper, Labor Defender*, the *New Masses*, the *Daily Worker*, and *The Woman Today*. In print, she reminisced about her time with the IWW and commented on current events. She profiled female labor leaders, such as Ella Reeve Bloor, known as "Mother Bloor," a friend from the Workers' Defense Union and the Passaic strike of 1926, who was now a leading communist.[7]

Before she retreated from public life, Flynn had been celebrated as one of the best female orators in America, "as fine a speaker" as Emma Goldman, and equally "as forceful."[8] Back from her long hiatus, Flynn demonstrated renewed vigor. As an IWW "agitator," she had spoken from the "heart," using only her lungs to project her voice. She "gestured and "paced the platform," establishing "an electric unity" with her audience. Now she learned to stand still and use a microphone. She began to write her speeches to prepare for radio broadcasts, which required her to compress her remarks into several minutes.[9] Despite her initial fear of the microphone, Flynn adjusted quickly to the new, more "streamlined" style of public speaking. In small, informal settings where amplification was not used, her "sheer lung power" continued to impress. Flynn gradually extended her range of speaking engagements beyond New York City, traveling to Philadelphia, Boston, Baltimore, Passaic, and "Paterson and Lawrence again!"[10] A young man who saw her speak in the late 1930s in upstate New York recalled that once she got going, "a reservoir of words" seemed to "flood out of her like the Susquehanna at thaw time."[11] Like her writing, her speeches became a source of income. From August 1936 until December 1937, Flynn wrote forty-one articles and gave eighty-three speeches, for which she earned a total of $296.50, less than $5,000 in today's dollars, but more than she had earned during the previous ten years.[12]

Flynn began to support herself, even if she generally felt "broke." During her first year and a half back in New York City, a $100 contribution from a friend helped Flynn cover her expenses.[13] Active and working again, she felt happier than she had in years. Leaving behind her comfortable life with Equi, Flynn realized "that economic security, [a] good house, fine furniture, clothes, comforts, money to spend, <u>are not what a person like me wants</u>." Instead, like Virginia Woolf, her British contemporary, Flynn wished for a room of her own, a feminist aspiration that crossed class lines. Even with money tight, Flynn reflected, "One's liberty, one's own life, one's own work is all important, even living in one room, with a bed, a chair, a table to write on, shelves for books, can suffice."[14] In a letter to her old friend Mary Heaton Vorse, Flynn reported in March 1937 that she was "beginning to be active again and . . . enjoying it immensely."[15]

In February 1937, Flynn joined the CP, experiencing "the same feeling of dedication and profound emotion" as when she had joined the IWW at age sixteen. She invested in both organizations as vehicles for building a socialist America. Whereas the IWW was a decentralized and spontaneous movement open to all sorts of challenges to the status quo, the CP, however, expected its members to follow policies set by its national leaders, who took their cues from the Soviet-controlled Communist International, or Comintern. Despite these differences, many former Wobblies became communists and embraced the Soviet Union as a positive example of a socialist society. In reality, the American CP encompassed a diverse set of priorities and organizing styles. Local communist leaders adapted party imperatives to local conditions, whether they were organizing railroad workers in Chicago, dockworkers in San Pedro, tenants in Harlem, or sharecroppers in Alabama.[16] Communists pursued alliances with progressive groups, and they provided the language to frame the most pressing social issues of the day, from the lack of jobs to African American inequality. In the 1930s, the American communist ideal of creating a more democratic and inclusive society inspired artists, writers, and dancers, and seemed strangely disassociated with actual conditions in the Soviet Union. Meanwhile, from 1936 to 1938, Stalin consolidated his power with the Moscow

Trials, which purged Soviet leadership of anyone he considered his adversary.[17]

Like most Americans who were attracted to the Communist Party, Flynn ignored charges that the Soviet Union had degenerated into a dictatorship. She wanted to be relevant, and communists were at the center of a "renaissance of American radicalism."[18] Even at the peak of the Popular Front, however, Flynn weighed her decision carefully. In the past, she had disliked the party's factionalism and doubted its leadership. Furthermore, she had been troubled by the treatment of political prisoners in the Soviet Union in the 1920s. By the 1930s, the American CP had become a far more effective organization than it had been earlier. Membership climbed to 100,000, and several times that number identified with the party and sympathized with its objectives. Communists played a crucial role in reviving the American labor movement. However, the treatment of dissenters within the Soviet Union remained as bad, or worse, than ever. Flynn set aside her earlier concerns, focusing instead on the CP's potential to bring socialism to the United States.

Making a list of thirty-seven reasons for joining the party in 1937, Flynn wrote at the top, "Organized and Varied Activity." She imagined the party as a sort of "yeast" that would catalyze "mass movements" and make them rise up to create a revolution. Flynn viewed the CP as inheriting the "best traditions" of the IWW. The party supported the creation of industrial unions, and it appealed to all workers regardless of race, gender, or ethnicity. Extending beyond the IWW, the CP reached out to farmers, housewives, and professionals.

Flynn signed on to the CP's new "identification" with the best of "Americanism." Earl Browder, the clean-cut, Kansas-born leader of the CP, coined the slogan "Communism is Twentieth-Century Americanism." Flynn's fame as an American labor leader made her valuable to the CP, which was eager to broaden its appeal beyond immigrant and foreign-born workers and to identify itself with the American radical tradition.[19] However communism and Americanism never fit together seamlessly. The CP shaped and reshaped its policies to conform to Soviet priorities. This made communists vulnerable to the charge that they were not truly loyal to the United States.

It seemed to Flynn that women had "equal status" in the "movement." Her assessment may have been overly optimistic, as the top national leaders of the CP were all men, and the party insisted on social class rather than gender as the fundamental category of concern. At the state and local level, however, women were pioneering the community-based organization associated with the Popular Front.[20] "Mother Bloor," a much-loved national figure, focused on working-class families and communities. Anita Whitney, a friend of Flynn's since the 1920s, built a strong, unified branch of the Communist Party in California that included Hollywood writers and actors, San Francisco longshoremen, and Mexicans and Asians who labored in the "inland empire" of commercial agriculture.[21] Bloor and Whitney, who were both a generation older than Flynn, remained active, vital, and engaged. Flynn regarded them as role models, women in leadership who were "loved and cherished as an invaluable part of the American labor movement."[22]

Flynn admired the principled stance the CP took on "Negro" rights. It fought for social, legal, and economic equality, as well as "protection from violence." Communists defended the "Scottsboro boys," nine black teenagers from Alabama who were falsely accused of rape in 1931. CP members also protested segregation and Jim Crow laws. They viewed African Americans as an oppressed, potentially revolutionary minority. Flynn's concern for African American rights stretched back to her visit to Ybor City, Florida, after the Paterson strike of 1913, and developed further during and after World War I, when she spoke out against lynching and other forms of racial violence.[23] The CP was the most integrated social movement of its era, and Flynn welcomed the opportunity to work with African American activists.

The CP endorsed political action as crucial to workers' movements. The IWW, in contrast, rejected meaningful political change as impossible to achieve within a capitalist society, and its members often refused to vote. In the early 1900s, Flynn's experiences as a leader of strikes and free-speech battles convinced her that the state served the needs of the ruling class at the expense of workers. But by the 1930s, with the New Deal getting underway, she felt that the state could improve workers' lives, both by regulating their conditions of labor and by providing social supports such as old-age insurance. The electorate had changed dramatically: women could vote, as could most workers, who were unlikely to be recent immigrants, owing to the immigration restrictions in effect since 1924. In November 1937, Flynn voted for the first time, casting her ballot for Mayor Fiorello LaGuardia, a Republican reformer and supporter of the New Deal. She jotted in her diary, "I cease to be a Wobbly!"[24]

The "<u>Discipline</u>" of the CP appealed strongly to Flynn, as she noted by underlining the term twice. A sense of solidarity knit the Wobblies together, but their rejection of hierarchy made it difficult for leaders to overrule the impulses of members, even when they were counterproductive. In Flynn's opinion, Bill Haywood had attempted to exercise control over the sprawling organization by becoming dictatorial. Perhaps a more disciplined group, like the CP, would enjoy more rational—if less inspired—leadership. Privately, she and her sister Kathie described Browder, a former accountant, as "boring" compared to the larger-than-life prewar labor leaders they had known.[25] As Flynn would later discover, demands for discipline among CP members made it all too easy for party leaders to become dictatorial, too, even as they pursued policies that damaged the organization.

Although her own private life remained unconventional, Flynn approved of the CP's abandonment of the "freakishness & bohemianism" of the prewar Left. She liked the CP's emphasis on "home" and "family," believing, perhaps, that these more conservative cultural values would make communism more appealing to the masses. By embracing these values, however, Flynn repudiated her own past, which included advocacy of free love and a long-term relationship with a woman. Conventional gender relations required women to subordinate themselves to men. As a result of having to conform to the CP's more conservative values, Flynn's romantic life became limited to a series of short-term, secret relationships.

At the end of her list of reasons, Flynn concluded, "Definitely decided my place [is] in the CP."[26] If Flynn made a counter list of reasons *not* to join the CP, she did not save it. Her decision to join the party shaped every aspect of her life from this point forward. Flynn became a national organizer, joined the CP's Women's Commission, and was quickly elected to the CP's National Committee.[27] She invested the party with all of the energy and idealism she had devoted to previous causes, from leading strikes for the IWW to defending workers targeted by the Red Scare. Eventually, however, Flynn's loyalty to the CP linked her to an organization that failed to deliver on its democratic promise and that remained hopelessly tied to a corrupt Soviet regime.

Flynn avoided being pulled into the rivalry between two top leaders of the party, Earl Browder and Bill Foster. Browder, who was about Flynn's age, proved adept at making communism appealing to many Americans who were critical of capitalism during the Depression and who were searching for alternative forms of economic organization. Foster, who was about a decade older than Browder and Flynn, hewed to a revolutionary hard line. A lanky former IWW and union organizer, Foster disliked the CP's drift away from the language of class warfare.[28] Flynn worked closely with both Browder and Foster. Her warm personality and ready sense of humor, along with her unique position as the sole woman on the National Committee, enabled her to escape some of the infighting that plagued the CP.[29] Party regulars considered her a "mass figure" who was skilled at reaching the public, but excluded from the close and contentious circle of top leaders who traveled to Moscow each year to take direction from the Comintern.[30]

Flynn's new membership in the CP thrilled her, but old friends differed bitterly over whether communism fulfilled or betrayed socialist ideals. Many liberals, socialists, trade unionists, and civil rights activists were disillusioned by the Moscow Trials, and later, in 1939, by the Nazi-Soviet Non-Aggression Pact.[31] Anarchists who had been exiled to Soviet Russia, such as Emma Goldman, had warned of Soviet brutality in the 1920s, and Soviet repression of dissent under Stalin continued into the 1930s. Lack of a free press within the Soviet Union meant that the full story of Stalin's brutality would not become known until twenty years later. Like most communists, Flynn assumed that the capitalist press was exaggerating the negative stories about Stalin in order to discredit the Soviet

Union. The communist press generated its own newsfeed, lauding the accomplishments of the Soviet Union in achieving rapid industrial development, avoiding economic instability, and banishing differences of class and gender.[32]

Three of Flynn's oldest friends, Carlo Tresca, Joe Ettor, and Arturo Giovannitti, urged her to reconsider her choice to join the CP. Like many anarchists and syndicalists, they sympathized with Leon Trotsky, a Bolshevik leader who had been exiled to Mexico City in 1929 and then brutally murdered by Soviet assassins in 1940. As antifascist Italians, Tresca, Ettor, and Giovannitti were also disillusioned by Soviet participation in the Spanish Civil War. Soviet troops in Spain seemed more concerned with liquidating Spanish anarchists and other noncommunists than with restoring the elected government.[33] Most American antifascists were ignorant of these details and viewed the Soviet Union's intervention in support of the Spanish republic as heroic.[34] Flynn's sisters, Kathie and Bina, found the CP rigid and unappealing. But according to Flynn's nephew, Peter Martin, once Flynn joined the party, "she never looked back."[35] In a letter to Vorse, Flynn announced, "We are living in great days—dreams coming true." She felt sorry for old friends like Tresca who rejected the CP and failed to see the significance of the CIO. Flynn concluded, "We can't go on forever on past reputations and dead organizations. Life goes on."[36]

In the spring of 1937, the CP featured Flynn as a speaker at a wide range of events in New York City. In April, she joined the author John Dos Passos at a mass rally at the Mecca Temple on West 55th Street to honor the Abraham Lincoln Brigade, a group of mostly communist American volunteers fighting the fascists in Spain. The rally featured a radio hook-up to Madrid that enabled Dolores Ibárruri, a leading Spanish communist, to address the gathering.[37] In May, Flynn spoke to a sold-out crowd of 20,000 people at Madison Square Garden. Wearing a black velvet dress made by her mother, Flynn demonstrated her renewed "ability to hold a crowd spellbound" through the simplicity of her language and drama of her voice. Flynn shared the stage with Earl Browder, Bill Foster, Mother Bloor, and Angelo Herndon, an African American labor organizer who had been recently released from prison in Georgia. Herndon had been charged under a Reconstruction-era law with inciting an "insurrection" after organizing a march of unemployed workers in Atlanta.

On May Day of 1937, Flynn climbed onto the reviewing stand in Union Square to watch a ten-hour parade. Surrounded by representatives of socialism and labor, she must have relished the display of unity and appreciated the relaxed attitude of city police, who had once treated labor protesters as criminals.[38] Photographs show a smiling Flynn wearing a stylish felt hat and a tailored coat. Her renewed activity showed on her face and her body: she appeared younger than she had in a photograph taken four years earlier in Arizona. Although Flynn remained heavy, she looked trimmer and more energetic. She stood next to Bill Foster, who wore a suit and tie. Whereas communists had once dressed as workers, and Wobblies often dressed flamboyantly, these conservative clothes communicated respectability. Under Browder's direction, the CP formed the left wing of the New Deal coalition. They supported President Franklin D. Roosevelt's programs for reform, and they pushed him to go further in offering federally financed jobs and housing.[39]

Flynn enjoyed being back in the spotlight, but she was not content to address workers from a stage. She wanted to participate in their struggles and talk to them "face to face." In 1938, with her mother's encouragement, she embarked on an intense, ten-month assignment as a field organizer for the CP in Pennsylvania. Being a communist in New York felt easy, "comfortable." Half of the members of the CP lived in New York City—the rest were concentrated in California and Chicago, or clustered in smaller industrial cities around the country.[40] Basing herself in Pittsburgh, Flynn jumped into campaigns to bring miners and steelworkers into CIO unions. She urged working-class voters to support New Deal candidates in the 1938 election. Flynn offered courses at workers' schools in Pittsburgh and Philadelphia, outlining the history of the American labor movement. Workers' economic and political demands were "Inseparably Intertwined," Flynn argued. She joined meetings of women's auxiliaries, which played a key role in the success of the CIO. *Woman of Steel*, a local newsletter, noted that whereas Flynn had been a powerful but singular female figure in past decades, women were now organized and working together, giving them a new sense of collective power.[41]

May Day in Pittsburgh in 1938 seemed to Flynn to be the flowering of the work that had been so brutally interrupted by World War I and the Red Scare. She felt proud to be the lead speaker at events where workers had so much to celebrate: the surge of the CIO, the growth of collective bargaining, and workers' participation in the political process. Under the combined influence of the CP, the CIO, and the New Deal, workers were "changing industrial feudalism into a real commonwealth." In a radio address that preceded a parade and picnic, Flynn explained how nineteenth-century struggles for shorter working hours had inspired the first May Day parade in Chicago in 1886. Recent laws making eight hours a day's work came after decades of pressure from organized labor. This long struggle showed "that every right the people enjoy in America today has been hard won and should not be lightly held." Flynn reminded her audience that workers' rights—to organize, to strike, and to picket—had once been declared an "illegal conspiracy." Likewise, workers' civil liberties and right to free speech had been "challenged innumerable times." Flynn urged her audience to remember the "men and women" who had been "denied work, blacklisted, deported, arrested, beaten, even killed, to assert these rights for the American people." None of labor's victories had been handed to them "on a silver platter." Workers must be prepared to fight for these rights "to maintain them."[42]

Influenced by Marxist theory, Flynn placed special significance on the organization of industrial workers by the CIO. Communists built unions in basic industries such as steel, rubber, automobiles, meatpacking, and electrical products. Back in New York City, however, Flynn's organizing focused on women and extended in new directions. She frequently attended meetings of the Domestic Workers' Union (DWU), a predominantly African American union of domestic workers based in Harlem that was fighting for better wages and working conditions and challenging the exclusion of domestic workers from state and federal labor legislation.[43] The DWU was affiliated with the AFL, indicating expansion and change in an organization formerly identified exclusively with skilled white male workers. Flynn

reached out to barbers and "Beauty Culturists" in Brooklyn and Manhattan, workers who had traditionally been excluded from the labor
movement, but now showed interest in joining a CIO union in order
to gain a say in their hours and working conditions.[44] Flynn also accepted invitations to speak to department-store workers, a previously
unorganized sector of the labor force.[45] Nationwide, membership
in unions doubled during the 1930s, rising to about 28 percent of
American workers by 1940.[46] Flynn took pride in the role that she
and other communist organizers were playing in rebuilding the labor
movement.

Flynn's public life seemed to be a string of triumphs in the late
1930s. Her personal life, in contrast, seemed tentative. While working
in Pittsburgh, she mused about "how to accept the autumn of one's
life." Like spring, her youth had been "wild and wayward," rushing
"so heedless by in ecstatic dreams." The World War I era seemed like
the summer, "high noon of work beyond measure." But "the thunder
and lightning of great struggles" had ended in a "blinding crash" that
left her "bruised and spent." In Pittsburgh, she finally felt recovered.
She promised herself that her mind remained her "living core" and
would save her from her "wild tempestuous heart." She compared a
love affair with an unnamed man in June 1938 to a "desert spring"
that cooled and healed, contrasting it to the "mad love" of her youth
that flamed, seared, and blinded. Her new lover was an organizer
for the CP. Flynn imagined this relationship as "Red love, Bolshevik
love." It would be "calm and creative" rather than fiery and destructive, as her relationships with both Tresca and Equi had been. But the
organizer moved on and the lovers parted ways.

In her private moments, Flynn, venturing into poetry, struggled
to keep her "dual minds apart / The mind of reason and the mind
of heart." She tried "not to possess and therefore not to lose / Not
to be possessed and once again be lost." But she soon fell passionately in love with another man. He was Jewish, and she described
him as having "the swift slender hands of an artist" and the "smolder-
ing romantic eyes of a poet." Just as she had idealized Tresca's Italian
background, so, too, she imagined "a thousand years of subtle racial
sensitivity" in her new lover. He seemed bred to be "a martyr" and "a

fighter." But with these stronger feelings came pain and the "sharp hurt of anger." She resolved to fill her mind with work, writing, "I lock my heart against you—throw away the key, I cannot spend my mind or strength on you, or anyone." But, Flynn and this young man, whose name she left blank in her poems, continued their sporadic relationship through World War II, when he enlisted as a fighter pilot. Another poem written around the same time despaired at men's preference for weak women. "Afraid to be overshadowed, possessed, dwarfed out," they seemed threatened by a "proud, intelligent, passionate woman."[47] Flynn's liaisons provided pleasure but left her without steady emotional support.

Flynn felt even more alone after her mother's death in 1938. Riding east on the train from Pittsburgh, she remembered all the times she had eagerly returned home, anxious to see her mother and "to tell her all I did and saw." Now Flynn struggled to come to terms with the loss, writing in her poetry notebook, "<u>She is not there; she never will be there</u>!" Flynn remembered her mother as "young, beautiful and sad" as well as "old, happy and tolerant." In her later years, Flynn's mother had seemed "serene, proud of us, but always slightly amused." Flynn admired her father's long-standing commitment to radical causes, but she and her sisters faulted him for making their mother unhappy.[48] Musing on her mother's legacy to her daughters, Flynn reflected, "If we have independent spirits, inquiring minds, the courage of our convictions, and a revolutionary outlook, we can thank our Mother."[49]

Flynn's own feelings about motherhood remained conflicted. Since having her son, Buster, at age nineteen, she had struggled to reconcile motherhood with revolutionary activism. She did not always succeed. Her earnings as an organizer helped keep her family afloat, but she was absent for much of Buster's childhood, leaving for months at a time to lead strikes or work on behalf of labor defense. Once Flynn moved to Oregon she became even more removed. She missed milestones in her son's life, such as his eighteenth birthday and his 1928 graduation from Stuyvesant High School, where he was an honor student.[50] After graduation, Buster traveled out to Oregon to visit her. They vacationed together at Crater Lake. However, they soon had a falling out. She wanted him to go to a public college in New York City. However, he had his heart set on the University of Michigan. Kathie, who had been a more active caretaker than Elizabeth, promised to help pay Buster's tuition, but she could not afford to keep supporting him once the Depression hit. Buster received high marks, especially in math and statistics, but he seemed more interested in playing chess than in pursuing his studies. He left school six months shy of a degree. Elizabeth doubted the value of college, but she confessed disappointment in Buster's lack of interest in "radical affairs." Buster stopped writing to his mother for several years, to her "very great sorrow."[51]

The death of Flynn's mother may have spurred Flynn to rebuild her relationship with her son. Laid off from his job after Congress cut funding for the Works Progress Administration, Buster moved back to New York City to live with his mother, Aunt Kathie, and cousin Frances. Now in his late twenties, Buster and his mother became friends. Buster, who had curly dark hair and blue eyes, shared his mother's keen sense of humor. They stayed up late listening to the radio and drinking beer. They discussed politics. Buster became active in the American Labor Party, a political party that endorsed candidates favorable to labor. In the summer of 1939, he took her to a baseball game at Yankee Stadium. Reflecting on the fun she had going to the game with Buster in one of her weekly columns for the *Daily Worker*, Flynn regretted that she had missed out on getting to know her son earlier. They spent Christmas of 1939 and New Year's of 1940 together.[52] A Valentine's Day card from Buster to Elizabeth read, in part, "Slushy phrases and all the rest; Still you are the one that I love the best." Thus, it came as a terrible shock when Buster told his mother at dinner on March 4, 1940, that he had lung cancer. He entered Beth Israel Hospital for an operation on March 20, but died nine days later.[53] Having so recently regained her son, Flynn felt his loss acutely.

Grief struck Flynn at a particularly difficult time politically: in August 1939, the Nazi-Soviet Non-Aggression Pact had ended the CP's easy camaraderie with liberals and intellectuals.[54] Many people who had sympathized with the Popular Front and supported the fight

*Fred "Buster" Flynn as an adult,
in a photo taken by his Aunt Kathie.*

NP18-67, EGF Photographs,
Tamiment Library, NYU

against fascism felt betrayed by the Soviet Union when it cut a deal with Germany to avoid invasion. When Flynn ran into an Italian friend from her days defending Sacco and Vanzetti, he greeted her with a "Heil Hitler" salute. American communists painted World War II, like World War I, as an imperialist conflict and called for peace. But their stance seemed hypocritical when the Soviet Union invaded Poland, Estonia, Latvia, Lithuania, and Finland in the fall of 1939.[55] At a CP rally in Baltimore in December, war veterans, many of them Jewish, "hissed, booed, cat-called and shouted" at Flynn when she tried to defend Soviet actions.[56] The American Legion disrupted meetings that Flynn held in Davenport and Des Moines, Iowa.[57]

The Nazi-Soviet Non-Aggression Pact sparked a mini Red Scare, but anticommunism had already intensified during the New Deal. Business and religious leaders viewed communism with hostility. The national leaders of the AFL continued their long animosity toward socialism and criticized their rivals in the CIO for their communist connections.[58] President Roosevelt's consolidation of executive power and his administration's sympathy for workers and African Americans antagonized both northern Republicans and southern Democrats, who sought to paint the New Deal as a communist plot. In May 1938, Representative Martin Dies, a Democrat from Texas, formed a Special Committee on Un-American Activities to investigate "subversive activities."[59] The Dies Committee assumed a broad mandate to question suspects about communist ties and find them guilty by association. Anxious to avoid censure and disillusioned by the Nazi-Soviet Non-Aggression Pact, many liberal organizations that had been part of the Popular Front resolved to rid themselves of communists.[60]

Flynn became a victim of this new upsurge of anticommunism. In January 1940, the ACLU adopted a resolution declaring it "inappropriate for supporters of so-called totalitarian dictatorships to serve on the governing committees and staff of the union." They expected Flynn, the sole member of the CP who remained on the board of the ACLU, to resign quietly. She refused. Instead, she wrote articles for the *Sunday Worker* and the *New Masses* defending herself. Flynn expressed disbelief that she would be asked to resign from the ACLU due to her membership in an organization: a practice the ACLU had *"continuously protested against"* since its founding twenty-three years earlier. Once composed of "heretics" and "non-conformists," she complained, the board of the ACLU now consisted of wealthy "lawyers, business men, [and] ministers" and included "not a single representative of organized labor." Damning liberals' conceptions of themselves as neutral mediators between opposing interests, Flynn accused the board of having become "class conscious." The board was intimidated, Flynn argued, by a strong, powerful labor movement that made demands rather than asking for favors.[61] Flynn suspected that she was being sacrificed in order to "wash out the red" and spare the ACLU negative scrutiny by the Dies Committee.[62] The ACLU added further charges against Flynn for insulting the organization in print. One union leader who supported Flynn quipped, "Hitler's crusade to save the world from 'Communism'—momentarily compromised by his treaty with Russia—has been taken up by the American Civil Liberties Union."[63]

As allegations of fascism flew, former friends became enemies. Margaret De Silver, a major contributor to the ACLU, who had been offended by Flynn's attacks on Tresca as a "Trotskyite," resigned in protest over the ACLU's tolerance of communists. De Silver indicated that she might return if Flynn were removed. De Silver's actions suggested personal as well as political animosity toward Flynn.[64] Roger Baldwin, who had been a friend of Flynn's since World War I, knew that her son, Buster, was dying of lung cancer. Yet he insisted on holding a "trial" for the board of the ACLU to weigh the evidence against Flynn and decide whether to expel her. In personal correspondence, Baldwin and John Haynes Holmes, the chairman of the board of the ACLU, urged Flynn not to take the charges personally, a notion she dismissed as absurd.

For Flynn, the struggle for civil liberties was personal: she had watched men beaten and imprisoned for daring to speak freely in Missoula and Spokane in 1909 and 1910. She had tried to save foreign-born dissenters from deportation during and after World War I. She had watched families literally being torn apart by the deportations and had seen the health of political prisoners permanently damaged. Her friend Frank Little had been lynched in Montana for organizing miners and speaking out against World War I. The death of yet another promising young man—in this case, her son, Buster—may have

ACLU to Act on Red's Ouster
Baldwin Says Resolution Means What It Says

The board of directors of the American Civil Liberties Union will consider the expulsion of Elizabeth Gurley Flynn, member of the national committee of the Communist Party at its meeting Monday at the City Club, it was learned today.

On Feb. 5 the union passed a resolution barring supporters of totalitarian governments from the union's governing bodies or staff.

Urged to Resign

Miss Flynn was urged privately to resign. Instead she issued a statement last week to the Daily Worker declaring:

"I am not quitting. Communis are not quitters.

"I was a charter member of the ACLU. When I joined the Communist Party three years

ago I informed the directors of that fact though I was under no

ELIZABETH GURLEY FLYNN

compulsion to do so, and the ACLU directors said they were glad to have a Communist on the board.

"I was re-elected to the board a year ago and my term has two years more to run."

Baldwin Statement

Roger N. Baldwin, ACLU director, said in a statement:

"Any report that the resolution (barring Communists from office) adopted by the union does not mean what it says is wholly incorrect.

"Under our by-laws, when a member of a governing committee affected by the resolution declines to resign, there is a legal procedure of disassociating the member from the union. Obviously, the legal procedure takes time."

Flynn's expulsion from the ACLU drew headlines.

EGF Papers, Tamiment Library, NYU, Box 2, Folder 59

brought these feelings to the surface, making Flynn even more determined to fight this betrayal of principles and of friendship.

Flynn had helped to build the field of civil liberties defense, and she resisted being pushed aside by professional men who judged her too radical to serve the cause. Flynn's "trial" took place on a rainy Tuesday evening in early May at the City Club of New York at 55 West 44th Street. Corliss Lamont, a philosophy professor at Columbia, and a member of the board who later published a book about the trial, remembered Flynn as "a handsome woman, straightforward and hard-hitting in argument, whose face and voice gave the impression of great strength and sincerity of character." For more than three decades, according to Lamont, Flynn "had been one of the staunchest fighters for the Bill of Rights in America." No one on the board could match her record of activism, or offer a single example in which she had betrayed the principles of civil liberties due to her membership in the CP. And yet John Haynes Holmes, the chairman of the board, who ran the meeting, acted more as a "Grand Inquisitor" than a judge, overriding all of Flynn's objections to the process and the substance and the charges. The same people who brought the complaint against Flynn now judged the merits of the case, violating the spirit of due process. After a "long and acrimonious discussion" that dragged on until 2:20 a.m., Flynn was asked to leave the room so the board could deliberate. Holmes cast the deciding vote in favor of her expulsion. However, no one bothered to call Flynn back in to tell her the verdict. Instead, she found out as members of the board straggled into the Algonquin Bar next door, where Flynn had retired for a drink.[65]

In the end, the trial damaged the reputation of the ACLU more than it damaged Flynn's. Baldwin embarrassed himself further by claiming that the ACLU had never tolerated communists, a blatant lie. Flynn received a flood of letters of support. A telegram from Harvard professor Harry Dana assured Flynn, "ALL OF US WHO KNOW YOU AND ROGER [BALDWIN] WILL STAKE YOUR INTEGRITY AGAINST HIS ANY TIME."[66] The proceedings revealed the undemocratic nature of governance within the ACLU. Many members resigned in protest. The attempt by ACLU leaders to rid themselves of communists did not, in fact, save them from further scrutiny from the federal government, but, as Lamont argued, instead "became a precedent and a model for all sorts of other organizations and for government agencies." The leaders of the ACLU, the strongest organization devoted to defending civil liberties in America, now suggested that communists did not deserve the same protections of free speech and political association as other Americans—a dangerous precedent whose full dimensions would become apparent only after World War II during the McCarthy era.[67] In the immediate aftermath of the trial, Flynn felt deeply injured, and she resolved never to trust liberals again. Her expulsion from the ACLU ruptured alliances that she had built over decades, making the CP her sole source of political identity.[68] Made freely, Flynn's choice to become a communist now seemed iron clad.

8

Flynn Fights Fascism—
World War II

Germany invaded the Soviet Union in June 1941. The United States entered the war six months later. Almost overnight, the CP switched from advocating peace to supporting "the complete harnessing of our nation's economy to the war effort."[1] CP leaders built a new Popular Front determined to win the war, even if meant toning down their critique of capitalism and condemning workers who broke no-strike pledges. The alliance between the United States and the Soviet Union ended the Red Scare that began in 1939 and allowed American communists to be patriotic.

During World War II, Flynn addressed a larger and broader audience than ever before. Establishing a strong base in New York City, where she supported communist candidates for city council and ran for US Congress, she built a national reputation through speaking tours and radio addresses. Her reach became international when she traveled to England and France immediately after the war to attend a women's peace conference. Surprisingly, perhaps, Flynn used wartime mobilization to pursue feminist goals. She advocated women's equality and empowerment in politics, the workforce, labor unions, and the CP. For Flynn, the fight against fascism justified a battle within America against both sexism and racism.

Flynn during the World War II era,
when she was on the road almost constantly for the CP.

NP18-29, EGF Photographs,
Tamiment Library, NYU

With the Soviet Union as a US ally, American communists gained new acceptance within the United States. Movies and magazines pumped out heroic portrayals of Russian soldiers, who bore much of the brunt of the fighting in Europe.[2] Anticommunism went into remission, but it did not go away. Like other leaders of the CP, Flynn remained under FBI surveillance during and after the war; she was secretly classified as "dangerous" and identified as a subject for possible internment.[3] The CP marred its otherwise strong record on civil rights during the war by raising no opposition to the internment of Japanese Americans in concentration camps on the West Coast. Communists did not question the commonly held notion that Japanese Americans might engage in subversion. Nothing could be allowed to interfere with the war effort.[4]

Flynn's win-the-war message made her a welcome speaker at union halls, public schools, and civic clubs across the country. When Flynn had shown up to lead labor conflicts or free-speech fights in the early 1900s, local officials had often called the police. Now they welcomed her. In May 1943, a local newspaper columnist in Denver remarked on how times had changed. In the early 1900s, Flynn had been "the brilliant juvenile of an all-star cast" that included Bill Haywood, John Reed, and Emma Goldman. "What a collection that was of penetrating and independent minds!" he marveled. "What a terrific price most of them paid for their independence!" Forty years later, Flynn was still going strong. Equally as impressive, she had not "abandoned or even relaxed in her devotion to basic principles." Flynn described herself as a "home-grown communist" whose determination to share the nation's wealth among its workers grew out of her long career of labor activism rather than directions from the Soviet Union.[5]

Flynn showed a remarkable mastery of local issues wherever she spoke, and newspapers described her as an outstanding orator. As an aging woman, however, she no longer drew acclaim for her beauty. On her fiftieth birthday, she declared herself untroubled by the appearance of wrinkles and grey hair. She described women's preoccupation with looking young as a capitalist affliction, since most women still relied on men for economic support.[6] As a female speaker, however, Flynn remained subject to far greater scrutiny of her appearance than a man. A reporter from Denver found it "easy to envision" Flynn as "pretty" in her youth, but he described her now as "ample mid-fiftyish in build, inclined to be the grandmother type with flowered dresses and graying hair."[7] References to Flynn as "grandmotherly" may have been condescending, but they did not diminish her popularity. Those who knew Flynn, heard her speak, or read her columns cared more about what she had to say than how she looked.

World War II tilted Flynn toward the most gender-conscious phase of her career. Fascism presented an image of women happily subordinate to men in all areas of life. The Nazis perpetrated atrocities against Jewish women and expected German women to serve as breeders for the war machine. Flynn framed the fight for women's equality as antifascist. Like her fellow communist Susan B. Anthony II, a niece of the famous suffragist, Flynn insisted on "the right of all adults to work [and] to participate equally in public affairs" as a tenet of "basic democracy."[8] Flynn highlighted the obstacles African American women faced in exercising their right to vote in the South, or in moving beyond jobs as domestic servants in the North. She distinguished communist ideas of women's equality from those of the National Women's Party, which was still pushing for an Equal Rights Amendment (ERA). Like female trade unionists and members of the Women's Bureau, Flynn opposed the ERA because she believed it threatened to invalidate state laws protecting women from working long hours or being asked to work at night.[9] Real equality, Flynn insisted, would abolish discrimination against women at work while expanding social support for working mothers.[10]

Flynn advanced a bold new set of demands to equalize the position of women in the labor force and to maximize their ability to contribute to the war effort. "Womanpower is manpower today," Flynn announced in 1942. Mobilization for war produced more than 10 million new jobs. With about 16 million men serving in the military, women's workforce participation soared. Six million women took paying jobs for the first time. The number of women in labor unions doubled, rising to 3 million in 1944, which represented one-fifth of all union members. Most unions remained male dominated, however. In a memo to Earl Browder, Flynn expressed frustration that, like the federal government, most male union leaders viewed women's increased employment as temporary and thus refused to devote resources to organizing them.[11]

Flynn countered the tendency to discount female workers in her popular pamphlet *Women in the War*, which was directed at union members and distributed at defense plants throughout the nation.[12] She presented the movement of women "out of the kitchen on to the assembly line" as the acceleration of a trend that had begun before the war and would continue once it ended. The rise of industrial production was making old distinctions between "men's work" and "women's work" meaningless, she argued. A government survey of twenty-one key war industries found that women could perform 80 percent of the jobs. Women could now be found testing tanks and machine guns, transporting airplanes, rigging parachutes, and assembling radios. Picking up on the popularity of "Rosie the Riveter," Flynn described "the glamour girl of today, the woman in the news," as "the working woman." Thus, she was disappointed by organized labor's failure to discuss "the needs of these millions of new women workers," such as providing locker rooms and child-care facilities. As a result, 12 million female workers remained unorganized. "Let the labor unions launch a campaign with the vigor and enthusiasm with which the C.I.O. was started, with women organizers, special literature, posters, conferences, meetings," she promised, "and results would follow immediately."

Hoping to inspire union leaders to take a more active role in organizing millions of new workers, Flynn outlined the special challenges women faced. First and foremost, women needed to be given an "equal opportunity to work" regardless of race. Outmoded union rules excluded women and African Americans from jobs as welders and blacksmiths. These old regulations must be repealed, Flynn argued. Long-standing prejudices against hiring black men and women for industrial jobs should no longer be tolerated or accommodated through segregated workplaces. Flynn described married women and African American men and women as a "reserve army" who could help win the war and called on her fellow Americans to live up to their ideals of democracy by eliminating discrimination. "Let us overcome our past shortcomings now in the white heat of a war for human liberation," Flynn argued.[13] Appeals to the public to join the CP to fight against fascism and to support equality for women and African Americans showed results. Membership in the party increased from 44,000 in 1942 to 65,000 in 1945.[14]

Flynn called on organized labor to consider the fact that millions of workers were also mothers. "Child care is a legitimate trade union concern," she insisted. She encouraged unions to fight for more federal money to open child-care centers that provided safe, affordable care close to women's workplaces. Extending the arguments of the Popular Front and reflecting women's local activism within the CP, Flynn prodded labor unions to start paying attention to housing. "Homes are working places" for women, explained Flynn. Women carried "the burden of domestic duty after a day's work" in the factory. The lives of female wage earners would be easier, and their loyalty to their unions secured, if they could "come home to a modern, comfortable government project house with all the facilities for a quick bath, a dinner already prepared in the Frigidaire or partly cooked in an electric stove." Here was an updated version of Flynn's earlier call for communal kitchens to ease the burdens of housework. Flynn did not challenge the assumption that cooking, cleaning, and caring for children inevitably fell to women. But she did urge union men to encourage their female coworkers to "speak up" and "elect them to positions of responsibilities." Female union leaders would represent women's interests in setting union priorities.[15]

Flynn further developed her ideas about women's equality in her run for representative at large to the US Congress from New York State in 1942, a position that enabled candidates to draw voters from throughout the state. The sole woman on a slate of communist candidates, Flynn made women's equality the centerpiece of her campaign. She presented herself as a legislator who would speak "for the working women, mothers, housewives, and consumers" of the state. She saw no conflict between her communism and her feminism, explaining, "It's traditional with the Communist Party to fight for the rights of women." Flynn asked all women to support her, if only to help change the balance of power in Washington, DC. Just six women served in

Congress, along with more than five hundred men. At a campaign rally in Staten Island, she described women's lack of representation more than twenty years after gaining the vote as "disgraceful." She argued that reluctance to hire African Americans for industrial and skilled work deprived the nation "of the intelligence, ability, and patriotic determination of the Negro people." On a swing through upstate cities including Troy, Buffalo, and Schenectady, Flynn's campaign secretary remarked, "You could see that [Flynn] spoke the minds of the hundreds of women who attended her meetings." Flynn received more than 50,000 votes.[16]

Flynn did not win the election, but she kept her promise to continue campaigning for child care. In the *Daily Worker*, a communist newspaper that enjoyed a daily circulation of about 50,000 during the war, Flynn urged action on the issue. Women were being called upon to sign up for war work in magazines and newspapers, on the radio, and in government-sponsored newsreels. Feeling the pull of patriotism, and sensing new opportunities to prove themselves, women were stepping up to "take over the home front, to work on farms, in factories, shops and shipyards." Many of these new female workers had children. Without safe, affordable day care, they faced constant anxiety about their children's welfare and often had to miss work to care for them. Flynn urged unions to "demand wartime childcare centers financed and supervised by the government, such as they have in England." As an American example, Flynn pointed to Seattle, where five hundred nurseries had been opened to care for the children of defense workers. Working mothers should be able to collect their children, "bathed and ready for their mothers at the end of the day to be taken home and put to bed."[17]

Flynn brought her message directly to the masses by embarking on numerous speaking tours. In 1943, for example, she traveled to Birmingham, Alabama; Norfolk, Virginia; Oklahoma City; Tacoma, Washington; Butte, Montana; and cities in Colorado and California. Reporting on Flynn's talk in Norfolk, the local newspaper explained that the communists' main concern was national unity and winning the war. Based on Flynn's speech, a local reporter had the impression that with the men away fighting, "the Communist organization is now practically in the hands of women." The party was now focused on recruiting women to work in war industries, demanding equal pay for equal work, and establishing nurseries for working mothers. Flynn recommended "adequate care, not only for the very young children, but also for the school children who need supervision after school hours." Flynn was encouraged by women's rising rates of unionization. She lauded the autoworkers for promoting equal opportunities for women, and she praised the electrical workers for their active recruitment of female members. She did not moderate her insistence on equal opportunities for African Americans when speaking in the South. In Norfolk, she pled for an end to "discrimination against Negro men and women, especially the women, who have two prejudices against them."[18] In Oklahoma City, she addressed a mixed crowd of African Americans and whites, still an unusual event in wartime America.[19] Flynn pushed for equality for African American women in both civilian and military work throughout the war, sharply critiquing the practice of limiting African American nurses to caring for African American soldiers.[20]

In California, which continued to be a stronghold for the CP, Flynn participated in a drive to increase the presence of women in the party. She joined her old friends Mother Bloor and Anita Whitney in signing a "special appeal" to women, explaining that the party had "fought uncompromisingly for equal opportunities for women in all spheres of human activity; against the degrading fascist concept of women; against discrimination practiced toward Negro women." Comrades in California gave Flynn's tour significant publicity, advertising her speaking dates in Oakland, Marin County, San Francisco, San Diego, and Los Angeles. They described her as "one of the foremost and best beloved women in our Party" and a leading recruiter of new members. "To hear Elizabeth Gurley Flynn is to love her and to gather new strength for the great historic task of winning the war and for building our Party," they promised.[21] The efforts of Flynn and other female leaders of the CP to recruit women bore fruit. By 1943, women made up half of all party members, up from about one-third in 1940.[22] The number of women in local leadership also increased, but Flynn demanded equality. In her columns in the *Daily Worker*, she bemoaned the lack of female representatives at national communist conventions and highlighted promising young female leaders, such as Dorothy Healey in California and Ann Burlak in Massachusetts.[23] Flynn was not afraid to critique the party when it came to women's issues, and no one challenged her authority on the subject.

In 1942, Flynn took the lead in organizing huge birthday celebrations for Mother Bloor, who was turning eighty, and Anita Whitney, who would be seventy-five. Based in Pennsylvania and California, respectively, Bloor and Whitney were both national figures. The event reprised Popular Front tactics, gathering the names of prominent progressive women who sent birthday greetings. Flynn wrote a widely distributed pamphlet celebrating these two "daughters of the American Revolution," native-born women from comfortable circumstances who had devoted their lives to advancing the interests of the working class. She urged local party leaders to use these birthday celebrations, which were scheduled throughout July and August, as recruiting opportunities, suggesting that they organize discussions highlighting the role of women in the labor movement and the CP while dramatizing women's role in winning the war. To Flynn, celebrating Bloor and Whitney meant "planning the training and promotion of women in our Party."[24]

Flynn encouraged mothers, housewives, and wageworkers to join the CP. Her attention to women's paid *and* unpaid labor had its roots in the community-based organizing she had practiced for the IWW and in the feminist and socialist theory she had been reading steadily since she was a teenager. In the early 1940s, she pondered the writings of Mary Inman, a California communist, who argued that housework should be considered "productive" labor. Flynn ultimately disagreed with this feminist deviation from traditional Marxist theory, but she agreed that housework had economic value.[25] Flynn's most direct insights into the politics of housework came from her sister Kathie, who volunteered for the Office of Price Administration (OPA), a federal agency that rationed scarce food, such as meat and sugar, and sought to control prices. Kathie had been a public school teacher in the Bronx for many years, but she had been forced to retire during the war on the pretense that she had become hard of hearing. In fact, it seems that Kathie had been pushed out of her job because of her leadership in the teachers' union and because of her sister's prominent position within the CP.[26]

After Kathie lost her job, she, Elizabeth, and Kathie's daughter, Frances, moved to a third-floor walk-up apartment in Manhattan on East 12th Street, just a few blocks away from the headquarters of the CP. Kathie's work for the OPA often took her to the Essex Street Market, where she encouraged mom-and-pop businesses to post their prices and helped to organize drives to gather used clothing to send to Europe. Elizabeth wrote up many of Kathie's experiences and turned them into a popular column for the *Daily Worker*, "Sister Kathie Says." Peppered with witty observations about the Lower East Side, which was still a predominantly Jewish and Italian neighborhood, the articles detailed women's daily labor of shopping, cleaning, and mending. The column dignified working-class women's unpaid labor, suggesting that it was crucial for family survival. Flynn used stories of women dealing with wartime shortages to give their work patriotic value. Characteristically, Flynn made fun of her own limited cooking skills—and her love of potatoes and beer, regardless of their effects on her figure. She gently teased Kathie about encouraging people to eat tripe, confessing that after she got home from a long day at work she would rather just boil an egg.

Kathie was Elizabeth's closest companion during the 1940s. If Elizabeth continued to have short flings, she covered her tracks or destroyed the evidence. Flynn's family dwindled in 1942 when her sister Bina died at age forty-four after a heart attack. Flynn's father died from a stroke soon thereafter. In January 1943, Flynn's former partner, Carlo Tresca, was gunned down on the corner of 15th Street and Fifth Avenue while he was leaving the office of his newspaper, *Il Martello*. His old friend Max Eastman remarked that Tresca would have been disappointed if he had died in his sleep. Historians think Tresca was killed by Carmine Galante, a mobster, whose boss Tresca had insulted. But at the time, suspicions focused on fascists and communists, both of whom Tresca had declared his sworn enemies. Tresca's funeral attracted 5,000 mourners and turned into a protest against "totalitarianism," a term used by anticommunists to describe both fascism and communism. In the *Daily Worker*, Flynn described Tresca's murder as "a dastardly crime" committed, no doubt, by a fascist assassin.[27]

In a poem she wrote shortly after Tresca's death, Flynn reflected, "How strange it seems that you are dead / Who were so long the other half of me." Tresca's death brought Flynn's "memories long suppressed" of their "young rebellious love" to the surface. She sometimes romanticized Tresca as her great, lost love, but her feelings were complicated. Flynn never forgave Tresca for the affair he had with her sister Bina. She was alienated by Tresca's anticommunism and perhaps relieved to have a political reason to call him a traitor. Memories of a young Tresca still burned in Flynn's mind, but in person, he had lost his allure. The last time she saw him, he had seemed to be little more than "an old weary disillusioned shadow of the man I knew."[28] Flynn's nostalgia for their romance may have been, in part, a longing for her lost youth and the freewheeling culture of the Wobblies prior to World War I.

During the World War II era, Flynn seems to have found the rational "Bolshevik love" she had sought in the late 1930s in extended rather than intimate relationships. An article in the *Daily Worker* by Sergeant Ralph Friedman, one of about 15,000 communists who enlisted in the military during World War II, revealed that he was one of at least nineteen soldiers with whom Flynn corresponded regularly. Friedman had written to Flynn while he was deployed in Europe, and to his delight she wrote back and sent stacks of reading material that included everything from Irish poetry to political theory. Friedman felt that he knew Flynn well enough to stop by her apartment at 7:00 a.m. one morning after he arrived home in New York City. Instead, he met her sister Kathie, who recognized Friedman's name from his letters, but apologetically declined to wake Elizabeth up to meet him. Elizabeth had just arrived home from a trip to West Virginia a few hours ago, Kathie explained, and she needed her rest.[29] But Flynn did meet some of the other servicemen with whom she exchanged letters. She and Kathie invited several of these men to join them celebrating Thanksgiving and Christmas. These relationships seem to have been maternal rather than romantic; they may have helped fill the void Flynn had felt since Buster's death in 1940.

Although Flynn fully supported the war effort, she was immensely relieved when the war ended with Allied victory in Europe in May 1945 and in Japan in August. Like many people around the world, however, she was also horrified by the destructive power of the atomic bomb. More than 60 million people were killed in the war, half of them civilians. In November 1945, "before the ashes of war were cold," she traveled to Paris to attend the International Congress of Women (ICW), a weeklong women's peace conference organized by French communists.[30] The ICW concluded by creating a new, permanent organization, the Women's International Democratic Federation (WIDF).[31]

International women's organizations had long made peace a central issue, but the ICW, which drew 850 delegates from forty nations, was one of the first to include a truly global group of women in its discussions. Whereas most international women's organizations drew primarily from the developed nations of Europe and North America, the ICW included representatives from Algeria, Ceylon, China, Egypt, India, Indonesia, Korea, and Morocco.[32] The organization had a strong antifascist orientation and connected fighting for women's equality with strengthening democracy around the world.

Flynn participated in the ICW as a member of an American delegation that became the nucleus of the Congress of American Women, a cross-class, racially integrated organization. The group included Muriel Draper, an elegant interior decorator who advocated Soviet-American friendship; Gene Weltfish, an anthropology professor at Columbia University; Charlotte Hawkins Brown, an African American educator; and Thelma Dale, a leader of the National Negro Congress. Flynn thought their "biggest shortcoming as a delegation" was their lack of "trades unionists." The organizers of the delegation had asked "progressive trade unions" to nominate a female representative to send to Paris, but their request was met with "indifference and lack of cooperation." Flynn remained frustrated that trade unions did not devote more resources to their female members, but the problem was partially remedied by the addition of Sergeant Ann Bradford, a journalist affiliated with the CIO who was just completing a tour of duty in France.[33]

Airplanes did not yet fly directly from New York City to Paris, so Flynn flew first to England, using a one-day stopover in London to attend a Congress of the British Communist Party. The sheer scale of the destruction of World War II seemed much more immediate in Europe than it had in the United States. Walking from her London hotel to the communist congress, Flynn saw "bombed areas, buildings totally wrecked and ruins partly cleared away." The people of London looked "tired, exhausted and nerve-wracked." Their clothes were "old and worn" and food was "sparse." Yet the British Communist Party seemed energetic, and its newspaper enjoyed a circulation of 110,000, more than twice the number of the *Daily Worker*.[34]

Traveling on to Paris by train and boat, Flynn felt "increasingly conscious" of her "warm clothes, good shoes," and spending money. Paris was chilly in late November, but there was no heat, except in the Metro. Lights flickered on and off. The Parisians seemed "grim" but "proud." The American delegation lodged at the Hotel Lutetia, which until recently had been the headquarters of the Gestapo. Makeshift memorials had sprung up around the city to the victims of the Nazis. Children looked underweight and traumatized. Parisians struggled with severe shortages of milk, butter, meat, sugar, and even soap. "It's hard for us in far off America to visualize the human suffering and misery in these ruined and exhausted countries," Flynn explained in an article for the *Daily Worker*; "Victory did not bring happiness."[35]

At the ICW, which met for five days at the Palais de la Mutualité, each national delegation reported on women's work in the fight against fascism. The damage inflicted by the Nazis was overwhelming. Flynn jotted notes: The Soviet Union had lost 20 million people. Six and a half million Jews had been "exterminated." These estimates increased in later years. Survivors included Marie-Claude Vaillant-Couturier, a communist photojournalist who had helped to organize the meeting. Vaillant-Couturier, who spoke English, greeted the Americans and sat with them at lunch on their first day. She looked "very thin" and "very frail," Flynn noticed, with her "blonde hair braided around her head." Flynn was surprised when Vaillant-Couturier pushed up the sleeves of her thin, green cardigan, "revealing a large number, stamped in indelible ink, on her arm." Someone asked her what it was, and she explained that she had been in a concentration camp. During the Nazi occupation of Paris, she had been arrested, placed in solitary confinement for five months, sent to Auschwitz, and then transferred to Ravensbrück. Vaillant-Couturier described starvation, dysentery, hard labor, and the gassing of Jews unloaded from freight cars. She had been completely cut off from contact with her family, including her young daughter, who did not recognize her when she returned to Paris more than two years later. Vaillant-Couturier then discovered that her husband had been one of 75,000 French communists killed by the Nazis.[36] Encounters like this shocked Flynn and convinced her that communists were the world's most courageous fighters against facism.

The ICW ended with a huge public meeting at the Vélodrome d'Hiver featuring Flynn and Dolores Ibárruri, "La Pasionaria," the legendary Spanish antifascist in exile in the Soviet Union.[37] Flynn was proud to share the stage with Ibárruri. "It was worth coming half way around the world just to look at her," Flynn claimed.[38] Flynn concluded the conference with a host of new contacts and ideas. She continued to deny any universal quality to women as a group, but she now thought that peace might be the one cause that could unite them. The ICW established the Women's International Democratic Federation, which became the largest international women's organization of the postwar era. The WIDF continued to hold international congresses every three years to vote on policies.[39]

The ICW produced a sweeping set of resolutions. Claiming that women had shown "their worth" in the fight against fascism, as well as "their abilities as mothers, citizens, and workers," the ICW called for "equality of rights" for women as essential for both "democracy" and "freedom." They focused on women's status in the workforce, demanding a "right to work" for all women as well as "access on the same terms as men, to all trades and professions." They also called for "equal pay for equal work" and an equitable system of social security and unemployment insurance. They advocated day care and supervised after-school activity for children. They asked for new, modern housing for workers, along with rent control. These resolutions affirmed Flynn's gender-conscious agenda during the war and framed it as part of a worldwide effort to fight fascism. They not only asserted women's equality but also demanded that areas traditionally identified as women's concerns, such as housing and child care, be taken seriously. Furthermore, the ICW urged "all democratic women's organizations of all countries to help the women of the colonial and dependent countries in their fight for economic and political rights."[40]

When the ICW ended, the members of the American delegation found themselves stranded in Europe. Pan American, the airline they had flown, had cut flights to twice a week, and ships were packed with soldiers eager to arrive home in time for Christmas. The better-connected women lobbied the American ambassador to provide the delegation with priority passage on a US Army ship. But Flynn enjoyed the delay. She found her way around Paris and met leaders of the Resistance. Flynn especially enjoyed meeting about twenty-five American communist soldiers stationed in Paris, who sought Flynn out when they read in the *Paris Post* that she was in town. Accompanied by Thelma Dale, Flynn went to meet the men at their mess hall. Flynn spent two evenings talking to the men about their experiences and the postwar prospects for the CP. Boundaries of class seemed more significant to Flynn than those of race: she seemed more comfortable spending her free time with Dale, who was African American, than with some of the more elite white members of the American delegation.[41] Dale remembered her time in Paris as an "exhilarating experience."[42]

At a reception at the Soviet embassy, Flynn met the top leaders of the French Communist Party, including Jacques Duclos, who "chuckled" as he asked, "How is Browder's utopia in America these days?"[43] In April, an article by Duclos had accused Browder of turning the American CP into an organization devoted to reform rather than revolution. Flynn had initially defended Browder, but she soon lined up with other party leaders to support Foster, who took control of the party in July. Historians have discovered that the Soviet Union initiated and approved the change in leadership.[44] Flynn hoped the crisis would make the party more tolerant to different points of view, but the party remained undemocratic and hostile to dissent.[45] By writing about her meeting with Duclos for the *Daily Worker*, Flynn cemented her allegiance to Foster. She genuinely respected Foster's experience as a labor organizer, but she had appreciated Browder's efforts to make communism appealing to American workers. Foster's more doctrinaire approach helped to marginalize the party.[46]

The American delegation to the ICW secured passage back to the United Sates on December 17, 1945. Flynn boarded the USS *Alexander* in Le Havre optimistic about the prospects of communism worldwide. The ship carried 4,404 enlisted men and 166 officers. The women who had served in the war included 4 Women's Army Corps officers and 547 nurses. Flynn and the other American delegates to the ICW were among 41 nonmilitary passengers, including Red Cross personnel and USO troops. On Christmas, Flynn enjoyed crowding into the ship's smoky recreation room to see a show featuring black and white soldiers. The campy revue was "toned down for the ladies," but it had enough "stag humor" to satisfy the men. Otherwise, the ship was segregated. Enlisted men were barely allowed above decks, and black soldiers were fed worse food than white soldiers. Flynn's time aboard the ship suggested that although the Nazis had been defeated, the fight against fascism had not yet eradicated racism. Sexism seemed to be part and parcel of army culture.[47]

While crossing the Atlantic, Flynn kept up with events back home by reading the ship's newspaper, *The Crow's Nest*. Labor conflict had returned. The CIO and the United Auto Workers were leading massive strikes. Federal officials warned that widespread labor unrest was limiting "industrial output" and delaying the production of many "consumer goods." A detailed grid of government benefits available to veterans, from education grants to home loans, seemed calculated to produce peace at home. The last issue of the newspaper from the voyage warned that the ship was running out of fuel, and thus at risk of capsizing when it landed. Passengers were warned to stay in their places as they entered New York Harbor. They must resist the urge to see the Statue of Liberty or get closer to the bands playing on the "Welcome Home Boats."[48] The journey ended safely, but the ship's tense arrival foreshadowed the quest for security that would soon obsess most Americans. After 1945, the federal government shifted from an uneasy alliance with American communists like Flynn to prosecuting them as enemies.

9

Liberty Denied—
The Cold War

The Statue of Liberty looked cold and lonely to Flynn in January 1949. From the Staten Island Ferry, the "lady with a lamp" seemed frozen in place on her small island. Her posture appeared "awkward," her torch dim in comparison to the neon signs advertising Colgate and Standard Oil. Lower Manhattan's "temples of finance" blotted out the sky and overshadowed this beacon to the oppressed of all lands. Still, Flynn saw "something majestic, uncompromising, noble" in this monument to American freedom. Nevertheless, when she traveled to Paris in 1950, Flynn warned her French hosts not to be surprised if the United States sent the Statue of Liberty back to France. As the United States and the Soviet Union battled to shape the world order during the Cold War, peace and internationalism seemed suspect, and American communists became internal enemies.

The prospects for American communism had seemed more hopeful at the end of World War II. American workers had launched the biggest strike wave in US history. Five million people had walked off their jobs, demanding wages that would keep pace with inflation.[1] The CP had channeled this upsurge of discontent into a recruiting drive, and Flynn had played a leading role in this initiative. By the fall of 1946, the party had 80,000 members. Catching up with Flynn, who was hoarse from weeks on the road, a reporter for the *New Yorker* found "a hearty, bespectacled woman of fifty-six" who was not just a CP leader, "but a public speaker in a class with "the "brass-lunged giants of Chautauqua days." In her forty-year career, Flynn had given nearly 10,000 speeches. She was earning $57 a week, the same pay as Bill Foster, the head of the CP. With Browder out and Foster in, the CP revived the language of class conflict. Flynn pronounced herself pleased that, when she gave a speech about capitalism, she was "free to give it hell." When she was not "attacking entrenched greed" or attending meetings, she was reading Irish poetry and working on her memoirs.[2]

In February 1946, Flynn celebrated the fortieth anniversary of her first speech, on women and socialism, by joining picket lines. She recounted her experiences in an article for the *Daily Worker*. In Westinghouse, Pennsylvania, she rallied striking electrical workers. In other Pennsylvania cities, including Bethlehem, Homestead, and Pittsburgh, she saw huge steel factories "idle" and "dead," but she found life "in all these working class towns, in union halls, on picket lines." In Philadelphia, she met the "fightingest bunch of women." They proudly told her how they had prevented replacement workers from crossing picket lines and breaking their seventeen-week strike against the American Tobacco Company. Flynn emphasized the international dimensions of their struggle. Based on her trip to Paris in 1945, she explained that women "all over the world" were "fighting for the same things," the chance to work on an equal basis with men and to be fairly compensated for their labor. Flynn's international framing of these local problems made the strikers feel that they were "not alone" and belonged to "something big."[3]

In 1946 and 1947, Flynn was on the road almost constantly, speaking to strikers, reaching out to local communists, and addressing groups of women. Many working people struggled as inflation soared and labor unions exercised their renewed right to strike, and many women, Hispanics, and African Americans were laid off from their wartime jobs. In addition to expanding its ranks, the CP sought to preserve and extend the gains working people had won during the

New Deal and World War II. The CP and organized labor faced politicians and a business community that were eager to roll back these provisions by labeling them as socialist, communist, or "un-American."

Flynn evaluated the turbulent political scene during a stop in Pittsburgh in June 1946. Having traveled up and down the West Coast and across the Midwest, she found workers "restive" and looking for change. "Wartime expectations of a long-term partnership with capital" and with government had "been shot to hell in the last year." Flynn was signing up new members every day. However, she saw "stormy days ahead." President Harry S. Truman had just called out the army to halt a railroad strike. For Flynn, "the marching feet of armed men arouse[d] somber echoes" of earlier patterns of government intervention favoring employers. "Workers had begun to believe this was all a thing of the past," but recent events showed that the "class struggle" continued.[4]

Flynn not only spoke; she listened. A lengthy memo sent back to CP headquarters the following year summarized a three-month tour. Leaving New York City in March 1947, Flynn visited Michigan, Illinois, Indiana, Washington, Oregon, California, Arizona, Utah, Colorado, and Nebraska. Based on her meetings with local organizers, she worried that the national leaders were out of touch. CP organizers in Arizona were doing a "bang up job." Despite "a ferocious campaign of red-baiting," they were supporting striking copper miners and African Americans fighting for a civil rights bill. When local organizers asked for Spanish-language material to help organize agricultural workers, however, the national office had supplied a statement from Bill Foster on Puerto Rican independence. This seemed irrelevant to Mexican American workers, and "they were greatly disappointed." Local efforts to enroll Spanish-speaking workers foundered because of a national failure to respond to local conditions. Organizers across the country complained that the CP's pamphlets "all look alike." Even English-speaking workers did not understand the language. Departing from Browder's program of making communism more American, Foster directed the party to educate workers in Marxist and Leninist theories of revolution. Flynn agreed with Foster's revolutionary objectives, but she found his strategy and tactics flawed.

Flynn had little interest in theory for its own sake. Since working with Bill Haywood in the 1910s, she had followed his advice about using simple, direct language to reach workers. "What matters how learned and profound it sounds to you if your audience does not understand you?" Flynn asked.[5] Flynn complained to Foster that his emphasis on theory was alienating rather than attracting workers. She followed Foster's orders by dropping references to "the classics" into her speeches and articles. But she used these references for her own purposes. In an article for the *New Masses*, Flynn critiqued the failure of the Left to pay attention to women's issues since the end of the war. She cited Lenin, who she believed "had a real sympathy with women in their struggle for equality," and Marx, who commented in 1868 that "anybody who knows anything of history knows *that great social changes are impossible without the feminine ferment.*"[6]

In her report from the road, Flynn identified another problem with the CP: local leaders and party members felt detached from the national leadership in New York City. Flynn urged Foster and other national leaders to "make a trip around the country to meet the Party." Flynn knew travel could be "wearing," but it was "worth it." Even if they were not great speakers, national leaders needed to meet informally with local comrades. "Closer ties, bonds of confidence, yes, and affection, must be built between our leaders and members, such as exists in other Communist Parties," Flynn argued. She described the national leadership as "too remote" and "too depersonalized." This lack of connection, Flynn warned, "has elements of danger in this period."[7] Some disaffected CP members became informants for the FBI. Rather than becoming more open and accessible, as Flynn recommended, however, the national leaders became more closed and cut off from their base. The building housing the CP on East 12th Street began to feel more like a fortress than the vibrant center of a mass movement.[8]

As it contracted, the CP devoted fewer resources to organizing women. Flynn's pamphlet *Women's Place in the Fight for a Better World* sought to strengthen weakening links between labor and feminism. Flynn urged women to support organized labor, which was now under attack by the 80th Congress, "an unholy alliance" of southern

Democrats, who were intent on disenfranchising African Americans, and northern Republicans, who were subservient to big business. To explain the stakes involved in preserving unions, she emphasized that they "raised wages, shortened hours, and fought for decent living and working conditions." Furthermore, unions gave workers a voice, and were thus "part of democracy."[9] Flynn chided labor and the CP for failing to reach out to women as effectively as the Republican Party and the National Association of Manufacturers did. These organizations at least provided "Program Notes" for women's clubs. "The fight for the full rights of women is an important part in winning all democratic rights," Flynn declared. Extending an analysis of the potential militancy of women that she had developed decades earlier, Flynn characterized women as "a dynamic force when aroused to fight for peace, security, democracy for themselves and for their families." To fail to reach out to women "in today's life and death struggle" seemed, to Flynn, tantamount to "criminal negligence."[10]

The increasingly loud drumbeat of anticommunism soon drowned out Flynn's proposals for better connecting the national leadership of the CP with local members and for expanding the labor movement to more fully encompass women's concerns. Countering Republican allegations that he was "soft" on communism, Truman, a Democrat, issued an executive order in March 1947 requiring federal employees to swear they were not members of the CP or sympathetic to its aims. Many states passed similar legislation. These new laws set off a witch-hunt in which any public employee suspected of communism could be fired. Private employers followed suit. Thousands of people lost their jobs, were blacklisted, or were classified as security risks.[11] In June 1947, the Taft-Hartley Act, passed over Truman's veto, eroded New Deal protections for organized labor by outlawing the closed shop and allowing states to pass "right-to-work" laws. Furthermore, Taft-Hartley required all union officials to sign affadavits swearing they were not communists in order to be recognized by the National Labor Relations Board. Flynn thought that the requirement "would be really funny if it were not so serious." Organized labor objected on principle, but most complied eventually. National leaders of the AFL had always been hostile to communism. Communists had helped build the CIO, but the national leadership of the organization now shifted in a more conservative direction.[12] Foster's uncompromising radicalism made communism less appealing to American workers than it had been during the Browder years. To most Americans, the Soviet Union now seemed like a dangerous, expansionistic, and repressive regime rather than a model for a more egalitarian society.

Within a few years, the nation was in the midst of a full-blown Red Scare. Flynn found the atmosphere "far more hysterical and fear laden" than it had been during and after World War I, "when the IWW was the national bugaboo."[13] Outside a May Day meeting in Milwaukee where Flynn spoke in 1950, a would-be vigilante remarked, "We ought to kill them now. It will make that many fewer to kill when we fight Russia."[14]

Flynn fought the assertion that communists were not patriotic. She wrote proudly of her trips across America, describing it as "a beautiful country, rich in resources" that should be owned by "the people" rather than by the small number of wealthy families who controlled the nation's major corporations. Flynn's vision of "the people" remained broad, encompassing African Americans and expanding to include Mexican Americans and Native Americans.[15] She proudly invoked her "militant Irish ancestry" as an important element in the American working class. She envisioned class as a category that could transcend ethnic and racial differences by creating solidarity among American workers. At the same time, she intensified her feminist analysis by identifying certain common problems faced by professional and working-class women, such as the double day of wage work and housework.

Flynn identified American communists with earlier protest movements. Abolitionists and feminists had campaigned to increase democracy in America by correcting glaring social inequalities. Both of these movements had once seemed marginal, but they had spearheaded sweeping social change, culminating in constitutional amendments outlawing slavery and granting women the right to vote. Flynn hoped American communists could follow a similar trajectory from opposition to acceptance.[16]

Flynn renewed her efforts to explain socialism (the basis of communism) in speeches, pamphlets, and on the radio. She described capitalism as a system in which a small group of "men and women" owned "the land, natural resources and the industries of our country, which they use to make tremendous profits on the labor of others without working themselves." This unjust distribution of resources could be changed, as communist revolutions in Europe and Asia had demonstrated. To Flynn, capitalism was "no more the last word in human progress than was savagery, barbarism, or feudalism."[17] Socialism would establish "collective ownership by the whole people" of "land, natural resources, industries, railroads, banks, communications, etc." Furthermore, a "planned economy" would "guarantee an ample supply and equitable distribution of all commodities and services to all people." Using the Soviet Union as a model, Flynn championed collective ownership and government direction of the economy in the interest of abolishing unemployment and providing "work for all, under healthy and safe conditions."[18] Flynn idealized life and labor in the Soviet Union. However, she rightly pointed out that American workers bore the brunt of the nation's frequent economic downturns and shared relatively little of the wealth they produced.

As she had throughout her life, Flynn identified with the struggles of working people. The CP, she argued, recognized workers "as the majority and real foundation of America." Cleansed of the profit motive, which led to "unemployment, war and fascism," America could develop a more collective ethos in which "the benefits of the worker" came "first." On the radio, she explained that this communal impulse was expressed in the name "communist," emphasizing the "u," which J. Edgar Hoover, the head of the FBI, continued to mispronounce as "Comminist." Hoover exaggerated claims about the dangers of communism, she believed, in order to expand the powers and the budget of the FBI. Contrary to Hoover's claims, communists had no plans to overthrow the government. Rather, they were "trying to persuade the majority of the American people that Socialism would be a happier, more secure and peaceful, more just and equitable system of society than capitalism is or can be." Like the socialists of her parents' generation, Flynn explained, communists hoped to win socialism through the ballot box rather than through a violent revolution.[19] Flynn's description of communists as a nonviolent political party seemed more in tune with the programs of Earl Browder, the previous leader of the CP, however, than with Bill Foster's vision of an apocalyptic revolution following the Bolshevik model.[20]

Increasingly, anticommunism became the center of American foreign policy. In March 1947, President Truman persuaded the American Congress of the need for worldwide "containment" of communism through a combination of economic assistance to foreign nations and military alliances to counter the expansion of Soviet influence. In the 1948 presidential election, the CP supported Henry Wallace, FDR's first vice president, who ran on the Progressive Party ticket. Wallace promised to extend the New Deal and called for cooperation rather than confrontation with the Soviet Union. The CP expected leaders of the CIO to line up behind them in support of Wallace, but most refused, remaining loyal to the Democratic Party. Flynn later realized that the CP had followed the "wrong labor policy" in 1948. It had "alienated friends in leadership" by demanding that they conform to "party patterns."[21]

President Truman's determination to fend off a challenge from Wallace led him to step up his attacks on domestic communism. Early in 1948, the Truman administration targeted more than two hundred noncitizens for arrest and deportation. Victims included Flynn's friend Claudia Jones, a charismatic young organizer of African descent who had been born in Trinidad. Thousands more foreign-born radicals were threatened with deportation as well. Flynn organized a series of women's rallies on Jones's behalf. She traveled to Miami to raise money to fight the deportations, hoping, perhaps, to interest Jewish Americans who might remember the forced exile of Russian émigrés who sympathized with the Bolshevik Revolution.

Press coverage of Flynn's trip provides a snapshot of the growing hysteria around communism. A reporter and two photographers from the *Miami Herald* crashed Flynn's meeting at a South Beach hotel. The newspaper published photographs of the crowd, knowing that people identified as communists could lose their jobs.[22] Meanwhile, in Congress, the House Un-American Activities Committee (HUAC), formerly known as the Dies Committee, investigated communist influence in Hollywood. Senator Joseph McCarthy convened a similar committee in the Senate in the early 1950s. It seemed to one contemporary that "the Democrats and the Republicans are now racing each other for the anti-communist stakes."[23]

On July 20, 1948, FBI agents stormed the headquarters of the American CP on East 12th Street and arrested Bill Foster, the head of the party, along with Eugene Dennis, his second in command, and three other leaders. Within a week, all twelve members of the National Board of the CP had been arrested and charged with conspiring to "advocate the overthrow and destruction of the Government of the United States by force and violence."[24] The twelve men were charged under the Smith Act, an internal security measure passed in 1940.[25] Flynn had worked closely with the indicted men for years. She was particularly fond of Dennis, whom she regarded almost as a son. Dennis, who had been born in Seattle in 1905, had organized farmworkers and dockworkers in California before joining the national leadership of the CP. Although Flynn was not a member of the National Board during the three-year period of the indictment, she felt "embarrassed" not to be included in the group of top leaders and joked that she felt "discriminated against by Uncle Sam."[26] Seeking to avoid a backlash against the excessive use of government force, the FBI and the Department of Justice proceeded slowly and methodically. They regarded this first round of communist indictments under the Smith Act as a test case.[27]

The *New York Times* trumpeted the arrests of the twelve leaders in an "anti-U.S. plot." The CP had no actual plans to overthrow the government. Rather, as Flynn explained, communists wanted to expand the power of the government by taking public ownership of private property—a premise offensive to most Americans, but hardly a dangerous revolutionary plot. Timed just before the Progressive Party convention, the arrests of the twelve CP leaders undermined support for Wallace, who won less than 2.5 percent of the popular vote. Truman's victory over the Republican, Thomas Dewey, showed that the communists lacked effective political power. Anticommunism proved to be a potent political tool when wielded by Democrats and Republicans alike.

The Wallace debacle formalized the separation of the CP from the labor movement. In 1949 and 1950 the CIO purged itself of communists, expelling eleven affiliated unions with a million members. Among them were many of the unions most committed to promoting workplace equality for women and for racial minorities. The expulsions weakened the CIO and limited the range of political debate within the organization. Under the pressure of anticommunism, the CP lost allies in the movements for peace, civil rights, and women's equality, and those movements, like the labor movement, lost talented organizers and strong voices for economic justice.

The dissolution of the Congress of American Women (CAW) provides a case study of the unraveling of progressive alliances the CP had built during the Popular Front and World War II. Flynn had helped launch the CAW in the hopeful moment when she returned from Paris in 1946. The CAW included black and white women, some, but not all, of whom were communists. Branches formed in New York, Chicago, Cleveland, Seattle, Portland, Los Angeles, and Washington, DC. The CAW combined women's international aspirations for peace with local activism centered on community concerns, such as building playgrounds and desegregating public swimming pools. Nationally, the CAW lobbied for federal funding for child care, equal pay for equal work, and an alternative to the Equal Rights Amendment that would preserve labor protections for women. The CAW celebrated International Women's Day on March 8 with plays and parades. Its leaders critiqued superficial images of women in popular culture and launched an investigation into the condition of "the American Negro Woman," which they planned to present to the United Nations.[28] Given the crisis within the CP, Flynn had little time to devote to the CAW, but she and Claudia Jones both served on its national committee.

The participation of Flynn and other communists doomed the CAW, however. The FBI infiltrated the group. In 1947, the US attorney general included the CAW on its list of "subversive organizations." In 1949, HUAC issued a withering 114-page report charging that the CAW did not represent a genuine women's movement but was instead "a Communist-front organization." HUAC characterized the CAW's calls for peace as part of "a campaign to disarm and demobilize the United States" in order to render it "helpless in the face of the Communist drive for world conquest." The report quoted liberally from Flynn's articles about her 1945 trip to Paris in the *Daily Worker* to paint the CAW as part of an international communist conspiracy. The group disbanded within a year rather than face prosecution. Members of the CAW, some of whom became feminist activists in the 1960s and 1970s, tried to erase their participation in the group.[29] Flynn made no public comment about the CAW's demise, but it must have pained her, given the hopes she had pinned on feminist internationalism after the war.

A wave of popular attacks on feminism, epitomized in Marynia Farnham and Ferdinand Lundberg's popular book *Modern Woman: The Lost Sex*, seemed to Flynn like evidence of creeping fascism and the authoritarian, right-wing movements exemplified by Hitler.[30] Flynn, like other communists in postwar America, tended to refer to all of her opponents as fascists. This binary opposition between communism and fascism harked back to the fight against the Nazis. However, it also distorted the political landscape and tended to make communists seem paranoid and hysterical. By this point, many, if not most, Americans equated communism with fascism and saw communism as the more urgent threat.

The CP's response to the anticommunist crusade intensified the damage. The CP stopped recruiting and purged thousands of members who questioned party leadership. A new policy excluded homosexuals, contending, like the US government, that they could be subject to blackmail to hide behavior widely judged as deviant. Before becoming a communist, Flynn had lived in Portland for a decade with a woman identified as a lesbian. However, Flynn did not object to this policy, fearing, perhaps, that she would be identified as homosexual. The party began internal campaigns against "white chauvinism" and "male chauvinism." These initiatives reflected legitimate concerns about the status of African Americans and women within the party, but they became divisive and accusatory.[31] The broader goal of building a better world shrank to making sure party members followed the rules.

In the midst of this crisis, Flynn found herself pushed into a more direct position of leadership. She was the head of the Women's Commission, but up until this point, she had spent most of her time on the road, bringing the party's message to the masses. In August 1948, she was elected as the thirteenth member of the National Board—and she was the only one not under indictment. In her election speech, Flynn urged her fellow communists to stand and "fight for [their] democratic and constitutional rights."[32] However, Bill Foster, who remained in control despite a debilitating stroke, rejected a civil liberties defense for the twelve leaders indicted under the Smith Act.[33] In characteristically stilted language, Foster demanded that those on trial attack capitalism and champion the CP as "an organic part of the whole question of the eventual establishment of socialism in this country."[34] This ill-advised legal strategy prevented Flynn from building a united front like the one she had assembled in the 1920s to defend political prisoners, to protest deportations, and to publicize the cases of Sacco and Vanzetti. Although Flynn now had a great deal of responsibility, she had little real power.[35]

Communists saw the arrests of the twelve leaders as the onset of fascism. Hitler had begun by arresting labor leaders and outlawing the CP. Parties in France and Japan had gone underground in the 1930s and emerged to lead resistance movements. American communists had tried an "underground" strategy in the 1920s and it had been a disaster. Nonetheless, Foster decided to take the party "underground." Key leaders were ordered to disappear, change their names, and await instructions. Those who had been sentenced to prison were ordered to make themselves "unavailable." Flynn was one of several leaders who opposed the decision to go underground. When challenged, Foster accused his opponents of "Browderism," and they generally backed down. With the party under fire, leaders closed ranks.[36] Flynn did not disguise her disagreements with Foster, but she respected him and considered him a friend. She felt badly about challenging him when he was in poor health.[37] Even in these difficult times, however, she never considered leaving the party, which had been the main source of her identity since 1937. She felt loyal to her friends in the party, especially those in prison, and she remained convinced that communism constituted a viable alternative to capitalism.

Flynn plunged back into her old work of labor defense. Foster disparaged the work as a distraction from the real task of building socialism, but Flynn viewed it as essential and knew that no one else would do it. Drawing on her experience from the 1920s, she explained, "Labor defense is never successful nor are political cases won unless the principle of the United Front is applied on every level." In February 1949, Flynn launched a "Communist Committee to Defend the 12" to raise money for bail and lawyers and to bring the issues raised by the indictments "to the people." She tracked all the relevant legal developments, printed pamphlets, and outlined a campaign to repeal the Smith Act.

Flynn laid out an ambitious defense program. The twelve defendants should speak on their own behalf and become better known as individuals. The rights of the CP should be firmly identified with the rights of all Americans to speak freely and join whatever political association they chose. People did not need to agree with the communists, but needed "to make common cause [with them] to defend the Bill of Rights." This course would build a "broader and wider movement," that included trade unions and professionals, and it would draw international support.[38] Foster's firm rejection of a civil liberties strategy, however, coupled with the vehemence of anticommunism, made it impossible for Flynn to assemble a united front that could even come close to the defense movement she had built in the 1920s.

By the fall of 1948, Flynn felt exhausted. A fragment of a poem that she wrote the day before Thanksgiving showed her despair at having "no time" for life, rest, love, or tears. Still, Flynn hoped "to make a world where all may live and love and rest, may sing and dance and laugh, where none need weep, [nor] grieve."[39] These utopian aspirations seemed far removed from the grinding work of labor defense. Flynn gained energy from speaking, traveling, and meeting workers, but she found defense work draining. She did manage a trip to San Francisco to raise money. A newspaper reporter facetiously asked her whether the twelve CP leaders felt lucky to be charged with the overthrow of the government in the United States rather than in the Soviet Union or one of its "satellites." Flynn responded, "I am not prepared to say they would not get a fair trial elsewhere—or will get a fair trial here."[40] In their fight to preserve American democracy against the dangers of Soviet expansion, anticommunists created a consensus on the view that American communists did not deserve civil rights because Soviet citizens did not enjoy them. Several high-profile espionage cases gave credence to the assertion that American communists were agents of a hostile foreign power that was willing to use any form of subversion to undermine the security of the United States.[41]

Flynn attended the ten-month trial of the twelve CP leaders, which began in January 1949 at the federal courthouse in Foley Square in Lower Manhattan. J. Edgar Hoover, the head of the FBI, had spent three years compiling material for the case. In all this time, however, FBI agents had not been able to find any evidence of the defendants committing or advocating violence. Lacking a credible case against any one individual, the Justice Department charged all twelve of them with conspiracy, a legal strategy that had been used to prosecute labor organizers since the nineteenth century. Material to support the indictments consisted of clippings from Marxist classics and party literature advocating the overthrow of capitalism. Paid informants, such as Louis Budenz, a former editor of the *Daily Worker*, testified in support of the government. The case against the communists was extensive but insubstantial. The judge was openly hostile, and the jury returned a guilty verdict within hours. Eleven of the twelve defendants were convicted, sentenced to five years in prison, and fined $10,000 each. Prosecution of Foster, the twelfth, was postponed on account of his poor health.[42]

By October 1949, Flynn was the only member of the National Board left standing. A reporter from the *New York Times* tracked her down at CP headquarters at 35 East 12th Street. He rode the "wheezing elevator" up to the ninth floor, which was painted green and decorated with portraits of Marx and Lenin as well as presidents Jefferson, Lincoln, and Franklin Roosevelt. Flynn had taken over Foster's office. Her desk, he wrote, was "piled high with letters and contributions from party members and sympathizers who want to help the defense fund." Since the convictions, the party had received $15,000 in cash and $25,000 in pledges. Refusing to admit defeat, Flynn argued that people would join the CP as a protest. The CP planned to appeal, and Flynn predicted that the Supreme Court would invalidate the Smith Act as violating the right to free speech. It seems unlikely that Flynn believed this, but she used the interview to make people think about the democratic rights being violated by the prosecutions.

Arthur Garfield Hays, a lawyer for the ACLU, provided a more pessimistic reading of the significance of the Smith Act prosecutions. He thought the convictions would stand, and that as a result, "'only fanatics and martyrs' would dare to stay in the party." Employers would fire employees suspected of being communists, "and people would generally become afraid to voice any unpopular ideas."[43] Hays viewed the Smith Act and the convictions of the communist leaders as imperiling American civil liberties. But neither he nor anyone else associated with the ACLU would defend the communists.[44] The ACLU's leaders stuck to the anticommunist position they had developed in 1940. In a letter to the *New York Times*, Roger William Riis, who had served on the board of the ACLU with Flynn prior to her expulsion, described Flynn and her fellow communists as "malcontent, directed by and loyal to a foreign hostile dictatorship, striving by every device of sabotage, strike, espionage and untruth" to undermine American democracy.[45]

The legal noose around the neck of the CP tightened in September 1950, when Congress passed the McCarran Act, which required all communists to register with the US government. The CP's leaders called a mass meeting to protest the new law. For the first time since 1936, they failed to sell out Madison Square Garden. Addressing a crowd of 10,000, Flynn identified the CP's current struggles with the American people's long fight for freedom. Before ratifying the Constitution, people had demanded a Bill of Rights to guarantee free speech, a free press, free assembly, trial by jury, and reasonable bail. Today, she saw "these rights" as being put "in terrible jeopardy." The campaign against communism showed that "no right" was "static under capitalism." For strength in these trying times, Flynn looked abroad. Socialism was no longer the distant dream it had been when she had begun her career in 1906. In 1950, more than 800 million people in Europe and Asia had "left the orbit of capitalism."[46] Flynn's hopeful framing of socialist revolutions across the world ignored the failures of those new governments to guarantee civil rights to their citizens. She put a positive spin on developments that most Americans saw as profoundly negative: the falling of the "Iron Curtain" across Eastern Europe after World War II; the 1949 victory of communists in China; and the stand-off with communists in Korea that had led to a war that was at that moment escalating in the Pacific. Try as she might, Flynn could not make the communist worldview seem American.

Privately, Flynn drew strength from veterans of the grassroots struggles she had led, who continued to love and appreciate her. In August 1950, she celebrated her sixtieth birthday at Webster Hall in New York City. The event prompted hundreds of affectionate cards and telegrams from across the country and around the world. Many mentioned recent struggles for peace and civil rights in addition to longer battles on behalf of the working class. In one message, a woman named Sadie recalled meeting Flynn at the Passaic strike in 1926. My "confidence to speak in public came greatly from you," Sadie explained. She celebrated Flynn's life as proving "the indestructibility of women; and the equality of women in their strength and determination." A CP organizer from Pennsylvania thanked Flynn for her "fighting strength and warm, comradely devotion" to the "struggles" of workers in his state. Flynn had been there "with them on their picket lines and in their homes, in the coal patches and the steel towns." New York City's unions of bakers, fur workers, transit workers, metalworkers, shoe workers, and maritime workers gave Flynn gifts. Mike Gold, a communist author, sent her a telegram from Brooklyn: "YOU HAVE BEEN MY PERSONAL STATUE OF LIBERTY SINCE 1914 WHEN I FIRST HEARD YOU AT UNION SQUARE NOW THE LIGHTS ARE GOING OUT ONE BY ONE BUT FOR ME AND THOUSANDS OF OTHERS YOUR LIGHT IS SEEN CLEAR AND TRUE."[47] With the exception of Gold, most greetings came from ordinary people, a contrast with the luminaries who had feted Flynn at a celebration held in her honor by the League for Mutual Aid in 1926. Flynn's membership in the CP

had put her in the thick of working-class struggles, but it had separated her from most noncommunists.

As Hays predicted, the US Supreme Court upheld the convictions of the communist leaders under the Smith Act in *Dennis v.
United States*. On June 4, 1951, the Court ruled 6–2 that the right to
free speech was correctly limited in this case by the "clear and present
danger" to the US government posed by communism. In his dissent,
Justice Hugo Black reminded the Court that the communists had not
been charged with any actual crime, but rather with "conspiracy" to
advocate the overthrow of the government at some point in the future. This hardly seemed to meet the conditions of "clear and present
danger," and it violated the right to free speech. He hoped that "in
calmer times, when present pressures, passions, and fears subside,"
the Court would "restore the First Amendment liberties to the high
preferred place they belong in a free society." A second dissent, by
Justice William O. Douglas, questioned the validity of indictments
made according to books written by Marx and Lenin rather than because of any actual plans for "terror" or violence. Up until this point,
he wrote, "full and free discussion" of all ideas had been a hallmark
of American democracy. In this case, the Court had chosen to "exalt
order at the cost of liberty." The calculus seemed to be more Soviet
than American.[48]

Early on the morning of June 20, 1951, a knock came at the door
of Flynn's apartment. Her sister Kathie, who was making breakfast
for her daughter, Frances, opened it to find three FBI agents there.
They "roughly pushed their way past her" and presented Elizabeth,
who was still in her bathrobe, with a warrant for her arrest. She was
charged with conspiracy "to unlawfully, willfully, and knowingly, to
advocate and teach the duty and necessity of overthrowing the Government of the United States by force and violence."[49] Flynn did not
know it yet, but she was one of 109 "second-string" leaders of the CP
being indicted under the Smith Act in New York, California, Baltimore, Seattle, Hawaii, Pittsburgh, St. Louis, Detroit, Cleveland, and
Philadelphia.[50] Lawyers in the first set of Smith Act cases had been
charged with contempt of court and imprisoned, and they faced dis-
barment. Thus, it was extremely difficult for Flynn to find a lawyer.

After scores of inquiries, she found a small but dedicated group of attorneys willing to defend her and the other twenty communists who had been charged in New York. The group included Flynn's friend Claudia Jones.[51]

Flynn was forbidden from traveling to speak on her own behalf. Kathie, who had never liked the CP, may have been the one person to join the party to protest the Smith Act prosecutions. Kathie had been Elizabeth's steadiest supporter since Elizabeth had returned to political life in the 1930s, and now she mounted a defense campaign on behalf of her sister. Kathie published an appeal in the *Daily Worker* and sent out letters to possible supporters, explaining that Elizabeth's forty-five years of work on behalf of the labor movement had been "the outpouring of a keen mind and generous heart, of a woman who cares about what happens to people, hates poverty, exploitation, injustice and wants people free, peaceful and happy." This long record of service, Kathie argued, deserved a better finale than time behind bars. Kathie urged people to support Elizabeth, even if they disagreed with her views. The prosecution of the communists, she argued, threatened the "democratic traditions of our country and the rights of all its people."[52]

Flynn's case won few high-profile supporters, but a small group of women whose political consciousness had been formed during the Progressive Era did rally to her defense. Mary Dreier, a founder of the Women's Trade Union League, sent a check to help defray Elizabeth's legal expenses. Dreier wrote to Kathie, "When I think of your sister's life and how utterly devoted she has been to the over worked and exploited in our country it makes me sick at heart." Nora Stanton Barney, an architect who had been active in the CAW, characterized Flynn's refusal to compromise her principles as heroic. Barney, who was the daughter and granddaughter of suffrage leaders, classified Flynn with "those brave souls who chose to suffer martyrdom rather than abandon their opinions and convictions." Throughout history, Barney remarked, thousands of people like Flynn had been "crucified," "burned at the stake," and "imprisoned."[53] Alice Hamilton, a retired professor of medicine at Harvard who had pioneered the study of occupational diseases, wrote a letter to the *New York Times* praising Flynn "for her selfless idealism."[54]

Workers around the country rallied to Flynn's defense. Letters and donations in support of Flynn flowed into CP headquarters. Those who wrote and contributed included an "old timer" from Ohio, a union member from Oklahoma, housepainters from upstate New York, and a group of lumber workers from Tacoma, Washington. Women seemed particularly moved by Flynn's plight. A group of female hat workers in New York City held a dinner to raise money for the Smith Act victims. They presented Flynn with a new hat "made with love and admiration." Two elderly Jewish women from the Bronx raised money by cooking gefilte fish and knishes and selling them to neighbors. Wives of the Smith Act victims in Seattle described Flynn as a "standard-bearer for all freedom-loving Americans, whose precious Constitutional liberties are in jeopardy." Writing under the pseudonym "Betty Feldman," Eleanor Flexner, a pioneering historian of women, praised Flynn's "long fight to put the issue of women's rights" and women's leadership "in the forefront" of movements for peace, labor rights, and community improvement. Flexner saw Flynn as "the embodiment of what a fighting working-class woman can become."[55]

Despite this outpouring of support, Flynn found her eight-month trial "a monotonous repetition of the Dennis case." The charges were "practically identical," and the government used the same strategy of paid informants and quotations ripped out of context. "The newspapers lost interest" and "spectators dwindled." Judge Edward Dimock, whom Flynn viewed as more reasonable than the judge of the first set of Smith Act cases, charged Flynn with contempt of court for refusing to name CP members, who could lose their jobs as a result of being identified. As punishment, Flynn endured thirty days at the Women's House of Detention on Greenwich Avenue, a chaotic city jail filled with prostitutes, drug dealers, and petty thieves awaiting trial. She struggled to look presentable in court and had no files to help prepare her defense. Flynn spent Christmas of 1952 in jail. One hundred friends gathered outside the House of Detention to sing Christmas carols and Irish freedom songs. Given the political climate of the early 1950s, however, it is not surprising that a jury found Flynn and the other defendants guilty.[56]

I. F. Stone, an independent journalist who attended Flynn's trial, summed up the process and the outcome. The prosecution created a "semblance of a case" only by charging members of the group with conspiracy, which "always sounds sinister to a jury." However, the evidence was vague, at best: "General expressions of approval of certain Marxist classics were twisted into evidence that a defendant was proposing to do in the America of the 1950s what Lenin had advocated in the Russia of 1905." The trial was full of "logical fallacies." A subpoena of FBI records showed "that the most sensational of the informers had lied to the court." Members of the jury made comments that revealed their prejudice against communists. "The chief victim of the prosecution," Stone concluded, "is not the Communist Party but a growing list of historic constitutional and procedural safeguards." If the convictions stood, he predicted, "freedom of expression in America must dwindle, for by the standards being established in these prosecutions, there are few dissenters and little dissent which could not ultimately be brought within the nebulous purview of that strange thing called 'conspiracy to advocate.'"[57] The 1950s is remembered as one of the most repressive periods in American history. The aggressive prosecution of communists made all forms of dissent suspect.

Flynn left behind little personal insight into these painful years. The FBI bugged her phone and read her mail. Former friends turned up as informants. Flynn kept her feelings to herself. She concluded her 1952 datebook with the comment, "A Hard Year." But 1953 was worse. Confined to endless months in the office and the courtroom, she ate and drank to help relieve stress. Her weight ballooned to 250 pounds. She suffered from painful arthritis in her knees and high blood pressure. By 1955 she could barely walk around the block.[58]

As Flynn waited for her case to wend its way through the appeals process, she spent six months writing her memoir, *The Rebel Girl.* The book focused exclusively on Flynn's "first life," ending prior to her self-imposed exile in Oregon in 1927 and making no reference to communism. By focusing on her earlier years, Flynn granted herself a respite from the present, when the prospects for American radicalism looked bleak indeed. However, her present predicament shaped her story. She emphasized the "force and violence" used against workers.

She memorialized labor activists who "gave their lives, shed their blood, were beaten, jailed, blacklisted and framed, as they fought for the right to organize, to strike, and to picket." She traced American labor radicalism back to the Knights of Labor, the old Socialist Party, and the Industrial Workers of the World. She included women in her story of struggle. She looked back nostalgically on the "united front" of the 1910s and 1920s. She lamented the misdirection of the Wobblies under the pressure of government repression, worried, perhaps, that the CP was following a similar pattern.

On January 10, 1955, the Supreme Court announced its refusal to hear an appeal in Flynn's case. The next day, Flynn took a cab back to the Women's House of Detention to be transported to Alderson Female Penitentiary in West Virginia to serve twenty-eight months in prison.[59] Although she had been arrested at least a dozen times during the first twenty years of her career, Flynn had never spent more than a day or two behind bars. Times had changed. Flynn was no longer young and beautiful, and the prosecution of communists generated little public sympathy.

Flynn tried to steer a steady course through the turbulent decade that followed World War II. She continued to advocate socialism, identifying the CP as the best vehicle for achieving it. She sought to expand, improve, and defend the party. Using her own biography, she linked the CP to the American radical tradition. She explained the costs of capitalism to American workers. She argued that the strategy of containment warped American foreign policy, and that domestic anticommunism undermined civil liberties. Despite her powers as a public speaker and her talent as an organizer, however, Flynn could not fight the rising tide of anticommunism. Nor could she prevent the CP from making choices that facilitated its own destruction. From a position of relative strength during and immediately after World War II, the CP plummeted in size and influence to become little more than a "sect."[60] In 1950, the CP had about 43,000 members. By 1955, the number had fallen to 22,600.[61] No longer able to recruit members, Flynn shifted back to her old work of labor defense. But she could not save the party—or herself.

10

"Mortal Enemy of Capitalism"—Last Years

Locked into a cell just three and a half feet wide by eight feet long at Alderson Female Penitentiary in West Virginia, Flynn wrote to her sister Kathie describing her frustration: "One's own life, especially if it is a life with a purpose, a social purpose like mine, is precious to one and at my time of life I can't spare too much time." Prison cut Flynn off from her family, her friends, and her work. When she wasn't in her cell, she spent her days in the basement of the prison hospital, mending sheets and making pillows. Claudia Jones, who served nine months in prison with Flynn prior to her deportation, wrote from England, "There sits this outstanding daughter of the American working class, who at 65 years of age has so much more to contribute to the nation's progress."[1]

Flynn endured her twenty-eight months behind bars, from January 1955 until May 1957, by focusing on the positive. She put herself on a strict diet. She caught up on books she had never had time to read. Reflecting on the past, present, and future of radical movements in the United States, she realized that she needed to rebuild alliances destroyed by anticommunism and by the party's own rigidity. After her release from prison, she continued her defense work and traveled to the Soviet Union. In the early 1960s, Flynn saw revived movements for peace, civil rights, and women's rights as signs that young people were ready, once again, to challenge the status quo.

While she was in prison, Flynn's correspondents were limited to her lawyers and five additional people, who had to be approved by the FBI. Kathie was one of the latter, becoming Elizabeth's lifeline to the outside world. She kept her up to date on friends and co-workers, referring to them by first names or initials in order to evade the censors. Visiting monthly, Kathie made the eight-hour trip from New York City to Alderson by train and spent the night at a run-down hotel near the depot. Without the help of the Families Committee of the Smith Act Victims, a group Elizabeth had helped to launch in 1951, Kathie would never have been able to afford to visit so frequently.[2] Elizabeth's other correspondents were acquaintances, rather than friends. They included Alice Hamilton, a retired physician who protested Flynn's conviction under the Smith Act. When one of Flynn's other correspondents, Robert Lovett, a retired professor from the University of Chicago, died, Flynn replaced him with her nephew, Peter Martin. Flynn eagerly welcomed Martin, who was the son of her sister Bina and Carlo Tresca, as the "valiant voice of youth." Martin, who worked as an editor and publisher, belonged to the Beat Generation, a countercultural literary and artistic movement that was emerging to challenge the social conformity of the Cold War era.

The United States did not recognize the presence of political prisoners, but Flynn and Jones were both placed in the maximum-security area of the prison, a harsh assignment given their crime of "conspiring to advocate." A third communist, Betty Gannett, was housed in another part of the prison, making it difficult for Flynn to maintain contact with her. Gannett was Jewish and had grown up on the Lower East Side. Flynn and Gannett were both atheists, but they sometimes went to church to see each other.[3] Music appreciation classes provided another opportunity to meet. Flynn also felt some kinship with several Puerto Rican nationalists who were confined to Alderson. They, too, were political prisoners, but they were devout Catholics who spent hours praying. They were willing to use violence to further their cause, which Flynn viewed as counterproductive.[4]

Most prisoners at Alderson were women who had been found guilty of routine crimes that crossed state lines, such as theft, forgery, prostitution, and drug dealing. Many of the inmates were illiterate, and those who could write lacked powers of persuasion. Flynn helped many of them craft their appeals for parole and write letters to their lawyers. She viewed her fellow inmates as victims of bad circumstances rather than bad people, but she did not share their interests. They gossiped, played cards, and turned up the volume on the radio, except when the news came on, when they turned it off. None of them could understand why Flynn, Jones, and Gannett were there.

With few people with whom she could identify, Flynn locked herself into her cell every night from 7:00 p.m. to 9:00 p.m. She read more than two hundred books while incarcerated. Studying early America, she noted Rhode Island's status as a haven for dissenters, tracing the rise and fall of the Alien and Sedition Acts. She enjoyed autobiographies of Benjamin Franklin and Henry Adams. She wondered why people admired Marcel Proust, however, complaining, "I can't get interested in his gossip about decadent aristocrats."[5] Flynn had more patience for fiction by Thomas Mann, Henry James, Virginia Woolf, Theodore Dreiser, George Eliot, and George Sand. Remarking on the fact that Eliot and Sand both disguised their identities as women, Flynn wrote, "We'll never know how much women have contributed because so many of their efforts were taken over by some man who got all the credit."[6] She might have added that women often effaced themselves. In her autobiography, *The Rebel Girl*, Flynn wrote herself into American history, but she tended to foreground other people rather than highlight her own accomplishments.

In addition to reading history and literature, Flynn learned about the latest developments in science and technology. She was impressed with the promise of automation, but worried about the future, writing in a letter, "What will happen to workers eventually?" Recognizing the significance of the economic changes she had seen over the course of the twentieth century, she remarked, "We need a Karl Marx to analyze these modern capitalist trends."[7] Marx's "great contribution," Flynn explained, was his analysis of capitalism. "Tactics, methods, forms of organization and struggle change with each generation," she added.[8] Flynn must have reflected on the disastrous impact of anticommunism and the recent missteps of the party. To be successful in its fight for communists to exercise their "full constitutional rights" to free speech and free association, the CP would need allies. Flynn resolved to find them once she was freed.

Flynn's letters from prison were relentlessly upbeat. She adopted cheerfulness as a form of resistance. She would not be shamed, broken, or dissuaded from the righteousness of her cause. If anything, prison made her more committed than before. She took strength from Susan B. Anthony, who had been arrested for trying to vote. One day, perhaps, streets and stamps would be named for communists. Elizabeth assured Kathie (and herself) that she had served her country as best she could. She felt no guilt for trying to make it a better place.[9]

Refusing to reform or repent, Flynn vowed to reduce. Thanks to her "enforced absence" from the "delightful Italian menus" of her two favorite restaurants, John's and Mary's, and from the stress of her work, Flynn lost seventy-five pounds. Her blood pressure improved and her arthritis nearly disappeared. She felt more energetic and looked forward to getting out of jail and buying an entirely new wardrobe. She vowed never again to shop at "Lane Bryant's and all those abominable fat lady stores." But Flynn looked forward to enjoying a cocktail or two and a good steak dinner once she returned to New York City. And she looked forward to the company of men again, declaring herself thoroughly sick of women, having been surrounded by them in prison.[10]

Once released, however, Flynn had no interest in settling into married life. She laughed off suggestions from one of her correspondents, Clements France, a retired social worker, that she come live with him in Rhode Island. "I treasure my freedom too greatly at my age," Elizabeth wrote to Kathie.[11] Reflecting on the marriage of two of her good friends, Gene and Peggy Dennis, Flynn bemoaned women's tendency to "fall so easily into a secondary role of helping a man to the extent they efface themselves." Flynn considered Peggy, who had first become active in the CP in Los Angeles, "a good speaker" and a talented writer, but believed that by devoting her life to Gene, Peggy had "lost her personality and self-confidence."[12] Disappointed that she had not been able to find a steady partner when in her forties, Flynn seemed content to be single in her sixties.

Flynn's autobiography, *The Rebel Girl*, was published while she was at Alderson. Knowing that people were reading and discussing her book made her feel less isolated and "closer to the outside." She resolved to write a second volume of her autobiography as a reply to those who "admire my early life and are unwilling to admit that from 1936 on was its logical sequence."[13] But Flynn had little time to work on the book. She could barely procure paper, and she could not compose a story that would be accepted by prison authorities. Flynn's literary output during these months was limited to three letters a week along with several poems and an Independence Day article for the prison newspaper, the *Eagle*, published on July 4, 1956.

Flynn's article, "On the Declaration of Independence," celebrated the American revolutionary tradition and explained the democratic principles articulated in the Bill of Rights. Using sources from the prison library, Flynn described the events that had led the United States to declare independence from Great Britain in 1776. Since then, she wrote, the Declaration of Independence had "served as a model" to "many colonial and oppressed people seeking independence and self-determination." Flynn quoted from the Preamble, which stated, "We hold these truths to be self-evident, that all men are created equal." The Declaration described all people as entitled to "Life, Liberty and the pursuit of Happiness." People formed governments to ensure those rights. If a government undermined those rights, then "the people" had a right "to alter or abolish it." Flynn went on to discuss the Bill of Rights, especially its protection of free speech. She urged her fellow Americans to read the Declaration of Independence and the Bill of Rights on the Fourth of July, arguing, "These are not just historical documents but lasting guarantees." Flynn could not say it directly, but she viewed the prosecution and imprisonment of communists as violating America's "democratic traditions."[14]

By age sixty-five, Flynn had made up her mind about the world. She did not have much interest in information that would challenge her point of view or cast doubt on the decisions she had made. Thus, in June 1956, she was deeply alarmed to read excerpts of a secret speech by Soviet prime minister Nikita Khrushchev. Leaked to sources in the US State Department, then published in American newspapers, the speech charged Stalin with constructing a "cult of personality" and committing brutal crimes. Thousands of Bolsheviks had been killed in the 1930s. Flynn found the revelations "quite ghastly—hard to understand." However, she read the speech as a condemnation of Stalin himself rather than of the Soviet Union or of communism. She thought Khrushchev had shown "great courage . . . to confess such terrible faults." Still, she found the information "terribly disturbing." "How could it happen and for so long a time?" she wondered. "We were too far away to know anything really of what was going on," Flynn rationalized. Like other communists, Flynn had refused to listen to former friends who had warned that the Russian Revolution had veered dangerously off course and was making a mockery of socialism. Flynn worried that Soviet confirmation of Stalin's atrocities would give "reactionaries" a "field day." But she stayed firm in her own commitment to the Communist Party.

Flynn wished that she could speak with Bill Foster and Gene Dennis, who had recently been released from prison, to find out what they made of this news.[15] By reading the newspapers and conferring with Kathie, Elizabeth must have discovered that her two friends were at odds: Foster resisted making changes in response to the revelations; Dennis urged the American CP to become more democratic and less subservient to Moscow. Once again, however, united opposition to Foster failed to coalesce. Late in the fall of 1956, the Soviet Union invaded Hungary to crush a popular uprising, stripping off any democratic gloss that might have remained on the Soviet Union from its fight against fascism during World War II.[16] Given the crisis in the CP, Flynn felt "anxious to get into the thick of things again, to help preserve and defend my views."[17]

As her prison term drew to a close, Flynn looked forward to being out among the people of America, "to meet them again, to travel again, to speak and to write again."[18] But once she got home she discovered that the CP—the main vehicle for her activism—was a mess. Foster was hanging onto power with a death grip. People who had sought change were leaving the party in defeat. They included John

Flynn at home, 224 East 12th Street, after her release from prison.
NP18-42, EGF Photographs, Tamiment Library, NYU

Gates, the editor of the *Daily Worker*, who, in an interview with television journalist Mike Wallace, condemned the CP's "unshaken faith" in the Soviet Union. The party had lost touch with the American people, Gates charged. As a result, its membership had dwindled to somewhere between 5,000 and 8,000. About half of these remaining party members lived in New York City; the rest were in Chicago and California. They were a mix of workers and housewives: the party did not appeal to young people.[19]

Despite these seemingly fatal shortcomings, Flynn stuck with the CP. To leave after her release from prison would be to admit that she had devoted her life to a failed cause. She scorned people like Gates and the novelist Howard Fast, who found large audiences for "tell all" books and articles. Despite the many glaring flaws now evident in the Soviet Union, Flynn held on to her hopes that it would demonstrate the viability of socialism as an alternative to capitalism.[20] She remained an idealist and soldiered on as a party stalwart.

Back from prison, Flynn attempted to rekindle the CP's work among women. "The consciousness of the status of women, the rights of women, and the role of women should be drawn like a thread through every aspect of Party work," she argued.[21] But Flynn had little success. She remained the sole woman among the national leaders of the CP, and the only one who had any real interest in prioritizing women's issues. The party had lost its sway among noncommunist women during the Red Scare. By the mid-1960s, a new women's movement was emerging. Many participants had learned to think about women's oppression from organizations associated with the Popular Front. However, the continued power of anticommunism prevented most liberal feminists from focusing on issues of social class.[22] Despite Flynn's efforts, the CP did little to attract women. The culture of the CP in the 1950s and 1960s seemed more stodgy and male-dominated than it had in the 1930s or 1940s.

Publicly, Flynn remained loyal to the CP, but privately, she recognized its flaws. Based on informants and surveillance, the FBI reported that Flynn "was very disgusted and disheartened with the situation in the CP." In the late 1950s, she requested a leave of absence to travel the Soviet Union; she also asked her coworkers to release her "from all CP duties so that she could just speak and write and not be involved in 'poolroom politics.'"[23] The FBI reports seem accurate on the topic of her disillusionment. Flynn affirmed these feelings in letters to Al Richmond, a communist newspaper editor in San Francisco, describing herself as "tired, fed up in fact," with most of her coworkers. The leadership of the national party remained insular and hostile to outsiders. After working with the CP leaders for years, she almost knew what they were "going to say." She wanted to retire, but she stayed on because she feared no one else would take on her legal defense work.[24]

In 1960, Flynn secured party sponsorship for a nine-month trip to Copenhagen, the Soviet Union, and Eastern Europe. In Copenhagen, she attended a huge celebration marking the fiftieth anniversary of International Women's Day. Flynn spoke at the event and reflected on its significance in an article for *Political Affairs*, a monthly magazine published by the CP. In the fifty years since the first Women's Day, American women had gained the right to vote and earned acceptance in the workforce. Stubborn inequalities persisted, however. Women had trouble finding skilled positions and gaining access to lucrative professions. They were clustered in areas of the economy that lagged in terms of labor organization. Even in organized sectors of the economy, such as making clothes, men dominated the unions and paid little attention to women's concerns. Women were active in politics at the local level, but their hours of labor rarely translated into positions of power. Only one woman served in the US Senate. What sort of legislation would the US Congress produce if it truly represented the nation in terms of race and gender? If women made up half of the legislators, Flynn argued, they would promote peace, spend less money on the military, and allocate more to social welfare. The dream of women's internationalism endured, but the Cold War divided most of the world into two hostile camps.

Flynn was prepared to love the Soviet Union, and her hosts made sure she was not disappointed. Writing to her nephew, Peter Martin, who was staying in her New York City apartment while she was traveling, Flynn reported in May 1960 that she liked Moscow "immensely—it is clean, quiet, no harsh ads or lurid electric signs."

She stayed at the Hotel Sovietskaya, a base for visiting party officials from around the world, where she was given a suite and treated to a sumptuous buffet breakfast each morning. She had a driver and a translator at her disposal. Not speaking Russian, she relied on them to help her find her way around Moscow, where she visited American exiles and "old Bolsheviks" who had survived Stalin's purges. She attended the circus, the ballet, and puppet shows. She had not done things like this in New York for at least thirty years, lacking time, money, and easy transportation.

Flynn's communism made her a criminal in the United States. In the Soviet Union and Eastern Europe, it made her a hero. *The Rebel Girl* had been translated into Russian, Hungarian, and German. On her trip, Flynn spoke on the radio and on television. She appeared at official events. She met Nikita Khrushchev and his wife, Nina, who spoke good English. "Mr. K.," as Flynn called the Soviet leader, seemed friendly and informal. He waved to Flynn whenever he saw her. Khrushchev, Flynn thought, "must be a great relief to the Russians after Stalin's severity." In the fall of 1960, Flynn was "caught up in a round of exciting festivities celebrating the Oct. Revolution of 1917." She watched a magnificent parade through Red Square from a seat at the tomb of Lenin and Stalin.[25] The following year, Flynn was invited back to Moscow to speak at Red Square, giving her the largest audience she had enjoyed in years.

Treated to an endless round of celebratory meals, Flynn packed on the pounds she had lost in prison. Her arthritis returned and her mobility diminished. After a three-and-a-half-hour examination, a Soviet doctor declared her "too fat" and put her on a diet. Instructing Flynn to avoid meat and potatoes and to substitute dry white wine for vodka, he sent her off to a health spa in Romania. Flynn soaked in mineral baths and got daily massages as well as hot paraffin treatments for her knees. The spa was located in a pine forest near the border of Bulgaria in a location where "rich villas and . . . sumptuous casinos" had been torn down to build "resorts for children and workers."[26] If it had not been for her painful arthritis, the lack of an audience, and the fact that they served only tea and mineral water to drink, Flynn might have been in heaven.

Flynn had traveled to the Soviet Union and Eastern Europe eager to compare the status of women under capitalism and socialism. Much of her information about women's disadvantaged position within the United States came from the Women's Bureau. The federal agency was a stronghold for feminist labor reformers who were determined to expose inequality in order to correct it. In the Soviet Union, the central government ran the economy. They permitted no real questioning of government methods or results. Soviet publications painted a rosy picture of women's lives under socialism. Articles and press releases enumerated the large number of female politicians and public employees. They reported that women made up half of all trade-union members and were well represented in trade-union leadership. They gave examples of female excellence in sports, education, and culture. The newspapers featured a female astronaut. Soviet propaganda celebrated legislation protecting female workers, including lengthy paid maternity leaves. Mothers benefited from free preschool for their children and pensions if they lacked male support. Flynn seems to have absorbed these statements without subjecting them to critical inquiry.

Reporting from Moscow, she announced that Soviet socialism had "abolished the domination of women by men." It "guaranteed to women an independent existence as a human being—a worker, a citizen, a wife and mother." Women in the Soviet Union had "the right to work, to vote, to an education, to participate in all public affairs, to rest and leisure, to medical and child care, to a peaceful old age—free from anxiety." She argued that, just as she had predicted in some of her first speeches, she now saw proof that state support of mothers and children could free women "from dependence upon individual men, either father or husband." Thus, the conditions of women had been "revolutionized."[27] Flynn had developed a sophisticated critique of women's conditions under capitalism, but she depicted women's conditions under socialism in idealistic terms. Privately, she admitted that traditional ideas about women's subservience to men died hard, but publicly she insisted that conditions were far better for Soviet women than they were for American women. The Soviet Union did go further than the United States did to promote women's equality in the workplace and provide social support for motherhood, but Flynn did not try to look behind the façade of equality to see whether Soviet women were satisfied. Flynn's treatment as a visiting luminary and the mediation of her translators insulated her from the realities of Soviet life.

Flynn's travels took her through Berlin, Prague, Bucharest, and Budapest. Everywhere she went, she received the "V.I.P. red carpet treatment." Her translators took good care of her, but they also made sure she stayed on a course designed to highlight the achievements of socialism. In Budapest, she was assigned her first male translator. He was just her type: a professor of philosophy who had been a steelworker and a partisan fighter against the Nazis. He treated her professionally, but when he realized she was not an uptight dignitary, they became "good friends." Deviating from the official program, they went to see a movie of "War and Peace in English." They "visited an open-air drinking and dancing place." They "went to the top of the highest mountain to see the city at night," where they shared "a bottle of their famous Tokay." Describing the encounter in a letter to her nephew, Peter, Elizabeth confessed, "I really hated to leave."[28] This intense but temporary relationship was much more to Flynn's taste than marriage.

Flynn may have returned home regretfully, but duty called. She was expected at a CP meeting in December. More urgently, Peggy Dennis wrote to tell her that Gene was dying of cancer. Gene's death in late December 1961 pained Flynn personally and dashed her hopes that he would inject new energy and flexibility into party leadership. Peggy deeply appreciated Flynn's presence. Party leaders squabbled for days over funeral arrangements. Flynn was the only one who "came to sit and talk and seek comfort."[29] As Dorothy Healey, a younger CP leader from Los Angeles, remembered, Flynn "was genuinely concerned about people in a way that most Party leaders were not." However, Healey was disappointed in Flynn's refusal to openly criticize party leaders or the Soviet Union.[30] Despite Flynn's personal warmth, she was embedded in an organization that seemed cold and hollow, even to its dwindling number of members.

Flynn found the transition from communism back to capitalism rough. "After being taken care of like a baby in a carriage in the Socialist countries for eight months," she lamented in the *Daily Worker*, "I landed with a thud alone on the sidewalks of New York."[31] Kathie was on an extended trip to Africa to visit her daughter, Frances, who had married a Nigerian. Elizabeth soon headed out to San Francisco. From a room with a view of the bay at the Hotel Powell, she wrote a book describing her experiences at Alderson. She hoped the book would build support for ending the prosecution of communists and improving conditions in women's prisons. In March 1961, Flynn was named chairwoman of the CP. It was the first time a woman had ever held such a position, but the promotion was largely symbolic. Gus Hall, who replaced Bill Foster, who had finally retired, held the levers of power in the party. Flynn got along fine with Hall, who had grown up in a Wobbly family of Finnish miners in Minnesota, but most people found him inflexible and resistant to change.

Flynn took time out from writing to survey the political scene in San Francisco and to see old friends. She visited City Lights, a bookstore Peter Martin had helped to start that had become a hub for the West Coast Beat community. She went out to dinner with Martin's sister, Roberta Bobba; visited Chinatown and Coit Tower with Peggy Dennis, who had moved to San Francisco; and saw her old friend Mike Gold. One sunny day in April, Flynn and Gold went to Union Square, where "a couple of thousand, mostly young people, gathered" at the end of a peace walk. They "sat on a park bench in the sun, to hear the speeches." By Flynn's standards, the speeches were "not so hot, a lot of piety." She missed the "burning eloquence" of early twentieth-century agitators like Eugene V. Debs. But Flynn thought "the youth everywhere" were "really O.K.," and she was pleased to see college students and their professors "fighting back."[32] Gold was dubious about this new generation of activists, however, because he thought they seemed concerned with abstract issues such as "values" and "identity," rather than the more concrete problem of class inequality. Flynn and Gold were both disappointed that young people showed so little interest in the CP.[33] Peggy Dennis blamed the national leadership. After 1960, she said, they "placed the Party in isolation from practically every new form of struggle that erupted in the ghettos, on the campus and in the street."[34]

Once she completed her book on Alderson, Flynn returned to New York City. She felt drawn back to defense work, and she needed to take care of her sister. Kathie had contracted a gastrointestinal illness in Nigeria; she returned home in August 1961, weighing just ninety-five pounds. Elizabeth now became Kathie's caretaker. Neither woman could manage the stairs to their walkup apartment. Just before Christmas of 1961, they moved to the Madison Square Hotel. Kathie died at the end of February 1962. Elizabeth dedicated her book on Alderson to Kathie, "who by her courage, cheerfulness, understanding and great sense of humor, helped make my time at Alderson more bearable and my whole life, at all times, easier and happier."[35] Elizabeth could not have pursued her career without Kathie, who had raised Elizabeth's son, carried her family through the Great Depression, and provided endless assistance to Elizabeth after her return to public life in 1936. Elizabeth moved to the Chelsea Hotel, a haunt of artists, writers, and musicians. She still felt at home among bohemians, even though she had officially embraced conservative cultural values when she had joined the CP. By this point in her life, Flynn did not care too much about what people thought of her.

Meanwhile, in Flynn's words, the CP continued to be "harassed, persecuted, stripped of its right to function, bankrupted financially, denied the use of halls, deprived of its rights of speech, press, and assemblage, subjected to lengthy and expensive legal proceedings, [and] practically illegalized."[36] In March 1962, the federal government indicted Gus Hall and Ben Davis for failing to register under the McCarran Act. Davis, an African American attorney who had been born in Atlanta, had joined the party during the Popular Front era, and he had become an important figure in Harlem. Flynn headed the Davis-Hall Defense Committee, which raised money for bail and appealed the indictments. Like Flynn, both men had already served time in prison under the Smith Act. In addition, the government fined the CP $10,000 a day for failing to register as a communist organization. The CP stuck to its vow not to comply with this section of the

McCarran Act: to do so would have required turning over membership lists to the FBI.

In July 1962, Flynn received a letter from the US Department of State revoking her passport. The letter cited a provision of the McCarran Act denying passports to known communists. J. Edgar Hoover, the head of the FBI, continued to track Flynn closely. He notified reactionary groups when she gave speeches so that they could protest. Hoover had tried to block Flynn's application for a passport. He was outraged when she continued to travel internationally even though she had been indicted under the Smith Act. Flynn was determined to fight for her right to travel. She found support from her old friend from the ACLU, Corliss Lamont, who directed the Emergency Civil Liberties Committee.[37]

Flynn used her fight to have her passport reinstated to rebuild alliances with liberals that had ruptured when she had been ousted from the ACLU in 1940. In an article for *Political Affairs*, she argued that the CP's leaders needed to start cooperating with other forces on the Left if they wanted to make progress. Flynn was one of at least five communists whose passports had been revoked. The right to travel, Flynn pointed out, was included in the Universal Declaration of Human Rights, which had been adopted by the United Nations in 1948. To be denied this right was to be imprisoned "within the borders of the U.S.A." The right to cross national borders seemed quintessentially American. Most Americans were descended from people who had traveled from other nations to find freedom. This formulation inadvertently excluded African Americans and Native Americans, but to Flynn, the passport cases showed that the McCarran Act was "strangling the Bill of Rights."[38]

Flynn used the 1963 publication of her book *The Alderson Story: My Life as a Political Prisoner* to continue to mend fences with liberals and to fight against the McCarran Act. She sent an inscribed copy to John Haynes Holmes, who had presided over her expulsion from the ACLU. Holmes responded, "We have fought many good fights— sometimes for and sometimes against one another—but always with mutual respect and honor."[39] Norm Thomas, the head of the Socialist Party, also swung behind Flynn. "You know how sorry I was when an old-time Wobbly like you joined the Communists," Thomas wrote to Flynn. "But," he added, "that was no reason for putting you in jail." "Whatever our differences," Thomas concluded, "please think of me as your friend."[40] When the Belmont Plaza Hotel in Manhattan canceled Flynn's book reception because she was a communist, Thomas issued a press release arguing that Flynn had "lived a significant life" and had the right to express herself freely. To imprison her, deny her right to travel, or cancel her book reception was to subvert "the freedoms of speech, press and assembly which lie at the heart of democracy." The hotel relented after the Emergency Civil Liberties Committee secured an "injunction barring the hotel from breaching its contract."[41]

On Friday, March 29, 1963, at 7:30 p.m., "over 400 guests crammed the ballroom" of the Belmont Plaza Hotel on Lexington Avenue and 49th Street to celebrate Flynn and her book on Alderson. Speakers included Dorothy Day, the editor of the *Catholic Worker*, who recalled hearing Flynn speak in 1917 on behalf of striking miners on the Mesabi Range. Mary van Kleeck, the first director of the Women's Bureau, framed Flynn's life as a fight for democracy "against the forces, which recurrently have sought to weaken or destroy it."[42] Mike Gold praised Flynn's publication as demonstrating a "new compassion and understanding of humanity."[43] At age ninety-four, Alice Hamilton was too frail to attend the party, but she congratulated Flynn on her book. Hamilton regretted that she would "not live to see a real rebirth of our old ideas of freedom," but she added, "I do believe it will come."[44] Toward the end of the *Alderson Story*, Flynn had written, "It takes a long time to get prison out of one's mind and heart."[45] The letters from friends and the crowd of well-wishers at the Belmont Plaza must have helped.

Flynn's fight to keep her passport continued. The Department of State agreed to use appeals by Flynn and by Herbert Aptheker, a communist and a pioneering scholar of African American history, as test cases. In February 1964, the US Court of Appeals ruled in favor of Flynn and Aptheker. "The McCarran Act is cracking," Flynn announced, and at last "the fog of McCarthyism" seemed to be lifting.[46] On June 8, the Supreme Court nullified the requirement that the CP register with the federal government. On June 22, the Court invalidated the provision of the McCarran Act denying passports to communists. Both decisions cited the Fifth Amendment, which protects citizens from self-incrimination and guarantees individual liberty. Newspapers around the country ran a picture of Elizabeth Gurley Flynn smiling. She looked radiant in victory. According to an editorial in the *Washington Post*, the Supreme Court decisions revealed the fundamental problem with the McCarran Act: "It seeks security by discarding liberty." The editors described the McCarran Act as "a blemish on American history."[47] Flynn must have heartily agreed.

In July 1964, with her passport secured and a major legal battle won, Flynn resolved to make progress on the second volume of her autobiography. She gathered her notes and clippings and set off for the Soviet Union. On August 7, she celebrated her seventy-fourth birthday in Moscow. Greetings came from friends around the world and from "Mr. K." himself, who praised the American CP for standing "firm under attacks that few parties faced." After receiving a white bust of Lenin, Flynn spoke briefly, highlighting the CP's recent "victory" over the passport section of the McCarran Act. Although the American CP was "small," she said, it had "made a good fight—and won." Liberal allies had provided important assistance.[48] Flynn must have hoped that the decision in the passport cases marked a decline in official anticommunism and an end to the CP's isolation from other forces on the Left.

Flynn did not live to see this dream fulfilled. Within a week of her birthday, she collapsed from exhaustion and was rushed to the Kremlin Hospital. In a letter to Peter Martin, she described her large, quiet room overlooking a courtyard in an old building in the center of Moscow. She felt relieved to get away from "telephones, parties, [and] interviews." Even here, she assessed women's status under socialism. The doctors and nurses were all women, but "the Head" was a man. Tests revealed sugar in Flynn's blood and urine, a sign of diabetes. She described her condition as the result of being "overworked" and "overweight." She worried that her "poor book seems doomed" by "interruptions and distractions." With characteristic humor, she compared herself to "an old hen" who wanted to lay an egg but could not find a place to settle down and do it.[49] Flynn fell into a diabetic coma and died on September 5, 1964.[50]

True to her final role as a Soviet heroine of the American working class, Flynn was given a huge state funeral. As her body lay in state in the Hall of Columns in Moscow, a spokesman for the Soviet CP hailed Flynn "as one of the brightest figures of the 20th century." Dolores Ibárruri, the chair of the Spanish Communist Party in exile, who had first met Flynn in Paris in 1945, lauded Flynn's "fighting spirit," noting that even in prison, Flynn "never bowed her head." Using his restored passport, Herbert Aptheker traveled to Moscow to deliver a eulogy. He lauded Flynn's long fight to keep the Bill of Rights alive and praised her position "on the firing line of labor battles" for most of the twentieth century. To Aptheker, it seemed that "every victim of capitalism and racist oppression found in her a passionate defender." It took eight hours for 25,000 people to file past Flynn's casket, which was piled high with flowers. Mourners included Russians, American exiles, and students studying in Moscow "from Africa, Asia, Haiti, [and] Latin America." Mrs. Khrushchev served as a pallbearer. Mr. Khrushchev joined the honor guard prior to Flynn's cremation. A band played the Internationale, as an urn containing half of Flynn's ashes was placed at the base of the Kremlin wall, to be interred near the remains of Bill Haywood. The rest of Flynn's remains were sent back to the United States to be buried at Waldheim Cemetery in Chicago, a resting place of American radicals since the Haymarket Affair of 1886.[51]

Flynn's obituary ran on the front page of the *New York Times* and in hundreds of other newspapers across the United States. The press described the pomp and circumstance of the Moscow funeral. As always, reporters contrasted Flynn's appearance with her message. As one obituary explained, Elizabeth Gurley Flynn looked like "an old-fashioned docile grandmother," until she opened her mouth and began to speak, reminiscing about "bloody strikes" and championing communism. Reflecting gendered expectations for female behavior, newspapers noted with approval that Flynn had smiled more often as she had grown older. However, all agreed that she remained a "fiery orator."[52] An old-timer from the Mesabi Range remembered Flynn as "a firebrand, a consummate rabble rouser" who had no equal. One reporter wondered whether Flynn ever doubted devoting "so much time, talent and energy" to "an alien creed and country."[53] Another accused her of trying "to substitute the hammer and sickle for the Stars and Stripes." He could not understand how Flynn could mix two seemingly incompatible systems: communism and Americanism.

Loyalty was a major theme in Flynn's life, but in more nuanced ways than obituaries written during the waning years of the Cold War acknowledged. Throughout her career, Flynn tried to balance her loyalty to ideals, people, and organizations. The socialist principles she eagerly grasped as a teenager remained her guiding light. She believed in empowering working people and in establishing a new society that guaranteed the material well-being of all. She envisioned socialism as guaranteeing women's equality. She defended her right to preach unpopular ideas by citing the freedoms of speech and association guaranteed by the US Constitution. To act on these ideals, however, she joined an organization that turned out to be fatally flawed. In becoming a communist, she set aside her earlier concerns about Soviet violations of human rights. In remaining a communist, she clung to the Soviet Union as an example of a utopian, socialist society long after it had revealed itself to be a repressive, dictatorial regime. Ultimately, she was trapped by her loyalty to the people with whom she worked and by her refusal to admit the failure of the Soviet experiment.

Flynn believed in change, but she could not make it happen on her own. Thus, she spent most of her life working within organizations whose principles she shared, but whose direction she sometimes doubted. Both the IWW and the CP generated stiff opposition and faced intense government repression, creating almost insurmountable challenges for their leaders. Flynn cared deeply about the people she led in strikes, free-speech battles, and other confrontations with employers and government authorities. She believed that the victims of unequal power relations, whether they were workers, women, African Americans, or colonial subjects, had to develop a consciousness of their oppression and organize to liberate themselves. She worked tirelessly to bring this message to the masses through her speeches, writings, and organizational efforts. She remained loyal to her friends and her family and to her vision of an essentially noble but deeply wronged American working class. Her unusual status as a woman advocating radical political and economic ideas inspired many people who were unhappy with the current social order, but to some degree limited her power in both the IWW and the CP.

Flynn did not achieve her life's goal of bringing socialism to America. But her sustained critique of capitalism, developed over six decades of social activism, brings to light problems that remain to be solved. These include continued gender inequality, the fate of workers in a globalized society, dramatic disparities in income between the rich and the poor, and the power of the federal government to monitor people and organizations judged subversive. Flynn would see these issues as opportunities for critical examination, organization, and change.

Primary Sources

The following documents include a mix of sources designed to illustrate Flynn's evolution as a speaker and a writer, to highlight her public image, and to reveal some of her private feelings.

"YOUNG WOMAN LEADS THE WAITERS' STRIKE," NEW YORK TIMES, JANUARY 14, 1913, 7. PROQUEST HISTORICAL NEWSPAPERS

This article illustrates some of the rhetoric and techniques Flynn used as an IWW organizer.

Miss Elizabeth Gurley Flynn, the I.W.W. organizer, . . . was the principal speaker at a mass meeting of the Hotel Workers' Union in Bryant Hall last night. . . . Miss Flynn is the power behind the hotel workers. . . . It is largely she who is organizing the cooks, scullions, and waiters into an efficient fighting body, and she believes in the fullest publicity. . . .

Last night's meeting was held for the purpose of cheering up the drooping spirits of the men, and to prepare them for the mass meeting to be held to-morrow night, at which the men are to be asked to vote for or against the continuance of the general strike. In her speech last night, Miss Flynn indicated a new line of attack on the hotel proprietors by the union.

"I want every waiter and every cook who knows anything about the adulteration of food, about sending back food refused by one guest to another guest, about highly flavored sauces to disguise unfit food, to come to headquarters at 11 o'clock to-morrow to make affidavits as to the rotten conditions in hotel kitchens. . . . We want to tell Mr. Capitalist what kind of a place his dinner comes out of. A nice cup of coffee coming out of most kitchens is like a nice lily coming up out of a mud hole. You may have to work there, but they have to eat there."

"You'll hit them right in the stomach, where they have their most sensitive feelings. These capitalists don't enjoy art, they don't enjoy literature; what they do enjoy is eating. If their meat were analyzed by a chemist it would be found to be five-sixths poison and the other sixth covering up." . . .

Miss Flynn then announced that the union would give an educational dance in the near future, at which the wives of the members would be gently converted to unionism. . . .

"We know that a lot of your wives don't understand the strike," she said, "and that they lecture you at home and keep asking you, 'Why don't you get a job?' We'll make them like the women of Lawrence. . . . Better go out and work with a pick and shovel on the streets than go back without winning the strike."

ELIZABETH GURLEY FLYNN, LETTER TO MARY HEATON VORSE, SENT FROM
PORTLAND, OREGON, MARCH 22, 1929. MARY HEATON VORSE PAPERS, WAYNE
STATE UNIVERSITY

*In this letter to a friend, Flynn alludes to her depression and describes some of her feelings
about her son, Fred, nicknamed Buster.*

Dear Mary:—I owe you a most humble and heartfelt apology for not writing sooner. But
whether it was a by-product of my long illness or pure laziness, I have the hardest time
forcing myself to write letters. I get so bad that actually I only wrote to my mother and Fred
for about six months, and that was an effort. At the time I received your last letters I was
so uncertain of my plans and so rushed because the Dr. [Marie Equi] was sick in bed with
flu-pneumonia, that I laid it aside, intending to reply shortly. She was so very ill just before
X-mas that I was compelled to telephone to Miss Whitney to bring her little girl up at once
from California and we really feared she wouldn't last till the child reached here. . . .

Then I have also been a great deal disturbed about Buster. He is a good enough boy
from all conventional standards—doesn't drink, smoke, run around with girls, etc. I guess
he's a reaction from my own wild youth. But my family, as usual, decides what he is to
do—My mother and father are too old to quarrel with—but the others should know better.
However, they sent him off to the University of Michigan—tho[ugh] where they expect to
get the necessary funds to see him through is beyond me. And they do not seem to realize
the importance of him getting a job and helping to pay his own way through. So I've been
quite upset by it all. But I suppose eventually it will work out alright. Buster will never be a
radical, I fear. He had too much of it when he was a child and it has no novelty or interest
for him. What he has heard is mostly criticism, unfortunately, which is destructive of
enthusiasm.

But lately, I have begun to feel like myself again. Suddenly, with the coming of Spring,
which is very beautiful out here, I felt better. Of course the heart specialists told me two
years ago that it would take that long to get the streptococcus infection out of my blood
stream, and I simply had to be patient. But I am glad to say I have spoken at two meetings,
one in Seattle for the Centralia I.W.W. men and one here for Mooney and Centralia, and
did not feel any the worse for it except a little tired. But of course, I'll have to take it easy
at first and not overdo. And I can never go at the pace I used to—that's certain. I guess it
won't delay the revolution any either!

How are you, Mary dear? I read a story of yours about the youngsters coming home
from Europe and was so glad to see that you are writing again.

I would be glad to hear from you and to know how you are and what you are doing. I
hope you are well and happy. How are your children? I hope you are doing your own work
again and conserving your energy.

With all good wishes and love to you, as ever, your affectionate friend,
Elizabeth

ELIZABETH GURLEY FLYNN, "ON WOMEN'S COM[MISSION]," N.D. ELIZABETH GURLEY FLYNN PAPERS, TAMIMENT LIBRARY, NEW YORK UNIVERSITY, BOX 7, FOLDER 23

In these undated handwritten notes, likely from late 1940s or 1950s, Flynn outlines the policies she pursued as director of the Women's Commission of the Communist Party during the 1930s and 1940s.

1. Concerned itself with activities of our women workers—to guarantee that they were not relegated to minor or clerical tasks that they were represented + elected on all levels of the Party organization and their talents + capacities developed + utilized to the full—against all concepts of male superiority.

2. That women political candidates were put forward by our own Party + demands made on other parties to do likewise.

3. That the t[rade] u[nion] women were granted equal status with men on committees + in officership of the union + that large unions of women should be officered by women. In a word—We stood for equality vs. male supremacy—

4. That equal opportunity was fought for in the shops + professions—for women, with equal pay for equal work, seniority rights in shops, etc. with provisions for rest periods, child care + maternity leaves.

5. Protective legislation for women + children workers—passage of a child labor amendment pending for years.

6. That discriminatory practices against Negro women be abolished—who were last to be hired and first to be fired. Right to enter all occupations.

7. Guarantee full rights of suffrage to Negro + poor white women in South—Especially affected by poll tax—to expose violence vs. Negro women . . .

8. We recommended to all our women workers + other women of the working class to register + to vote + to familiarize themselves with all political issues + to take a firm stand on all issues [and to] urge others to do the same.

9. To join organizations—such as Parent-Teachers; Consumers'—Tenants—T.U. [Trade Union] Auxiliaries—fraternal organizations—to be active [in] public affairs + concern themselves with welfare of women + children in all aspects of community life + to help all worth while efforts in these directions.

10. We conferred regularly with our women in different cities + states on programs to be advanced for welfare + family + community in relation to all these activities. [Organized] conferences . . . + conventions.

11. We helped organize the women of the CP to participate in all war efforts during war vs. fascism (Red Cross—Civilian defense-blood donors, etc.). Support O[ffice of] P[rice] A[dministration]—Rationing—Rent control, etc.

12. Since the war end[ed] Com[munist] women have joined + engaged in peace organizations; delegations to U.N. + to Wash[ington]

ELIZABETH GURLEY FLYNN, "WHAT DO I MISS—YOU ASK," AUGUST 21, 1955.
ELIZABETH GURLEY FLYNN PAPERS, TAMIMENT LIBRARY, NEW YORK UNIVERSITY,
BOX 7, FOLDER 4

Flynn reminisces about her daily life in a poem written from Alderson prison.

Besides freedom, work, my friends and life, I'm sure you mean. To faithfully answer? The list grows—both great and small.

I miss the foghorns on the river at night and the pictures on the wall.

I miss the children playing on the sunny street, and the corner candy store with good neighbors whom I meet.

I miss my sleepy cat, my ugly cactus, my treasured books, and a long leisurely talky breakfast under Kathie's kindly looks.

I miss sleeping until I wake up and getting up when I can't sleep.

I miss turning on the light at my ease and turning off the radio when I please.

I miss walking alone at night and seeing the stars and returning to an open door, a window without bars.

I miss a key on the inside of the door and a soft wool rug, not rag, to cover the floor.

I miss a large bureau with capacious drawers and a long, wide mirror without flaws.

I miss nylon stockings and a colorful dressing gown and leaving the house at will to take a ride 'round the town.

I miss grapefruit and real hot coffee in my big blue French cup and eggs and strawberries and cream to sup.

I miss sardines, cheese, olives and beer with the "early bird" edition at midnight and Giovannitti and other friends, to cheer.

I miss real movies—unexpurgated—with an audience of men, women, and lively children, and soft voices and low-pitched laughter.

I miss talking to men—talk about politics, trade unions, families and friends.

I miss soft dresses and underwear and gay, bright scar[ve]s and my wristwatch, my zircon ring and fountain pen.

I miss my firm, wide bed, my thick walls, my privacy to sleep, unheard to read aloud, to sing a little—even to weep.

I miss my name spoken with the proper prefix because it is a long time since I was or felt like "a girl."

I miss the beauty parlor on University Place and Sonny asking "Wave or curl?"

I miss the Hudson River and the East River drive and the U.N. at night and I miss dear old Brooklyn Bridge and the Skyline all night.

I miss New York and the Statue in the bay, LaGuardia airport, Idlewild and Union Square in May.

I miss travelling—I miss America—the Mississippi, the Rocky Mountains, Puget Sound, the Pacific Ocean, and Philadelphia, Detroit, Pittsburgh and ever-lovely San Francisco.

Nothing and no one can take my country away from me. It is ever in my mind, my heart, my eyes. But most of all I miss people—my own kind of people—people with ideas, ideals, dreams, hopes of tomorrow.

I miss real talks, natural laughter, jokes, persiflage, a sense of humor; people who are objective, who can discuss without prejudice, debate without anger, reason without rancor.

I miss people who know what they believe, are willing to suffer and sacrifice for it cheerfully and be true to it, come what may.

I miss good plain workers, who go to work, belong to unions, help their fellows, love their kids and wives—fur and steel workers, miners and auto workers, who lead normal, useful lives.

Yes, in this strange hiatus, this temporary withdrawal from a living world—I miss still more the intangibles—hard to define—personal liberty, the search for happiness, the right to speak my mind.

But in my memory I have all I miss and in my thoughts—all I seek, so fear not their loss should make me sad or weak.

MICHAEL GOLD, "GREETINGS TO THE DINNER IN NEW YORK HONORING THE APPEARANCE OF ALDERSON, A BOOK OF PRISON MEMOIRS BY ELIZABETH GURLEY FLYNN," 1963. ELIZABETH GURLEY FLYNN PAPERS, TAMIMENT LIBRARY, NEW YORK UNIVERSITY, BOX 7, FOLDER 17

The author of Jews Without Money *reflects on Flynn's legacy.*

It was in tragic 1914, year of world war and unemployment[,] that I first heard the voice of Elizabeth Gurley Flynn sounding like a bell of gold through New York's Union Square.

She was then a young Irish-American goddess, a girl of twenty with a face of classic beauty who had become a national legend for the courage and clarity she displayed in the leadership of great and bitterly-fought strikes of the textile workers, shoe workers, miners, and other masses of starving workers.

Now she had become active in organizing the half-million unemployed in imperial New York. I was one of those, a jobless young Jewish-American truck driver who wandered quite by accident into a great demonstration in Union Square. The cops ended the peaceful gathering with a brutal and senseless assault. I was among those clubbed, I too received there a first lesson in the ABC's of capitalism.

Yet through these 48 years I remember best the magnificent voice of Elizabeth Gurley Flynn. We had no loud-speakers then, but she filled the big square and every heart with her courage, her clarity, her wisdom based on proletarian experience and common-sense. She took the sordid facts of their suffering and composed them into a broad symphony of socialism. . . . Elizabeth has been one of the greatest teachers of our time, and how grateful I am to have learned from her, too.

It is inspiring to read "Alderson," her book of prison memoirs just issued. The inspiration comes from the book's truthfulness. She is a fine reporter, who can see the unique facts that make a women's prison so different from the men's. The book contains a gallery of portraits of the damned, the prostitutes, thieves, killers and other misfits of the social system. Elizabeth paints them as they are, neither better [n]or worse, but always human.

Her life-long indignation against a cruel profit-system that arranges such lives flows through Elizabeth's new book. But it seems to me a new compassion and understanding of humanity have also grown in the "Rebel Girl."

Her book is more than a prison book, it is a lesson in the perfectibility of humanity, including lesbians and addicts.

In the colleges today troubled youth on every campus are searching for what they call "values," for what they call "identity," and other such abstractions. Let them study the realist values and identity of Elizabeth Gurley Flynn. Others have abandoned her socialist ideals, but have turned sour and impotent. . . . She has remained faithful, and thus creative, brave and beautiful. Long live / Elizabeth Gurley / Flynn! Long live the American people she has served so well! Long live the peace and creativeness / of the world!

GLOSSARY

Each of the general terms listed below has a multitude of meanings, and each idea and organization has a long history and can be viewed from many different perspectives. This glossary is meant to clarify the terms as they applied to Elizabeth Gurley Flynn's life and work.

AFL: *see* American Federation of Labor (AFL).

American Federation of Labor (AFL): the leading national trade-union organization in the twentieth-century United States. The AFL focused primarily on "bread-and-butter" issues such as higher wages and shorter hours. It emphasized the rights of skilled workers, who from the 1890s through the 1920s tended to be white men. The federation became more diversified during the 1930s and merged with the CIO in 1955. It was opposed to socialism in all forms. *See* Congress of Industrial Organizations (CIO).

Anarchists: members of a transnational movement seeking to abolish all forms of political and economic authority and to establish "a new society based on the voluntary cooperation of free individuals" (Paul Avrich, *The Modern School Movement: Anarchism and Education in the United States* [Princeton, NJ: Princeton University Press, 1980], iii). A small minority of anarchists endorsed the use of violence as retribution against government officials and employers who perpetrated violence against workers; these anarchists believed that symbolic acts of violence could spark revolution.

Capitalism: a system of producing and distributing goods and services based on creating a profit for property owners. In a capitalist economy, people buy and sell land, labor, and goods in a "free" market, although some government regulations may be imposed. Flynn saw capitalism as fundamentally unjust to workers, who did not fully reap the benefits of the profits created by their labor and were often exploited by their employers.

CIO: *see* Congress of Industrial Organizations (CIO).

Civil liberties: individual rights guaranteed to all US citizens under the Bill of Rights, such as freedom of speech, assembly, and the press.

Communism: the political and economic system constructed in the Soviet Union during and after the Bolshevik Revolution. Acting in the name of the working class, the state sought to control all economic, political, and cultural activity. Some people viewed communism as an extension and fulfillment of socialist ideals, while many others deplored its antidemocratic tendencies and viewed the Soviet Union as a dictatorship rather than a socialist society.

Communist parties: organizations that formed not only in the Soviet Union and Eastern Europe but also in the United States, Western Europe, Asia, Africa, and Latin America in the 1920s and 1930s that admired and supported the Soviet Union as a model for a socialist society. After World War II, not all communist parties or nations aligned themselves with the Soviet Union.

Congress of Industrial Organizations (CIO): a nationwide organization of industrial unions that sought to organize all workers within a given industry rather than focusing exclusively on skilled workers or on workers that performed one particular type of job. The CIO flourished during the 1930s. It expelled communists after World War II and merged with the AFL in 1955. *See* American Federation of Labor (AFL).

Direct action: a strategy endorsed by the IWW that focused on staging strikes and protests rather than negotiating contracts, seeking labor legislation, or electing pro-labor politicians to public office. *See* Industrial Workers of the World (IWW).

Fascist: dictatorships characterized by military rule and a cult of personality. The term was first used to describe Benito Mussolini's paramilitary organization in Italy, which was formed to fight against the Italian communists in 1919. It was later used to describe Francisco Franco's regime in Spain and Adolf Hitler's rule in Nazi Germany.

Feminism: a diverse, transnational movement claiming full human rights for all people regardless of sex or gender. Elizabeth Gurley Flynn's feminism included attention to inequalities of class and race.

Free love: the idea that men and women should choose their sexual partners based on attraction rather than be limited by marriage.

Industrial Workers of the World (IWW): an early twentieth-century labor organization that endorsed socialism and syndicalism. It sought to organize all workers within a given industry regardless of skill, ethnicity, race, or gender. *See* Syndicalism.

IWW: *see* Industrial Workers of the World (IWW).

Knights of Labor: a late nineteenth-century organization that sought to organize all "producers" and critiqued the growing power of corporations in politics.

Left, leftist, left wing: shorthand for people with radical politics; often used in contrast to the "Right" or "right-wing" to refer to people with conservative politics.

Liberals: people who believe that capitalism can be made more humane through better regulation. They are reformers rather than revolutionaries.

Marxist: someone who agrees with Karl Marx's critical analysis of capitalism and/or his prediction of an inevitable conflict between the bourgeoisie and the proletariat leading to a socialist revolution.

Socialism: an alternative to capitalism in which the production and distribution of goods and services is managed collectively or by the state on behalf of the common good. The term implies a redistribution of wealth and resources and the empowerment of the working class.

Socialist Party or Socialist Party of America: an American political party that fielded candidates for local and national office. Members believed that change in the United States could come through the ballot box rather than through revolution. Syndicalists in the IWW disputed this idea, calling instead for "direct action." *See* Direct action; Syndicalism.

Syndicalism: an international movement popular among radical workers in the early twentieth century that sought to abolish the state except as an extension of workers' organizations. Members of the IWW were syndicalists.

Vigilantes: citizens without formal law-enforcement authority who attempt to perform law-enforcement duties. In Flynn's time, the term was used for local citizens who attacked organizers for the IWW and other radical or labor groups, often with encouragement from local police.

STUDY QUESTIONS

1. How did Flynn's identity as a woman shape her leadership in the two major organizations to which she belonged, the Industrial Workers of the World (IWW) and the Communist Party (CP)?
2. How did Flynn's personal and political life influence each other?
3. Flynn's main concerns were empowering workers and overcoming inequalities of race and gender. How did she combine these commitments? Did they ever seem at odds with each other? If so, how did she resolve the tension?
4. During and after the Cold War, many people saw communism and American patriotism as antagonistic ideas. How did Flynn seek to reconcile these two seemingly opposed concepts? To what degree was she successful?
5. Flynn's poem "What Do I Miss" (in "Primary Sources" section) discusses her life in prison. What does it reveal about her daily life prior to her incarceration? What does she miss the most, and why?
6. How did Flynn's age and experience shape her political outlook during different eras of her life?

NOTES

INTRODUCTION

1. Dorothy Healey and Maurice Isserman, *Dorothy Healey Remembers: A Life in the American Communist Party* (New York: Oxford, 1990), 174.

2. "They Called Her the Rebel Girl," undated clipping, EGF Papers, Tamiment Library, New York University (Tamiment), Box 13.

CHAPTER 1: EAST SIDE JOAN OF ARC—EARLY LIFE

1. Elizabeth Gurley Flynn, *The Rebel Girl: My First Life, 1906–1926* (New York: International Publishers, 1986), 22, 62–63; Rosalyn Fraad Baxandall, *Words on Fire: The Life and Writing of Elizabeth Gurley Flynn* (New Brunswick, NJ: Rutgers University Press, 1987), 2; Early Newspaper Clippings, 1906–1907, EGF Papers (Tamiment), Box 1, Folder 8.

2. Flynn, *Rebel Girl*, 23.

3. Ibid., 26–29.

4. Lara Vapnek, *Breadwinners: Working Women and Economic Independence, 1865–1920* (Urbana: University of Illinois Press, 2009), 3, 43–48, 66–70.

5. Elizabeth Gurley Flynn, "Mother," clipping from *Daily Worker*, 1959, EGF Papers (Tamiment), Box 1, Folder 2.

6. Flynn, *Rebel Girl*, 30.

7. Flynn, "Mother."

8. Art Shields, "'Rebel Girl's' [*sic*] Father," *The Worker*, New York, January 31, 1943, clipping, EGF Papers (Tamiment), Box 1, Folder 1.

9. Flynn, *Rebel Girl*, 31–32.

10. Date of marriage from Dartmouth College Alumni Record, December 9, 1938, EGF Papers (Tamiment), Folder 1, Box 1.

11. Flynn, *Rebel Girl*, 36.

12. "High School Girl on Box Talks Socialism" and "Girl Socialist Tells of Aims," unidentified clippings, 1907, EGF Papers (Tamiment), Box 1, Folder 9.

13. Flynn, *Rebel Girl*, 37–40.

14. Ibid., 65.

15. Ibid., 38.

16. Ibid., 46–47.

17. Ibid., 33.

18. Ibid., 30.

19. "School Children in Debate Declare for Restoring the Rod," unidentified clipping, 1903–1906, EGF Papers (Tamiment), Box 1, Folder 6.

20. Elizabeth Gurley Flynn, "Early Compositions," 1902–1906, EGF Papers (Tamiment), Box 1, Folder 3.

21. Flynn, *Rebel Girl*, 53; Rosalyn Fraad Baxandall, "Elizabeth Gurley Flynn: The Early Years," *Radical American* 8 (1975): 100.

22. Flynn, *Rebel Girl*, 48.

23. Ibid., 49.

24. Ibid., 66–67; "Red Sunday Parade Was a Mild Affair," January 23, 1906, *New York Times*, 6, ProQuest Historical Newspapers.

25. Flynn, *Rebel Girl*, 67–68.

26. Flynn, *Rebel Girl*, 53–55.

27. Ibid., 54–55.

28. Elizabeth Gurley Flynn, "How I Became a Rebel," *Labor Herald*, July 1922, 23–24, clipping, EGF Papers (Tamiment), Box 1, Folder 44.

29. Clippings, 1906–1907, EGF Papers (Tamiment), Box 1, Folder 8.

30. *Philadelphia Public Ledger*, August 23, 1907, clipping, and unidentified clipping from Irvington, NJ, EGF Papers (Tamiment), Box 1, Item 8.

31. Emma Goldman, *Living My Life*, 1931, http://theanarchistlibrary.org/library/emma-goldman-living-my-life, 489.

32. Flynn, *Rebel Girl*, 49–50.

33. "Woman," notes for speech, 1907 or 1908, EGF Papers (Tamiment), Box 1, Folder 14.

34. Flynn, *Rebel Girl*, 49–50; "Woman."

35. "Women and Syndicalism," notes for speech, n.d., EGF Papers (Tamiment), Box 1, Folder 14.

36. Lara Vapnek, "The 1919 International Congress of Working Women," *Journal of Women's History* 26, no. 1 (2014): 161, 163, 174, 176.

CHAPTER 2: WOBBLY AGITATOR—FIGHTS FOR FREE SPEECH

1. Elizabeth Gurley Flynn, "Spokane," manuscript, 1910, EGF Papers (Tamiment), Box 1, Folder 21.

2. Elizabeth Gurley Flynn, "Memories of the Industrial Workers of the World," American Institute for Marxist Studies, 1977, available online at https://archive.org/details/MemoriesOfTheIndustrialWorkersOfTheWorldiww.

3. For the Wobblies' antipolitical stance, see Melvyn Dubofsky, *We Shall Be All: A History of the Industrial Workers of the World*, abridged edition, edited by Joseph A. McCartin (Urbana: University of Illinois Press, 2000), 89; James R. Barrett, *William Z. Foster and the Tragedy of American Radicalism* (Urbana: University of Illinois Press, 1999), 32–33; Bryan D. Palmer, *James P. Cannon and the Origins of the American Revolutionary Left, 1890–1928* (Urbana: University of Illinois Press, 2007), 52.

4. Dubofsky, *We Shall Be All*, 98–99; David M. Rabban, *Free Speech in Its Forgotten Years, 1870–1920* (New York: Cambridge University Press, 1997), 79.

5. Philip S. Foner, *History of the Labor Movement in the United States: The Industrial Workers of the World, 1905–1917* (New York: International Publishers, 1965), 29–30,

6. Dubofsky, *We Shall Be All*, 96.

7. Ibid., 277.

8. Vincent St. John, "The I.W.W.—Its History, Structure and Methods," 1917, University of Arizona, Special Collections, AZ 114, Box 1, Folder 1A, Exhibit 19, available online at www.library.arizona.edu/exhibits/bisbee/docs/019.html.

9. Paul Frederick Brissenden, *The IWW: A Study of American Syndicalism* (New York: Columbia University, 1920), 55; Michael McGerr, *A Fierce Discontent: The Rise and Fall of the Progressive Movement in America 1870–1920* (New York: Free Press, 2003), 140.

10. "Girl Socialist Tells of Her Aims," 1907, clipping, EGF Papers (Tamiment), Box 1, Folder 1.

11. Melvyn Dubofsky, *"Big Bill" Haywood* (Manchester, UK: Manchester University Press, 1987), 145.

12. "The IWW," Samuel Gompers Papers Project, University of Maryland, http://history.umd.edu/research/samuel-gompers-papers.

13. Flynn, *Rebel Girl*, 77.

14. Robert J. Embardo, "'Summer Lightning,' 1907: The Wobblies in Bridgeport," *Labor History* 30, no. 4 (1989): 531–532.

15. Flynn, *Rebel Girl*, 78.

16. Letter from Eugene V. Debs re: dinner, February 1, 1926, EGF Papers (Tamiment), Box 1, Folder 37.

17. Dubofsky, *We Shall Be All*, 80–81.

18. Clipping from *Chicago Inter-Ocean*, September 17, 1907, EGF Papers (Tamiment), Box 1, Folder 8.

19. Flynn, *Rebel Girl*, 81–83.

20. Quoted in Dubofsky, *We Shall Be All*, 72.

21. Flynn, *Rebel Girl*, 84–86.

22. Ibid., 86–88.

23. Helen C. Camp, *Iron in Her Soul: Elizabeth Gurley Flynn and the American Left* (Pullman: Washington State University Press, 1995), 21.

24. Brissenden, *IWW*, 178.

25. Flynn, *Rebel Girl*, 104.

26. Quoted in George A. Venn, "The Wobblies and Montana's Garden City,": *The Montana, Magazine of Western History* 21, no. 4 (1971): 22.

27. Ibid., 27; Flynn, "Notes on Missoula," undated manuscript, EGF Papers (Tamiment), Box 1, Folder 32.

28. Quoted in Venn, "Wobblies and Garden City," 25.

29. Flynn, *Rebel Girl*, 104.

30. Venn, "Wobblies and Garden City," 19.

31. Barrett, *Foster*, 39.

32. Gregory R. Woirol, "Two Letters on the Spokane Free Speech Fight: A Document Note," *Pacific Northwest Quarterly* 77, no. 2 (1986): 68–71.

33. Barrett, *Foster*, 41.

34. Dubofsky, *We Shall Be All*, 89.

35. Ibid., 102.

36. Benjamin H. Kizer, "Elizabeth Gurley Flynn," *Pacific Northwest Quarterly* 57, no. 3 (1966): 111–112.

37. Kizer, "Flynn," 112.

38. Jennifer Guglielmo, *Living the Revolution: Italian Women's Resistance and Radicalism in New York City, 1880–1945* (Chapel Hill: University of North Carolina Press, 2010).

39. Flynn, "Notes on Missoula."

40. Kizer, "Flynn," 112.

41. Flynn, *Rebel Girl*, 111.

42. Bill Haywood, *Bill Haywood's Book: The Autobiography of William D. Haywood* (New York: International Publishers, 1966), 239.

43. Flynn, *Rebel Girl*, 113.

CHAPTER 3: BUILDING SOLIDARITY WITH THE IWW—
LANDMARK STRIKES

1. Guglielmo, *Living the Revolution*, chap. 6.

2. Elizabeth Gurley Flynn, "Women and Syndicalism," undated manuscript, EGF Papers (Tamiment), Box 1, Folder 14.

3. Elizabeth Gurley Flynn, "IWW and Women," 1912, EGF Papers (Tamiment), Box 1, Folder 20.

4. Elizabeth Gurley Flynn, "Small Families a Proletarian Necessity," 1915, EGF Papers (Tamiment), Box 1, Folder 30.

5. Dubofsky, *We Shall Be All*, 137.

6. Ardis Cameron, *Radicals of the Worst Sort: Laboring Women in Lawrence, Massachusetts, 1860–1912* (Urbana: University of Illinois Press, 1993), 126.

7. Flynn, *Rebel Girl*, 135.

8. Ibid., 120.

9. Flynn, "Memories of the IWW."

10. Flynn, *Rebel Girl*, 131.

11. Mary Heaton Vorse, *A Footnote to Folly* (New York: Farrar and Rinehart, 1935), 8–9.

12. Dee Garrison, *Mary Heaton Vorse: The Life of an American Insurgent* (Philadelphia: Temple University Press, 1989), 51–61.

13. "IWW Call to Women," 1915, reprinted in Baxandall, *Words on Fire*, 104–108.

14. Flynn, *Rebel Girl*, 132.

15. Flynn, "IWW and Women."

16. Flynn, *Rebel Girl*, 150.

17. Ibid., 137–138; Bruce Watson, *Bread and Roses: Mills, Migrants, and the Struggle for the American Dream* (New York: Viking, 2005), 159.

18. "The Lawrence Strike Children," *Literary Digest*, March 9, 1912, 471–472.

19. Quoted in Dubofsky, *We Shall Be All*, 147.

20. Dubofsky, *We Shall Be All*, 164–167.

21. Flynn, *Rebel Girl*, 150–151; Kathy Ferguson, *Emma Goldman: Political Thinking in the Streets* (Lanham, MD: Rowman and Littlefield, 2011), 30–31.

22. Brissenden, *IWW*, 306–308.

23. Flynn, *Rebel Girl*, 149.

24. Nunzio Pernicone, *Carlo Tresca: Portrait of a Rebel* (Oakland, CA: AK Press, 2010), 2–3.

25. Dorothy Gallagher, *All the Right Enemies: The Life and Murder of Carlo Tresca* (New York: Penguin, 1988), 31, 37–39.

26. Inscribed copy of *Maiden of the Rock*, EGF Papers (Tamiment), Box 1, Folder 23.

27. Pernicone, *Tresca*, 84.

28. Diary, EGF Papers (Tamiment), Box 1, Folder 15.

29. Camp, *Iron in Her Soul*, 43.

30. Flynn, *Rebel Girl*, 152.

31. "Modern Joan of Arc Lectures," clipping from 1907, EGF Papers (Tamiment), Box 1, Folder 8; Flynn, "Women and Syndicalism."

32. Flynn, *Rebel Girl*, 152; Howard Kimmeldorf, *Battling for American Labor: Wobblies, Craft Workers, and the Making of the Union Movement* (Berkeley: University of California Press, 1999), 87–88, 93, 107.

33. Camp, *Iron in Her Soul*, 43–44.

34. Kimmeldorf, *Battling for American Labor*, 109.

35. Flynn, *Rebel Girl*, 152–153.

36. Elizabeth Gurley Flynn, *Sabotage: The Conscious Withdrawal of the Workers' Industrial Efficiency* (Chicago: IWW Publishing Bureau, 1917), 14–16.

37. Pernicone, *Tresca*, 58–62.

38. Camp, *Iron in Her Soul*, 43–44; Melvyn Dubofsky, *When Workers Organize: New York City in the Progressive Era* (Amherst: University of Massachusetts Press, 1968), 123–124; Kimmeldorf, *Battling for American Labor*, 116.

39. Flynn, *Rebel Girl*, 155–160.

40. Flynn, *Sabotage*.

41. Flynn, *Rebel Girl*, 162–165.

42. Steve Golin, *The Fragile Bridge: Paterson Silk Strike, 1913* (Philadelphia: Temple University Press, 1988), chap. 4.

43. Flynn, *Rebel Girl*, 169. Golin disagrees with Flynn's assessment in *Fragile Bridge*, 170–178.

44. Dubofsky, *We Shall Be All*, 156–165.

45. Christine Stansell, *American Moderns: Bohemian New York and the Creation of a New Century* (New York: Holt, 2000), 74, 77, 117, 151, 179.

46. Flynn, *Rebel Girl*, 172–173.

47. Ibid., 184–185; Nancy A. Hewitt, *Southern Discomfort: Women's Activism in Tampa, Florida, 1880s–1920s* (Urbana: University of Illinois Press, 2001), 6.

48. Nancy F. Cott, *The Grounding of Modern Feminism* (New Haven, CT: Yale University Press, 1987), 38–40.

49. Flynn, *Rebel Girl*, 279–280.

50. Elizabeth Gurley Flynn, "Men and Women," manuscript, 1915, EGF Papers (Tamiment), Box 1, Folder 34.

51. Flynn, "IWW and Women"; Flynn, "Small Families."

52. Baxandall, *Words on Fire*, 263–272.

53. Flynn "Men and Women."

CHAPTER 4: THE QUESTION OF VIOLENCE

1. Flynn, *Rebel Girl*, 233–234.

2. Dubofsky, *We Shall Be All*, 226–230; "Woman IWW Is Held," *Washington Post*, October 1, 1917; "Blow at IWW," Special to the *New York Times*, September 29, 1917, ProQuest Historical Newspapers.

3. Paul Avrich and Karen Avrich, *Sasha and Emma: The Anarchist Odyssey of Alexander Berkman and Emma Goldman* (Cambridge, MA: Harvard University Press, 2012), 2.

4. Flynn, *Rebel Girl*, 191.

5. Foner, *IWW*, 435–442.

6. Flynn, *Rebel Girl*, 182–184.

7. Foner, *IWW*, 442–448; "Tanenbaum's Men Testify for Him," March 27, 1914, and "Tannenbaum Guilty; Gets a Year in Jail," March 28, 1915, *New York Times*.

8. Vorse, *Footnote to Folly*, 70.

9. Paul Avrich, *The Modern School Movement: Anarchism and Education in the United States* (Princeton, NJ: Princeton University Press, 1980), 218.

10. Ferguson, *Goldman*, 35–36, 41, 57.

11. Elizabeth Gurley Flynn, "Violence," ms., 1915, EGF Papers (Tamiment), Box 1, Folder 32.

12. Beverly Gage, *The Day Wall Street Exploded* (New York: Oxford University Press, 2009), 69–70.

13. Flynn, *Rebel Girl*, 188.

14. Ibid., 188; Scott Martelle, *Blood Passion: The Ludlow Massacre and Class War in the American West* (New Brunswick, NJ: Rutgers University Press, 2007), 2–3, 175–181.

15. Martelle, *Blood Passion*, 223.

16. Gallagher, *All the Right Enemies*, 51.

17. Guglielmo, *Living the Revolution*, 177.

18. Pernicone, *Tresca*, 71, 78, 82.

19. Flynn, *Rebel Girl*, 187–189.

20. Letter from Elizabeth Gurley Flynn to Mary Heaton Vorse, July 5, 1914, Mary Heaton Vorse Papers, Walter P. Reuther Library, Wayne State University.

21. Avrich, *Modern School Movement*, 215, 217.

22. Flynn, *Rebel Girl*, 190.

23. Vorse, *Footnote to Folly*, 71.

24. Flynn, *Rebel Girl*, 190.

25. Letter from Elizabeth Gurley Flynn to Mary Heaton Vorse, July 17, 1914, Vorse Papers.

26. Flynn, "Patriotism and Preparedness," 1917 ms., EGF Papers (Tamiment), Box 1, Folder 33, and "War: Can Labor Be Neutral?" c. 1917, EGF Papers (Tamiment), Box 1, Folder 35.

27. Circular from Emergency Labor Conference, 1914, EGF Papers (Tamiment), Box 1, Folder 35.

28. Foner, *IWW*, 462.

29. Dubofsky, *We Shall Be All*, 200.

30. Ibid., 179.

31. Flynn, *Rebel Girl*, 191–194; William M. Adler, *The Man Who Never Died: The Life, Times, and Legacy of Joe Hill, American Labor Icon* (New York: Bloomsbury, 2011), 13, 277–280.

32. Foner, *IWW*, 490.

33. Letter from Elizabeth Gurley Flynn to Mary Heaton Vorse, July 24, 1914, Vorse Papers; Gallagher, *All the Right Enemies*, 55–59.

34. Dorothy Day, "Red Roses for Her," *Catholic Worker*, November 1964.

35. Haywood, *Bill Haywood's Book*, 291–292; Camp, *Iron in Her Soul*, 73–75; Pernicone, *Tresca*, 92–93.

36. Gallagher, *All the Right Enemies*, 59.

37. Patrick Renshaw, *The Wobblies: The Story of the IWW and Syndicalism in the United States* (Chicago: Ivan R. Dee, 1999), 93–94.

38. Flynn, *Rebel Girl*, 221.

39. Dubofsky, *Haywood*, 92–93.

40. Flynn, *Rebel Girl*, 163, 221.

41. Ibid., 232.

42. Ibid., 232–233; Dubofsky, *We Shall Be All*, 215–225.

43. Haywood, *Bill Haywood's Book*, 302–303.

44. Quoted in Dubofsky, *We Shall Be All*, 233.

45. Flynn, *Rebel Girl*, 236.

46. Morris R. Preston, "The Smith-Preston Case: A Review of the Trial," 1915 EGF Papers (Tamiment), Box 1, Folder 24.

47. "IWW Cases," 1917, EGF Papers, Wisconsin Historical Society (WHS), 1917–1923.

48. Pernicone, *Tresca*, 98.

49. Camp, *Iron in Her Soul*, 78–83.

50. Flynn, *Rebel Girl*, 237.

CHAPTER 5: DEFENDING WORKERS DURING THE RED SCARE

1. Letter from Elizabeth Gurley Flynn to "All Liberty-Loving Workers," May 12, 1920, EGF Papers (WHS).

2. Flynn, *Rebel Girl*, 283–286.

3. Ibid., 265, 267.

4. Ibid., 241–242.

5. Robert C. Cottrell, *Roger Nash Baldwin and the American Civil Liberties Union* (New York: Columbia University Press, 2000), 31–32.

6. Flynn, *Rebel Girl*, 244.

7. Camp, *Iron in Her Soul*, 81.

8. Flynn, *Rebel Girl*, 245.

9. Eugene Lyons, *Assignment in Utopia* (New York: Harcourt, Brace, 1937), 12–13; Flynn, *Rebel Girl*, 282.

10. Flynn's work on these cases is documented in the EGF Papers (WHS).

11. Letter from Harry Weinberger to Elizabeth Gurley Flynn, March 2, 1920, EGF Microfilm Collection, 1918–1926, Manuscripts and Archives, Yale University Library (Yale).

12. Flynn, *Rebel Girl*, 247–248; EGF Papers (WHS).

13. Flynn, *Rebel Girl*, 238–239.

14. NARA M1085, Case No. 371117, Investigative Case Files of the Bureau of Investigation, 1908–1922, accessed on www.fold3.com.

15. Flynn, *Rebel Girl*, 50.

16. Goldman, *Living My Life*.

17. Kate Richards O'Hare, *In Prison* (New York: Knopf, 1923), 12.

18. Flynn, *Rebel Girl*, 292–294.

19. Workers' Defense Union, "Resolution Against Deportation," 1919, EGF Papers (WHS).

20. Memorandum for Mr. Hoover re: the Deportees' Defense Committee, April 20, 1920, Case #381677, National Archives, Investigative Files of the Bureau of Investigation, Old German Files, 1909–1921.

21. Bill of Fare, Ellis Island, July 24, 1919, and Letter from Workers' Defense Union to Frederick C. Howe, July 22, 1919, EGF Papers (WHS).

22. Gage, *Wall Street*, 26–27.

23. Camp, *Iron in Her Soul*, 97.

24. Louis F. Post, *The Deportations Delirium of 1920: A Personal Narrative of an Historic Official Experience* (Chicago: Kerr, 1923), 29–32, 91–93.

25. Ibid., 5–6.

26. Open Letter from Emma Goldman and Alexander Berkman, January 10, 1920, EGF Papers (WHS).

27. Ibid.

28. "Dear Friend," Letter from Eugene Lyons, December 24, 1919; Letter from Norman Thomas to Eugene Lyons, January 6, 1920; Letter from Henry Neumann, Brooklyn Society for Ethical Culture, to Eugene Lyons, January 8, 1920, EGF Papers (WHS).

29. Letter from William B. Wilson, secretary, US Department of Labor, to Mrs. Helen Todd, January 7, 1920, EGF Papers (WHS).

30. Letter from Elizabeth Gurley Flynn, raising money for the Steimer Relief Fund, May 14, 1920, EGF Papers (WHS).

31. Letter from Elizabeth Gurley Flynn to Harry Weinberger, November 25, 1919, EGF Microfilm (Yale).

32. Avrich and Avrich, *Sasha and Emma*, 305.

33. Paul Avrich, *Anarchist Portraits* (Princeton, NJ: Princeton University Press, 1988), 214–226; Richard Polenberg, *Fighting Faiths: The Abrams Case, the Supreme Court, and Free Speech* (New York: Viking, 1987), 344–345, 351, 355, 357, 359, 362–363.

34. Benjamin Gitlow, *I Confess: The Truth About American Communism* (New York: Dutton, 1940), 299; Palmer, *Cannon*, 91.

35. *New York Evening Herald*, July 5, 1928, clipping, EGF Papers (Tamiment).

36. Pernicone, *Tresca*, 118–119.

37. Lisa McGirr, "The Passion of Sacco and Vanzetti: A Global History," *Journal of American History* 93, no. 4 (2007): 1085–1115, 1103.

38. Bruce Watson, *Sacco and Vanzetti: The Men, the Murders, and the Judgment of Mankind* (New York: Penguin, 2007), 15–16.

39. Art Shields, *Are They Doomed?* (New York: Workers' Defense Union, n.d.), 29.

40. Flynn, *Rebel Girl*, 303–314.

41. Gage, *Wall Street*, 207–228; Pernicone, *Tresca*, 113–121; Avrich, *Anarchist Portraits*, 162–164, 167, 174–175.

42. Art Shields, "Their Courage Inspired Millions," *Daily Worker*, August 24, 1952, 3.

43. Letter from Elizabeth Gurley Flynn on behalf of Sacco-Vanzetti Defense Committee, December 20, 1924, EGF Papers (Tamiment), Box 1, Folder 64.

44. Elizabeth Gurley Flynn, Notes from Sacco-Vanzetti Conference held on Friday, July 9, 1926, at the Labor Temple, 243 East 84th Street, New York, EGF Papers (Tamiment), Box 1, Folder 64.

45. Handbill announcing Elizabeth Gurley Flynn's speech, "The Story of Two Working Men," 1920s, EGF Papers (Tamiment), Box 1, Folder 65.

46. Camp, *Iron in Her Soul*, 111–112; unidentified clipping, 1926, EGF Papers (Tamiment), Box 1, Folder 54.

47. "Radicals Hold Dinner," *New York Times*, February 15, 1926, clipping; "Extremists Join to Fete Labor 'Queen,'" *New York American*, February 1926, EGF Papers (Tamiment), Box 1, Folder 54.

48. *New York Telegram*, February 5, 1926, and *New York American*, February 1926, EGF Papers (Tamiment), Box 1, Folder 54; David Montgomery, "American Workers in the 1920s," *International Labor and Working-Class History* 32 (1987): 18.

49. Letter from Eugene V. Debs, February 1, 1926, EGF Papers (Tamiment), Box 1, Folder 37.

50. Letters and telegrams from Sidney Hillman, Mike Gold, Emma Goldman, and Bartolomeo Vanzetti, February 1926, EGF Papers (Tamiment), Box 1, Folder 54.

CHAPTER 6: "NO PRESENT PROSPECTS OF RETURNING EAST"— OREGON YEARS

1. Flynn, *Rebel Girl*, 333–334.

2. Dorothy Gallagher, Interview with Jane Bobba, n.d., Dorothy Gallagher Research Files, Tamiment Library, New York University (Tamiment), Box 1, Folder 2.

3. Gallagher, *All the Right Enemies*, 103–106; Pernicone, *Tresca*, 147–158.

4. Flynn, *Rebel Girl*, 335.

5. Letter from Bina Flynn to Carlo Tresca, April 4, 1925, Martin-Bobba Materials, Tamiment Library, New York University (Tamiment), Folder 2.

6. Gallagher, *All the Right Enemies*, 114–115; Camp, *Iron in Her Soul*, 112–113.

7. Mary Heaton Vorse, *The Passaic Textile Strike, 1926–1927* (Passaic, NJ: General Relief Committee of Textile Strikers, 1927); Garrison, *Vorse*, 196–203; Camp, *Iron in Her Soul*, 114–115.

8. Vorse, *Passaic*, 16.

9. Jennifer Luff, *Commonsense Anticommunism: Labor and Civil Liberties Between the World Wars* (Chapel Hill: University of North Carolina Press, 2012), 74–76.

10. Garrison, *Vorse*, 196.

11. Baxandall, *Words on Fire*, n. 90, 278–279.

12. Quoted in Camp, *Iron in Her Soul*, 117.

13. Dorothy Gallagher, Interview with Vera Burch Weisbord, April 12, 1979, Gallagher Research Files (Tamiment), Box 2, Folder 57.

14. Quoted in Camp, *Iron in Her Soul*, 118.

15. Card in EGF Papers (Tamiment), Box 1, Folder 36.

16. Quoted in Camp, *Iron in Her Soul*, 119.

17. Letter from Elizabeth Gurley Flynn to Mary Heaton Vorse, December 23, 1926, Vorse Papers.

18. Telegram from Carlo Tresca to Marie Equi, January 11, 1927, EGF Papers (Tamiment), Box 1, Folder 69.

19. Gallagher, Bobba interview.

20. Information on Equi comes from Nancy Krieger, "Queen of the Bolsheviks: The Hidden History of Dr. Marie Equi," *Radical America* 17, no. 4 (1983): 55–71; Tom Cook, "Radical Politics, Radical Love: The Life of Dr. Marie Equi," *Northwest Gay and Lesbian Historian* 1, no. 3 (1997); Michael Helquist, "Marie Equi," *The Oregon Encyclopedia*, www.oregon encyclopedia.org/entry/view/equi_marie_1872_1952_/; and Adam J. Hodges, "At War over the Espionage Act in Portland, Dueling Perspectives from Kathleen O'Brennan and Agent William Bryon," *Oregon Historical Quarterly* 108, no. 3 (2007): 474–486.

21. Krieger, "Queen of the Bolsheviks," 61.

22. Fragment, c. 1920, EGF Papers (WHS).

23. Lillian Faderman, *Odd Girls and Twilight Lovers: A History of Lesbian Life in 20th-Century America* (New York: Columbia University Press, 1991), 105–106; Margot Cannaday, *The Straight State: Sexuality and Citizenship in Twentieth-Century America* (Princeton, NJ: Princeton University Press, 2009), 174–175, 184–185.

24. Krieger, "Queen of the Bolsheviks," 69; Camp, *Iron in Her Soul*, 129–130.

25. Letter from the American Fund for Public Service to Elizabeth Gurley Flynn, February 16, 1928, and draft of letter from Flynn to International Labor Defense, July 29, 1929, EGF Papers (Tamiment), Box 1, Folder 69.

26. Letter from Elizabeth Gurley Flynn to Mary Heaton Vorse, May 16, 1930, Vorse Papers.

27. Baxandall, *Words on Fire*, 32.

28. Gallagher, Notes from AIMS, Gallagher Research Files (Tamiment), Box 2, Folder 6; Baxandall, *Words on Fire*, 32.

29. Letter from Elizabeth Gurley Flynn to Mary Heaton Vorse, January 12, 1931, Vorse Papers.

30. Gallagher, Bobba interview.

31. Letter from Elizabeth Gurley Flynn to Agnes Inglis, July 11, 1934, Agnes Inglis Papers, Special Collections Library, Labadie Collection, University of Michigan.

32. Letter from Bina Romolo to Carlo Tresca, October 22, 1931, Martin-Bobba Materials (Tamiment), Folder 2.

33. Gallagher, *All the Right Enemies*, 125.

CHAPTER 7: "MY SECOND LIFE"—THE COMMUNIST PARTY

1. Letter from Elizabeth Gurley Flynn to Agnes Inglis, September 10, 1936, Inglis Papers.

2. Kim Phillips-Fein, *Invisible Hands: The Businessmen's Crusade Against the New Deal* (New York: Norton, 2009), 4.

3. Elizabeth Gurley Flynn, "A Labor Leader Sums Up," *Woman Shopper*, February 1937, clipping, EGF Papers (Tamiment), Box 2, Folder 4.

4. Elizabeth Gurley Flynn, autobiographical notes for 1919–1946, EGF Papers (Tamiment), Box 3, Folder 28, p. 26; Elizabeth Gurley Flynn, "Memories of Oregon," c. 1939 Notebook of Poetry, EGF Papers (Tamiment), Box 2, Folder 5; Camp, *Iron in Her Soul*, 132.

5. Flynn, "Memories of Oregon."

6. Camp, *Iron in Her Soul*, 141–142.

7. Elizabeth Gurley Flynn, List of Articles and Speeches Since Return to NYC, August 1936 to December 1937, EGF Papers (Tamiment), Box 2, Folder 1.

8. Letter from Agnes Inglis to Elizabeth Gurley Flynn, September 19, 1936, Inglis Papers.

9. Elizabeth Gurley Flynn, "Recollections of Frame-ups," c. 1937 EGF Papers (Tamiment), Box 2, Folder 3, p. 6.

10. Flynn, "Memories of Oregon."

11. Tom Cawley, *Binghamton Press*, September 16, 1964, clipping, Martin-Bobba Materials (Tamiment), Box 1, Folder 8.

12. Flynn, List of Articles and Speeches, 1936–1937, EGF Papers (Tamiment), Box 2, Folder 1.

13. Ibid.

14. Elizabeth Gurley Flynn, autobiographical notes, 1946, EGF Papers (Tamiment), Box 3, Folder 28, p. 25.

15. Letter from Elizabeth Gurley Flynn to Mary Heaton Vorse, March 22, 1937, Vorse Papers.

16. Randi Storch, *Red Chicago: American Communism at Its Grassroots, 1928–35* (Urbana: University of Illinois Press, 2007), 139–141; Peggy Dennis, *Autobiography of an American Communist* (Westport, CT: Hill, 1977); Mark Naison, *Communists in Harlem During the Depression* (Urbana: University of Illinois Press, 2005); Robin D. G. Kelley, *Hammer and Hoe* (Chapel Hill: University of North Carolina Press, 1990).

17. Maurice Isserman, *Which Side Were You On?* (Middletown, CT: Wesleyan University Press, 1982), 21–25.

18. Barrett, *Foster*, 190–191.

19. James Ryan, *Earl Browder: The Failure of American Communism* (Tuscaloosa: University of Alabama Press, 1997), 103–107.

20. Van Gosse, "To Organize in Every Neighborhood," *Radical History Review* 50 (1991): 110.

21. Kathleen A. Brown, "The 'Savagely Fathered and Un-Mothered World' of the Communist Party, U.S.A.: Feminism, Maternalism, and 'Mother Bloor,'" *Feminist Studies* 25, no. 3 (Autumn 1999): 538–539, 547–552; Lisa Rubens, "The Patrician Radical: Charlotte Anita Whitney," *California History* 65, no. 3 (Sept. 1986): 166–170.

22. Elizabeth Gurley Flynn, *Daughters of America: Ella Reeve Bloor and Anita Whitney* (New York: Workers Library, 1942), 11.

23. Military Intelligence Division, Report on "Negro Activities," February 10, 1921, www.fold3.com/image/#183973435, and "Harlem Meeting of Socialist Party," June 6, 1921, www.fold3.com/image/#183975953.

24. Elizabeth Gurley Flynn, Notebook of Autobiographical Events, EGF Papers (Tamiment), Box 3, Folder 37, 1937–1948.

25. Gallagher, Bobba interview.

26. "List of Reasons Why I Became a Communist," c. 1936, Box 2, Folder 12; Comments on Browder, from Gallagher, Bobba interview.

27. Camp, *Iron in Her Soul*, 145. Flynn's election was unusual; most leaders were appointed. Baxandall, *Words on Fire*, 53.

28. Barrett, *Foster*, 178, 180, 188, 190, 207.

29. Dennis, *Autobiography of an American Communist*, 165.

30. Baxandall, *Words on Fire*, 52.

31. Larry Ceplair, *Anticommunism in Twentieth-Century America* (Westport, CT: Praeger, 2011), 45, 49; Fraser Ottanelli, *The Communist Party of the United States from the Depression to World War II* (New Brunswick, NJ: Rutgers University Press, 1991), 198–200.

32. Van Gosse, "To Organize in Every Neighborhood," 119–121. Thinking within the party can be partially recovered from memoirs by Dorothy Healy and Peggy Dennis cited in the annotated bibliography.

33. Gallagher, *All the Right Enemies*, 150–162; Pernicone, *Tresca*, 227–230.

34. Alice Kessler-Harris, *A Difficult Woman: the Challenging Life and Times of Lillian Hellman* (New York: Bloomsbury, 2012), 115, 118.

35. Dorothy Gallagher, Interview with Peter Martin, Gallagher Research Files (Tamiment), Box 2, Folder 27.

36. Letter from Elizabeth Gurley Flynn to Mary Heaton Vorse, March 22, 1937, Vorse Papers.

37. Clippings, 1937, EGF Papers (Tamiment), Box 2, Folder 10.

38. Camp, *Iron in Her Soul*, 139–140.

39. Ryan, *Browder*, 99, 106.

40. Flynn, Notebook of Poetry; Michael Denning, *The Cultural Front: The Laboring of American Culture in the Twentieth Century* (New York: Verso, 1996), 16.

41. Elizabeth Gurley Flynn, 1938 scrapbook, EGF Papers (Tamiment), Box 2, Folder 16; Elizabeth Gurley Flynn, Outlines for Classes on Labor History at the Workers' School, 1939, EGF Papers (Tamiment), Box 2, Folder 26A.

42. Elizabeth Gurley Flynn, Text of Radio Speech, Pittsburgh, May Day 1938, EGF Papers (Tamiment), Box 2, Folder 17.

43. Vanessa H. May, *Unprotected Labor: Household Workers, Politics, and Middle-Class Reform in New York, 1870–1940* (Chapel Hill: University of North Carolina Press, 2011), 147–165.

44. Clippings from Scrapbook, 1937, EGF Papers (Tamiment), Box 2, Folder 4.

45. Letters from Rebecca Grecht to Elizabeth Gurley Flynn outlining western tour, September–October 1940, EGF Papers (Tamiment), Box 1, Folder 12.

46. Robert VanGiezen and Albert E. Schwenk, "Compensation from Before World War I Through the Great Depression," January 30, 2003, US Bureau of Labor Statistics, www.bls .gov/opub/mlr/cwc/compensation-from-before-world-war-i-through-the-great-depression .pdf.

47. Flynn, Notebook of Poetry; Flynn, Notebook of Autobiographical Events, 1938–1939.

48. Camp, *Iron in Her Soul*, 132.

49. Elizabeth Gurley Flynn, "For Mother Gurley on St. Patrick's Day," clipping from *People's World*, March 14, 1959, EGF Papers (Tamiment), Box 2, Folder 8.

50. Letter from Stuyvesant High School, May 25, 1928, EGF Papers (Tamiment), Box 3, Folder 1.

51. Letters from Elizabeth Gurley Flynn to Agnes Inglis, January 17, 1931, and September 10, 1936, Inglis Papers.

52. Camp, *Iron in Her Soul*, 191–192.

53. Flynn, Notebook of Autobiographical Events.

54. Workers tended to stay with the party. Storch, *Red Chicago*, 216.

55. Isserman, *Which Side*, 45.

56. *Baltimore Sun*, December 9, 1939, clipping, EGF Papers (Tamiment), Box 2, Folder 30.

57. Flynn, Notebook of Autobiographical Events.

58. Luff, *Commonsense Anticommunism*, 74–75, 167, 188.

59. Ceplair, *Anticommunism*, 26–29.

60. Cottrell, *Baldwin*, 263.

61. Reprinted in Corliss Lamont, ed., *The Trial of Elizabeth Gurley Flynn by the American Civil Liberties Union* (New York: Horizon, 1968), 155–161.

62. Reprinted in Lamont, *Trial*, 151–154.

63. Lamont, *Trial*, 217.

64. Letter from Margaret De Silver to Elizabeth Gurley Flynn re: Carlo Tresca, October 31, 1939, EGF Papers (Tamiment), Box 2, Folder 27; Judy Kutulas, *The ACLU and the Making of Modern Liberalism* (Chapel Hill: University of North Carolina Press, 2006), 69–70.

65. Lamont, *Trial*, 11–17.

66. Telegram from Harry Dana to Elizabeth Gurley Flynn, March 16, 1940, EGF Papers (Tamiment), Box 2, Folder 47.

67. Luff, *Commonsense Anticommunism*, 187–188, 195–196.

68. Gallagher, Bobba interview.

CHAPTER 8: FLYNN FIGHTS FASCISM—WORLD WAR II

1. "War Economy Here Demanded by Reds," *New York Times*, August 31, 1942, ProQuest Historical Newspapers; Isserman, *Which Side*, 103–104, 107; Guenter Lewy, *The Cause That Failed: Communism in American Political Life* (New York: Oxford University Press, 1990), 65–66.

2. Healey and Isserman, *Dorothy Healey Remembers*, 86–87.

3. Camp, *Iron in Her Soul*, 193–195.

4. Ellen Schrecker, *Many Are the Crimes: McCarthyism in America* (Boston: Little, Brown, 1998), 32–34, 104; Isserman, *Which Side*, 136–138.

5. Lee Casey, "And the Girl Grew Older," op-ed, clipping, 1943, EGF Papers (Tamiment), Box 3, Folder 17.

6. Baxandall, *Words on Fire*, 256–258.

7. John C. Polly, "'Liz' Flynn's Been Waving the Red Flag Since 1906," May 24, 1943, *Rocky Mountain News*, EGF Papers (Tamiment), Box 3, Folder 17.

8. Flynn, "Our Country's Margin for Victory," *Daily Worker*, December 7, 1943, EGF Papers (Tamiment), Box 3, Folder 17.

9. Dorothy Sue Cobble, *The Other Women's Movement: Workplace Justice and Social Rights in Modern America* (Princeton, NJ: Princeton University Press, 2004), 60–68.

10. "Running for Representative-at-Large in N.Y.," unidentified clipping, 1944, EGF Papers (Tamiment), Box 3, Folder 24; Kate Weigand, *Red Feminism* (Baltimore: Johns Hopkins University Press, 2001), 31, 53.

11. Elizabeth Gurley Flynn, "Impressions of Recruiting Drive," n.d. (1940s), Earl Browder Papers, Special Collections Research Center, Syracuse University Library.

12. Camp, *Iron in Her Soul*, 172.

13. Elizabeth Gurley Flynn, *Women in the War* (New York: Workers Library, 1942).

14. Lewy, *Cause That Failed*, 307.

15. Flynn, *Women in the War*.

16. Clippings from Campaign, 1942, EGF Papers (Tamiment), Box 4, Folder 1, p. 7.

17. Elizabeth Gurley Flynn, "Talk of Child-Care? But We Need Action," *The Worker*, February 7, 1943, EGF Papers (Tamiment), Box 3, Folder 17.

18. "Communists Must Destroy Fascism," *Richmond Times-Dispatch*, February 22, 1943, clipping, EGF Papers (Tamiment), Box 3, Folder 17.

19. *Black Dispatch*, Oklahoma City, March 6, 1943, clipping, EGF Papers (Tamiment), Box 3, Folder 17.

20. Elizabeth Gurley Flynn, "Jim Crow Nurse Policy—A Betrayal of the Wounded," July 6, 1944, EGF Papers (Tamiment), Box 3, Folder 17.

21. "Special Appeal to Women," Announcement of Flynn's tour of California, 1943, EGF Papers (Tamiment), Box 3, Folder 17.

22. Weigand, *Red Feminism*, 23, 26.

23. Elizabeth Gurley Flynn, "Women Delegates at the Communist Convention," *Daily Worker*, August 8, 1945.

24. Letters, pamphlets, and clippings regarding Mother Bloor's birthday celebration, 1937–1947, EGF Papers (Tamiment), Box 3, Folder 32.

25. Weigand, *Red Feminism*, 38–40.

26. Camp, *Iron in Her Soul*, 192–193.

27. Ibid., 185–190; Gallagher, *All the Right Enemies*, 206–273; Pernicone, *Tresca*, 274–281.

28. Baxandall, *Words on Fire*, 45–46.

29. Sergeant Ralph Friedman, "Almost Met EGF," *Daily Worker*, January 4, 1946.

30. Elizabeth Gurley Flynn, "They Won't Let the World Forget," *The Worker*, January 20, 1946.

31. Francisca de Haan, "The WIDF: History, Main Agenda, and Contributions, 1945–1991," *Women and Social Movements, International* (Alexandria, VA: Alexander Street Press, 2012).

32. Leila Rupp, "From Rosie the Riveter to the Global Assembly Line," *OAH Magazine of History*, July 2004, 54; Weigand, *Red Feminism*, 47–59.

33. Elizabeth Gurley Flynn, "Gurley Flynn Meets Europe's Heroines," *Daily Worker*, December 21, 1945. For further discussion, see Amy Swerdlow, "The Congress of American

Women," in Linda K. Kerber, Alice Kessler-Harris, and Katherine Kish Sklar, eds., *U.S. History as Women's History: New Feminist Essays* (Chapel Hill: University of North Carolina Press, 1995), 296–312.

34. Elizabeth Gurley Flynn, "Gurley Flynn Meets the British Communists," *Daily Worker*, December 27, 1945.

35. Elizabeth Gurley Flynn, "A Cold and Hungry Noel in Paris," *Daily Worker*, January 2, 1946, and "They Won't Let the World Forget," *The Worker*, January 20, 1946.

36. Elizabeth Gurley Flynn, "French Woman Deputy: The Story of Mme. Marie Vaillant-Couturier," *Daily Worker*, December 30, 1945; Francisca De Haan, "Continuing Cold War Paradigms of Western Historiography," *Women's History Review* 19, no. 4 (2010): 563.

37. De Haan, "Continuing Cold War Paradigms," 558, 562.

38. "The Nazis Hunted These Women," *Daily Worker*, December 22, 1945; Flynn, "Gurley Flynn Meets Europe's Heroines."

39. De Haan, "Continuing Cold War Paradigms," 548.

40. Women's International Democratic Federation (WIDF), "Original Resolutions of the WIDF at the ICW, Paris, November–December, 1945," WIDF Records, Sophia Smith Collection, Smith College, Box 1, Folder 7, accessed on Women and Social Movements International, http://wasi.alexanderstreet.com.jerome.stjohns.edu:81/UIV/1460343.

41. Letter from Elizabeth Gurley Flynn to Kathie and Frances Flynn, December 10, 1945, Miscellaneous Notes, 1945, EGF Papers (Tamiment), Box 4, Folder 9.

42. Quoted in Erik S. McDuffie, *Sojourning for Freedom: Black Women, American Communism, and the Making of Black Left Feminism* (Durham, NC: Duke University Press, 2011), 155.

43. Letter from Elizabeth Gurley Flynn to Kathie and Frances Flynn, December 10, 1945, Miscellaneous Notes, 1945, EGF Papers (Tamiment), Box 4, Folder 9.

44. Harvey Klehr, John Earl Haynes, and Kyrill M. Anderson, *The Soviet World of American Communism* (New Haven, CT: Yale University Press, 2008), 95–97.

45. "Speech by Elizabeth Gurley Flynn," *Political Affairs* 24, no. 7 (1945): 614.

46. Elizabeth Gurley Flynn, "I Met a Great Leader of France," *Daily Worker*, February 3, 1946; Ryan, *Browder*, 253–255, 258; Barrett, *Foster*, 222.

47. Letter from Elizabeth Gurley Flynn to Kathie and Frances Flynn, December 10, 1945, Miscellaneous Notes, 1945, EGF Papers (Tamiment), Box 4, Folder 9.

48. Issues of the *Crow's Nest*, 1945, EGF Papers (Tamiment), Box 5, Folder 18.

CHAPTER 9: LIBERTY DENIED—THE COLD WAR

1. Isserman, *Which Side*, 235.

2. "Hoarse," *New Yorker*, October 26, 1946, 25.

3. Elizabeth Gurley Flynn, "Celebrates First Speech by Visiting Picket Lines," *Daily Worker*, February 18, 1946.

4. Elizabeth Gurley Flynn, "They Have Just Begun to Fight," *New Masses*, July 16, 1946.

5. Elizabeth Gurley Flynn, Notes on Public Speaking, 1940s, EGF Papers (Tamiment), Box 3, Folder 39.

6. Elizabeth Gurley Flynn, "The Feminine Ferment," *New Masses*, May 13, 1947, 6–9, www.unz.org/Pub/NewMasses-1947may13–00006.

7. Quotation of a letter Flynn sent to CP headquarters from Chicago, May 26, 1947, "FBI Material," EGF Papers (Tamiment), Box 13.

8. Isserman, *Which Side*, 239–240; Healey and Isserman, *Dorothy Healey Remembers*, 101.

9. Elizabeth Gurley Flynn, *Women's Place in the Fight for a Better World*, March 1947, http://archive.org/stream/WomansPlace-inTheFightForABetterWorld.

10. Flynn, "Feminine Ferment."

11. Schrecker, *Many Are the Crimes*, 266–273.

12. Lichtenstein, *Labor's War at Home: The CIO in World War II* (Philadelphia: Temple University Press, 1983), 234–237; Robert H. Zieger, *The CIO: 1935–1955* (Chapel Hill: University of North Carolina Press, 1995), 260–261.

13. Elizabeth Gurley Flynn, fragment of autobiography, 1953, EGF Papers (Tamiment), Box 8, Folder 24.

14. *Milwaukee Journal*, May 2, 1950, clipping, EGF Papers (Tamiment), Box 4, Folder 32.

15. Flynn, "They Have Just Begun to Fight."

16. Elizabeth Gurley Flynn, "Every Inch Is a Fight Back," clipping, September 19, 1950, EGF Papers (Tamiment), Box 4, Folder 27; Flynn, "Feminine Ferment."

17. Flynn, *Women's Place*.

18. Elizabeth Gurley Flynn, *Meet the Communists* (New York: Communist Party, 1946), accessed online at https://archive.org/details/MeetTheCommunists.

19. Elizabeth Gurley Flynn, Radio Script, Station WKXL, Concord, NH, April 12, 1947, EGF Papers (Tamiment), Box 3, Folder 34.

20. Isserman, *Which Side*, 241–242.

21. Elizabeth Gurley Flynn, "List of Mistakes," n.d., EGF Papers (Tamiment), Box 13, "Interparty" Folder.

22. Clippings, 1940s, EGF Papers (Tamiment), Box 3, Folder 10; Healey and Isserman, *Dorothy Healy Remembers*, 121–122; Fragments of *Miami News*, February 17, 1948, clippings, EGF Papers (Tamiment), Box 3, Folder 45.

23. Quoted in Geoffrey R. Stone, *Perilous Times: Free Speech in Wartime. From the Sedition Act of 1798 to the War on Terrorism* (New York: Norton, 2004), 328

24. Barrett, *Foster*, 235.

25. Stone, *Perilous Times*, 251.

26. Elizabeth Gurley Flynn, *The Alderson Story: My Life as a Political Prisoner* (New York: International Publishers, 1972), 12.

27. Schrecker, *Many Are the Crimes*, 190–191.

28. Weigand, *Red Feminism*, 46–49; Swerdlow, "Congress of American Women"; Jacqueline Castledine, *Cold War Progressives: Women's Interracial Organizing for Peace and Freedom* (Urbana: University of Illinois Press, 2012), 45–52; Katherine Moos Campbell, "The Congress of American Women: Feminism and Peace," unpublished paper, EGF Papers (Tamiment), Box 13.

29. FBI Intelligence Report, March 12, 1946, EGF Papers (Tamiment), Box 13; House Un-American Activities Committee (HUAC), "Report on the Congress of American Women," 1949, http://openlibrary.org/books/OL7145600M/Report_on_the_Congress_of_American_Women.

30. Elizabeth Gurley Flynn, "Hitler's 3K's for Women—an American Rehash," *Political Affairs*, April 1947, 376–381.

31. Barrett, *Foster*, 237, 240, 242; Weigand, *Red Feminism*, 103–107; Healey and Isserman, *Dorothy Healey Remembers*, 125–130.

32. Elizabeth Gurley Flynn, "On Arrests and Indictments," speech, August 6, 1948, EGF Papers (Tamiment), Box 4, Folder 25.

33. Isserman, *Which Side*, 247.

34. William Z. Foster, "Policies During Defense," 1952, EGF Papers (Tamiment), Box 4, Folder 50.

35. Baxandall, *Words on Fire*, 53–55.

36. Barrett, *Foster*, 239, 241; Baxandall, *Words on Fire*, 56.

37. Prison letters from Elizabeth Gurley Flynn to Kathie Flynn, February 11 and 26, 1955, EGF Papers (Tamiment), Box 7, Folder 7.

38. Minutes of Founding of the Communist Committee to Defend the 12, February 19, 1949, and "Life of the Party," November 18, 1949, EGF Papers (Tamiment), Box 6, Folder 27.

39. "Meeting," November 24, 1948, EGF Papers (Tamiment), Box 3, Folder 13.

40. "A World Apart . . . But Next Door," *San Francisco Chronicle*, September 23, 1948, clipping, EGF Papers (Tamiment), Box 3, Folder 10.

41. Schrecker, *Many Are the Crimes*, 161, 165–67, 190–191, 409.

42. Ibid., 190–200; Stone, *Perilous Times*, 395–398.

43. A. H. Raskin, "Communists Trying to Carry on 'as Usual,'" *New York Times*, clipping, 1952, EGF Papers (Tamiment), Box 4, Folder 41.

44. Letter from Arthur Garfield Hays to Elizabeth Gurley Flynn, October 9, 1951, Mary Metlay Kaufman Papers, Sophia Smith Collection, Smith College, Box 9, Folder 1.

45. Letter to the Editor from Roger William Riis, December 11, 1952, *New York Times*, EGF Papers (Tamiment), Box 5, Folder 1.

46. Flynn, "Every Inch Is a Fight Back"; "Communists Fail to Fill the Garden," *New York Times*, September 20, 1950, clipping, EGF Papers (Tamiment), Box 4, Folder 32.

47. Cards, letters, and telegrams from Flynn's Scrapbook, 1950–1951, EGF Papers (Tamiment), Box 4, Folder 32.

48. *Dennis v. United States*, 341 US 494 (1951), http://supreme.justia.com/cases/federal/us/341/494/case.html#579.

49. Flynn, *Alderson Story*, 9; "Text of Indictment of 21 Communist Leaders on Conspiracy Charges," *New York Times*, June 21, 1951, ProQuest Historical Newspapers.

50. *Amnesty Trumpet*, January 1954, clipping, EGF Papers (Tamiment), Box 6, Folder 26.

51. Flynn, *Alderson Story*, 13–14.

52. Appeal by Katherine Flynn, *Sunday Worker*, January 27, 1952, EGF Papers (Tamiment), Box 4, Folder 40. The same appeal was sent out as a letter.

53. Letter from Nora Stanton Barney to Committee of the Families of the Smith Act Victims, April 28, 1956, EGF Papers (Tamiment), Box 5, Folder 2.

54. Reprint of letter from Alice Hamilton to the *New York Times*, December 3, 1952, clipping, EGF Papers (Tamiment), Box 4, Folder 41.

55. Clippings, EGF Papers (Tamiment), Box 5, Folder 2.

56. Flynn, *Alderson Story*, 22.

57. I. F. Stone, "Second Round at Foley Square," *I. F. Stone's Weekly*, February 14, 1953, clipping, EGF Papers (Tamiment), Box 4, Folder 50.

58. Letter from Elizabeth Gurley Flynn to Kathie Flynn, January 13, 1956, EGF Papers (Tamiment), Box 7, Folder 7.

59. Elizabeth Gurley Flynn, Personal Account Book, 1946–1947, EGF Papers (Tamiment), Box 3, Folder 41.

60. Schrecker, *Many Are the Crimes*, 19.

61. Barrett, *Foster*, 251.

CHAPTER 10: "MORTAL ENEMY OF CAPITALISM"—LAST YEARS

1. "Claudia Jones Tells Dreary Round of Life in Prison," *Worker*, February 5, 1956.
2. Deborah A. Gerson, "Is Family Devotion Now Subversive? Familialism Against Mc-Carthyism," in Joanne Meyerowitz, ed., *Not June Cleaver: Women and Gender in Postwar America, 1940–1960* (Philadelphia: Temple University Press, 1994), 151–176.
3. Flynn, *Alderson Story*, 115–118, 185.
4. Ibid., 140–143.
5. Letter from Elizabeth Gurley Flynn to Mary M. Kaufman, January 28, 1956, Kaufman Papers, Box 9, Folder 7.
6. Letter from Elizabeth Gurley Flynn to Muriel Symington, July 28, 1956, EGF Papers (Tamiment), Box 7, Folder 8.
7. Letter from Elizabeth Gurley Flynn to Peter Martin, February 2, 1957, EGF Papers, Walter P. Reuther Library, Wayne State University, Folder 2.
8. Letter from Elizabeth Gurley Flynn to Muriel Symington, September 15, 1956, EGF Papers (Tamiment), Box 7, Folder 8.
9. Letter from Elizabeth Gurley Flynn to Kathie Flynn, July 24, 1955, EGF Papers (Tamiment), Box 7, Folder 7.
10. Letter from Elizabeth Gurley Flynn to Peter Martin, March 31, 1956, EGF Papers (Reuther), Folder 2.
11. Letter from Elizabeth Gurley Flynn to Kathie Flynn, October 8, 1955, Kaufman Papers, Box 9, Folder 7.
12. Letter from Elizabeth Gurley Flynn to Al Richmond, February 20, 1964, EGF Papers (Tamiment), Box 8, Folder 27.
13. Letter from Elizabeth Gurley Flynn to Kathie Flynn, August 27, 1955, EGF Papers (Tamiment), Box 7, Folder 7.
14. Elizabeth Gurley Flynn, "On the Declaration of Independence," *Eagle*, July 4, 1956, reprinted in *Alderson Story*, 217–221.
15. Letters from Elizabeth Gurley Flynn to Kathie Flynn, June 8 and 16, 1956, EGF Papers (Tamiment), Box 7, Folder 7.
16. Barrett, *Foster*, 253–256, 258, 260–261; Camp, *Iron in Her Soul*, 271.
17. Flynn, *Alderson Story*, 186.
18. Ibid., 181–189, 198.
19. Mike Wallace interview with John Gates, January 18, 1958, University of Texas at Austin, Harry Ransom Center, www.hrc.utexas.edu/multimedia/video/2008/wallace/gates_john_t.html.
20. Letter from Elizabeth Gurley Flynn to Muriel Symington, April 19, 1957, EGF Papers (Tamiment), Box 7, Folder 8.
21. "Resolution on the Work and Status of Women," Communist Party, December 1958, EGF Papers (Tamiment), Box 7, Folder 20.
22. Letter from Elizabeth Gurley Flynn to Al Richmond, March 16, 1964, EGF Papers (Tamiment), Box 8, Folder 37; Schrecker, *Many Are the Crimes*, 387–389.
23. Copies of FBI Reports, NY 100–1692 November 7, October 1, and October 29, 1958, FBI Material, EGF Papers (Tamiment), Box 13.
24. Letters from Elizabeth Gurley Flynn to Al Richmond, June 14, July 8, and September 7, 1963, EGF Papers (Tamiment), Box 8, Folder 37.

25. Letter from Elizabeth Gurley Flynn to Peter Martin, November 20, 1960, EGF Papers (Reuther), Folder 7.

26. Letter from Elizabeth Gurley Flynn to Peter Martin, July 4, 1960, EGF Papers (Reuther), Folder 5.

27. Elizabeth Gurley Flynn, "The Golden Jubilee of International Women's Day," *Political Affairs*, March 1960, 31–32.

28. Letter from Elizabeth Gurley Flynn to Peter Martin, August 10, 1960, EGF Papers (Reuther), Folder 6.

29. Dennis, *Autobiography of an American Communist*, 251–252.

30. Healey and Isserman, *Dorothy Healey Remembers*, 174.

31. Elizabeth Gurley Flynn, "From Moscow to 12th Street," *Daily Worker*, January 15, 1961.

32. Letter from Elizabeth Gurley Flynn to Peter Martin, April 2, 1961, EGF Papers (Reuther), Folder 8; Elizabeth Gurley Flynn, "The Voice of Gene Debs," *Masses and Mainstream*, November 1955, 27–31.

33. Letter from Mike Gold to be read at NYC dinner honoring publication of *The Alderson Story*, 1963, EGF Papers (Tamiment), Box 7, Folder 17.

34. Dennis, *Autobiography of an American Communist*, 266–267.

35. Flynn, *Alderson Story*, 4.

36. "The CP in the Dock," December 1962, clipping from *Political Affairs*, EGF Papers (Tamiment), Box 8, Folder 3.

37. Letter from US Department of State to Elizabeth Gurley Flynn, July 16, 1962; "Dear Friend" letter from Corliss Lamont, April 29, 1963, EGF Papers (Tamiment), Box 7, Folder 31.

38. Elizabeth Gurley Flynn, "The Borders Are My Prison," clipping from *Political Affairs*, November 1962, EGF Papers (Tamiment), Box 8, Folder 3.

39. Letter from John Haynes Holmes to Elizabeth Gurley Flynn, August 19, 1963, EGF Papers (Tamiment), Box 7, Folder 17.

40. Letter from Norm Thomas to Elizabeth Gurley Flynn, March 19, 1963, EGF Papers (Tamiment), Box 7, Folder 17.

41. Press release from Norm Thomas to Associated Press and *New York Post*, March 29, 1963, EGF Papers (Tamiment), Box 7, Folder 17.

42. Mary van Kleeck, Memo for Reception, March 29, 1963, EGF Papers (Tamiment), Box 7, Folder 15–16.

43. Press Release from International Publishers, April 3, 1963; Invitation to Reception; "Notables in Many Nations Greet Gurley Flynn's Book," *The Worker*, April 7, 1963, EGF Papers (Tamiment), Box 7, Folder 18.

44. Letter from Alice Hamilton to Elizabeth Gurley Flynn, March 17, 1963, EGF Papers (Tamiment), Box 7, Folder 15–16.

45. Flynn, *Alderson Story*, 190.

46. "First Victory over the McCarran Act," clipping from *Political Affairs*, February 1964, EGF Papers (Tamiment), Box 8, Folder 3.

47. "White Sepulcher," *Washington Post*, June 28, 1964, Martin-Bobba Materials (Tamiment), Folder 5.

48. Art Shields, "A Happy Birthday Dinner for Gurley Flynn," unidentified clipping, EGF Papers (Reuther), Folder 11.

49. Letter from Peter Martin to nephew, August 13, 1964, Martin-Bobba Materials (Tamiment), Folder 1.

50. Notes [from telephone conversation?], September 4, 1964, EGF Papers (Reuther), Folder 12.

51. "Miss Flynn Given Moscow Tribute," *New York Times*, September 9, 1964, Martin-Bobba Materials (Tamiment), Folder 6; "Reds Honor Memory of Comrade Elizabeth," *New York News*, September 9, 1964, Martin-Bobba Materials (Tamiment), Folder 7; "Thousands at Funeral in Red Square," *The Worker*, September 13, 1964, Martin-Bobba Materials (Tamiment), Folder 8.

52. *Albany Times-Union*, September 6, 1964, and *Garden Grove News*, September 6, 1964, clippings, Martin-Bobba Materials (Tamiment), Folder 7.

53. "Communist Old Guard Dying Out," *Times-Herald* (Newport News, VA), September 8, 1964.

ANNOTATED BIBLIOGRAPHY

In addition to citations within the chapters, the following sources may be useful to readers seeking further information about the individuals, organizations, and social movements discussed in this book.

Helen C. Camp's biography of Elizabeth Gurley Flynn, *Iron in Her Soul: Elizabeth Gurley Flynn and the American Left* (Pullman: Washington State University Press, 1995), provides a detailed look at Flynn's life. *Words on Fire: The Life and Writing of Elizabeth Gurley Flynn* (New Brunswick, NJ: Rutgers University Press, 1987), by Rosalyn Fraad Baxandall, includes a brief biography and a selection of primary documents. Flynn's autobiography, *The Rebel Girl: My First Life, 1906–1926* (New York: International Publishers, 1955, 1986), offers a firsthand account.

Emma Goldman makes an interesting counterpoint to Flynn. The many biographies of Goldman include Candace Falk, *Love, Anarchy and Emma Goldman* (New Brunswick, NJ: Rutgers University Press, 1990); Vivian Gornick, *Emma Goldman: Revolution as a Way of Life* (New Haven, CT: Yale University Press, 2011); and Kathy E. Ferguson, *Emma Goldman: Political Thinking in the Streets* (Lanham, MD: Rowman and Littlefield, 2011). The dual biography of Emma Goldman and Alexander Berkman by Paul Avrich and Karen Avrich, *Sasha and Emma: The Anarchist Odyssey of Alexander Berkman and Emma Goldman* (Cambridge, MA: Harvard University Press, 2012), can serve as an introduction to the history of anarchism.

Biographies of people associated with Flynn illuminate her life and times. These include two books about Carlo Tresca: Dorothy Gallagher, *All the Right Enemies: The Life and Murder of Carlo Tresca* (New York: Penguin, 1988); and Nunzio Pernicone, *Carlo Tresca: Portrait of a Rebel* (Oakland, CA: AK Press, 2010). Leaders of the CP and the IWW with whom Flynn worked closely are profiled in James R. Barrett, *William Z. Foster and the Tragedy of American Radicalism* (Urbana: University of Illinois Press, 1999); James Ryan, *Earl Browder: The Failure of American Communism* (Tuscaloosa: University of Alabama Press, 1997); and Melvyn Dubofsky, *"Big Bill" Haywood* (Manchester, UK: Manchester University Press, 1987). Dee Garrison's biography, *Mary Heaton Vorse: The Life of an American Insurgent* (Philadelphia: Temple University Press, 1989), provides a complementary point of view on many of the issues that concerned Flynn, as does *Left of Karl Marx: The Political Life of Black Communist Claudia Jones* (Durham, NC: Duke University Press, 2007), by Carole Boyce Davies.

Flynn was a major figure in radical and socialist movements in the United States. An overview of those movements can be found in Michael Kazin, "The Agony and Romance of the American Left," *American Historical Review* 100, no. 5 (1995): 1488–1512. For an accessible history of the Industrial Workers of the World, see Melvyn Dubofsky, *We Shall*

Be All: A History of the Industrial Workers of the World (Urbana: University of Illinois Press, 1988). The labor activism of Italian women and Jewish women is discussed, respectively, in Jennifer Guglielmo, *Living the Revolution: Italian Women's Resistance and Radicalism in New York City, 1880–1945* (Chapel Hill: University of North Carolina Press, 2012), and Annelise Orleck, *Common Sense and a Little Fire: Women and Working-Class Activism in the United States, 1900–1965* (Chapel Hill: University of North Carolina Press, 1995).

Flynn's activism can be contextualized within the broader story of labor and working-class feminism. For further discussion, see Lara Vapnek, *Breadwinners: Working Women and Economic Independence, 1865–1920* (Urbana: University of Illinois Press, 2009); and Dorothy Sue Cobble, *The Other Women's Movement: Workplace Justice and Social Rights in Modern America* (Princeton, NJ: Princeton University Press, 2004). For an introduction to feminism in the United States from 1945 to 1960, see the volume of essays edited by Joanne Meyerowitz, *Not June Cleaver: Women and Gender in Postwar America* (Philadelphia: Temple University Press, 1994). Kate Weigand considers the contentious history of feminism within the CP in *Red Feminism: American Communism and the Making of Women's Liberation* (Baltimore: Johns Hopkins University Press, 2001). Erik S. McDuffie, *Sojourning for Freedom: Black Women, American Communism, and the Making of Black Left Feminism* (Durham, NC: Duke University Press, 2011); and Dayo F. Gore, *Radicalism at the Crossroads* (New York: New York University Press, 2011), explore African American women's activism in the CP.

The radical milieu of New York City in the early decades of the twentieth century shaped Flynn's outlook. Tony Michels, *A Fire in Their Hearts: Yiddish Socialists in New York* (Cambridge, MA: Harvard University Press, 2005), describes the politics and culture of the Jewish Lower East Side. The cross-cutting currents of radicalism and reaction are explored in Thai Jones, *More Powerful Than Dynamite* (New York: Walker, 2012); and Beverly Gage, *The Day Wall Street Exploded* (New York: Oxford University Press, 2009). Christine Stansell reconstructs bohemian life in early twentieth-century Greenwich Village in *American Moderns: Bohemian New York and the Creation of a New Century* (New York: Holt, 2000).

Flynn's sexuality can be placed within a larger story of changing sexual mores, a topic discussed in John D'Emilio and Estelle B. Freedman, *Intimate Matters* (Chicago: University of Chicago Press, 2012). Margot Canaday outlines government regulation of sexuality and the definition of homosexuality as deviant in *The Straight State: Sexuality and Citizenship in Twentieth-Century America* (Princeton, NJ: Princeton University Press, 2009).

Flynn spent nearly thirty years within the CP, but she does not feature prominently within the historiography of communism. For the most part, this literature remains divided between "traditionalists," who see American communism as Soviet subversion, and "revisionists," who view communism as a legitimate, if flawed, American social movement. Key scholarship in the traditionalist camp includes Theodore Draper, *The Roots of American Communism* (New York: Viking, 1957); and Harvey Klehr, John Earl Haynes, and Kyrill M. Anderson, *The Soviet World of American Communism* (New Haven, CT: Yale University Press, 2008). Traditionalists tend to focus on national party leadership; since the opening of Soviet archives they have highlighted communist espionage. A more sympathetic, though still critical, view of the leadership of the CP emerges in the revisionist work of Maurice Isserman, *Which Side Were You On?* (Middletown, CT: Wesleyan University Press, 1982); and Fraser Ottanelli, *The Communist Party of the United States from the Depression to World War II* (New Brunswick, NJ: Rutgers University Press, 1991). Most revisionists focus on grassroots organizing. Books in this vein include Randi Storch, *Red Chicago: American Communism at Its Grassroots, 1928–35* (Urbana: University of Illinois Press, 2007); Robin D. G. Kelley, *Hammer and Hoe: Alabama Communists During the Great Depression* (Chapel Hill:

University of North Carolina Press, 1990); and Mark Naison, *Communists in Harlem During the Depression* (Urbana: University of Illinois Press, 2005).

Many books consider the impact of communism on progressive social and cultural movements. Michael Denning offers a broad assessment in *The Cultural Front: The Laboring of American Culture in the Twentieth Century* (New York: Verso, 1996). Daniel Horowitz traces the rise and fall of Popular Front feminism in *Betty Friedan and the Making of the Feminine Mystique* (Amherst: University of Massachusetts Press, 1998). Memoirs of former communists, such as Peggy Dennis, *Autobiography of an American Communist* (Westport, CT: Hill, 1977); and Dorothy Healey, who collaborated with Maurice Isserman on *Dorothy Healey Remembers*, republished as *California Red: A Life in the American Communist Party* (Urbana: University of Illinois Press, 1993), discuss their wide-ranging activism within the CP and reflect on the party's mistakes.

Flynn spent much of her career contending with anticommunism and fighting for civil liberties. The history of anticommunism is outlined in Larry Ceplair, *Anticommunism in Twentieth-Century America* (Westport, CT: Praeger, 2011); Jennifer Luff, *Commonsense Anticommunism: Labor and Civil Liberties Between the World Wars* (Chapel Hill: University of North Carolina Press, 2012); and Ellen Schrecker, *Many Are the Crimes: McCarthyism in America* (Boston: Little, Brown, 1998). Related issues of free speech and civil liberties are discussed in David M. Rabban, *Free Speech in Its Forgotten Years, 1870–1920* (New York: Cambridge University Press, 1997); and Geoffrey R. Stone, *Perilous Times: Free Speech in Wartime. From the Sedition Act of 1798 to the War on Terrorism* (New York: Norton, 2004).

INDEX

Abortions, 40, 95
ACLU. *See* American Civil Liberties Union
   (ACLU)
AFL. *See* American Federation of Labor
   (AFL)
Aguinaldo, Eduardo, 9
*Alderson Story, The: My Life as a Political
   Prisoner* (Flynn)
   publication/gift copies, 173
   reception at Belmont Plaza Hotel, 174
   writing/dedication, 171, 172
Amalgamated Clothing Workers of America,
   86
American Civil Liberties Union (ACLU)
   as anticommunist, 118–121
   Flynn (1936) and, 105
   Flynn's expulsion from, 118–121, 120
      (photo)
   See also specific individuals
American Federation of Labor (AFL)
   communism and, 90, 118, 142
   competition/differences with IWW, 23,
      24, 37, 39–40, 46, 57
   Flynn and, 92, 113
   unions/strikes and, 24, 46, 113
   women's issues and, 37
   See also specific individuals
American Labor Party, 116
American Railway Union, 22
American Tobacco Company, 139
American Woolen Company, 42
Anarchists
   assassinations (1880–1914) and, 57
   participation in demonstrations of
      unemployed, 56–57
   Flynn and, 57, 60, 79, 81
   free love and, 17, 56–57
   Tresca and, 58–59

See also specific individuals
Anniversary Party for Flynn (1926), 84, 85
   (photo), 86
Anthony, Susan B., 10, 162
Anthony, Susan B. II, 125
Appeal to the Young (Kropotkin), 18
Aptheker, Herbert, 174, 176
Are They Doomed pamphlet (Sacco-Vanzetti),
   82–83
Arrests/Communist Party leaders. *See*
   Communist Party (US) arrests (1948)
Arrests/Flynn
   on Broadway (1906), 7
   conditions/Spokane, 20
   conspiracy charges and, 30–31
   federal charges (1917) and legal strategy,
      53–54, 68–69, 70
   Missoula, Montana, 29
   Paterson, New Jersey, 50
   Spokane, Washington/trial, 19, 30–33
Arrests/Flynn 1951 and consequences
   appeal and, 158
   finding lawyer, 154–155
   imprisonment, 158–159, 160–162,
      163–164
   jail and, 156, 158
   other CP leader arrests and, 154, 156
   paid informants and, 156, 157
   Smith Act and, 154, 156, 160, 172
   supporters of Flynn, 155–156, 160
   trial/verdict, 156, 157
   *See also Alderson Story, The: My Life as a
      Political Prisoner* (Flynn)
Arrests/IWW
   Everett Massacre and, 65
   federal charges (Red Scare), 53–54,
      68–69, 70–71, 73, 74, 75
   Flynn helping prisoners, 69